The Adventures Of Thomas Pellow, Of Penryn, Mariner: Three And Twenty Years In Captivity Among The Moors...

Thomas Pellow

"Adventures are to the Adventurous."

BEACONSFIELD.

THE
ADVENTURE
SERIES.

THE ADVENTURE SERIES.

Illustrated.   Cr. 8vo, $1 25c.

1.

Adventures of a Younger Son.   By E. J. TRELAWNY. *With an Introduction by Edward Garnett.* Second Edition.

2.

Robert Drury's Journal in Madagascar. *Edited, with an Introduction and Notes, by Captain S. P. Oliver.*

3.

Memoirs of the Extraordinary Military Career of John Shipp. *With an Introduction by H. Manners Chichester.*

4.

The Adventures of Thomas Pellow, of Penryn, Mariner. *Written by himself, and Edited with an Introduction and Notes by Dr. Robert Brown.*

5.

The Buccaneers and Marooners of America. Being an Account of the Famous Adventures and Daring Deeds of certain Notorious Freebooters of the Spanish Main. *Edited by Howard Pyle.*

(OTHERS IN THE PRESS.)

MULEY ABD-ALLAH, EMPEROR OF MOROCCO (1745).

THE ADVENTURES OF THOMAS PELLOW, OF PENRYN, MARINER

THREE AND TWENTY YEARS IN
CAPTIVITY AMONG THE MOORS

WRITTEN BY HIMSELF, AND EDITED
WITH AN INTRODUCTION AND
NOTES BY DR. ROBERT BROWN

ILLUSTRATED

LONDON: T. FISHER UNWIN. NEW
YORK: MACMILLAN & CO. MDCCCXC

CONTENTS.

———◆———

PAGE

(1) EDITOR'S INTRODUCTION 7

(2) The Adventures of Thomas Pellow :—

CHAPTER I.

The Author; youth and schooling—He goes to sea—Is captured
by the Sallee rovers and wrecked on the bar of the Bouragreb
River between Sallee and Rabat—Escapes drowning only to
become a slave—Is sent to Mequinez with the rest of his
shipmates—They are attacked by the mob—They are taken
before the Emperor Muley Ismaïl—The author becomes the
slave of Muley Spha, the Emperor's son—He is beaten in
order to force him to change his religion—He " turns Moor,"
and is made an officer of the Emperor—He has a perilous
adventure with the latter—His uncle dies—The cruelties of
the Emperor—The terrible punishments inflicted by him—
The dreadful death of Larbe Shott, whose ghost appeared
unto Muley Ismaïl 47

CHAPTER II.

Mr. Pellow is better housed and higher in favour—He dines more
frequently off cuscassoo—How this dish is prepared—The
misery of the slaves—The arrival of Commodore Stewart to
ransom the English captives—The author, being excluded
from the provisions of the treaty, is left behind—Cruelties of
the Emperor—His character and the subservience paid him
—The danger of anticipating a remark—The drilling of
marksmen—He gets married—How weddings are conducted
in Morocco—He sets out on a military expedition—Curious
advice from a Moslem—The march—At Sharroot—Kill hundreds of wild boars—He takes command of the castle (or
Kasbah) of Tannonah—His lazy life during six years—He
marches to Morocco city—Expedition into the mountains . 66

CONTENTS.

CHAPTER III.

The Emperor's troops surprise the castle of Ehiah Embelide, and take vengeance upon the rebels—The march is continued and the revolted towns reduced to submission—Touching divers little places—A new mode of defence—A city is taken by storm—Fire and sword—The return to Morocco with hostages and booty—The Fast of Ramadan—The punishment of a Queen who failed to " nick the time "—Her expiation in the way of bridges and golden balls—Mr. Pellow attempts the madcap freak of trying to steal the latter—The palace gardens and the death of Muley Ar'scìd (Reschid)—The march to Mequinez, and a description of the intervening country—The amount of plunder brought back from the Expedition—Treatment of prisoners—An English executioner—The soldiers meet with their wives—Shooting and fishing—Feasts regardless of the law—Wild beasts and their ways   .   .   .   89

CHAPTER IV.

Mr. Pellow goes with the troops to Guzlan, and shares in the siege of that town—He is wounded—The place surrenders and a number of the inhabitants are beheaded—Our author is advanced in the Moorish service and returns to Tamnsnah —He is now inured to the cruel wars of the Emperor, and takes part in most of his attacks on rebellious tribes and towns—He goes across the Atlas to Tafilet, and enters the desert—How the Royal children are disposed of—The wild Arabs or Bedouins and their ways of life—Bashmagh the negro and his extraordinary adventures—He is sold and sold again by his own request, and always returns with a good horse and weapons—The return to Tafilet—The march to the borders of Algeria—The author often visits his countrymen at Sallee, and begins to meditate his escape—The death of Muley Ismaïl   110

CHAPTER V.

The rise of Muley Ismaïl—His character a mixture of vice and virtue and piety and cruelty—How he made himself master of the kingdom—He clears the country of robbers—His empire—His mode of government—How the governors of provinces are called to account—Degrading ceremonies incumbent on officials before they enter the Imperial presence —His supposed sanctity—His severity against law-breakers —His disturbed sleep—The terror his attendants had for telling him whom he had killed—His duel with a woman—

His Bokhari, or Black Guards—His esteem for them—His
fickleness—The story of an attempted assassination of him—
The influence of Maestro Juan over him—His mania for
building in an economical fashion—His attention to the
affairs of State—Civil war on his death—The contrast between
Muley Hamet Deby and his brothers—Character of Muley
Hamet—How Mr. Pellow's career was influenced by these
turmoils 134

CHAPTER VI.

Mr. Pellow makes a determined attempt to escape from Morocco
—He succeeds in reaching Mazagan, then in the possession
of the Portuguese—He unfortunately, however, mistakes the
Moorish outposts for the Christian, and is seized and sent to
Azamoor—He is thrown into a dungeon and is threatened
with execution—A friend saves him, and he is able to reach
his family in Agoory—The revolt of the Black Army—The
author takes part in the Siege of Fez—He is sent to Sallee
to bring new carriages for the field-guns—Arrived there, he
plots another attempt at freedom—Is betrayed by another
Christian renegado—He saves himself with difficulty, and
abandoning the plan returns to Fez with the gun carriages—
Is well received by Muley Hamet—The author is wounded,
and while thinking of returning to his wife and daughter
hears of the death of both 154

CHAPTER VII.

More uses for wine than one—Mr. Pellow and his renegade attendant find little difficulty in trying how far Malaga is potent
to cure wounds—He amazes his surgeon—Doctor and patient,
their adopted faith notwithstanding, have a merry evening
over the forbidden cup—The surrender of Fez—The humiliation and murder of Abdemeleck—A general beheading *more
Mauritiano*—Muley Hamid Ed-dehèbi is poisoned by Muley
Abdallah's mother—This prince seizes the throne—A new
master but old habits—War again—Fez once more in rebellion—A terrible siege of seven months—Famine compels the
Fasees to yield and meet their retribution—Hopes of escape
again disappointed by a fresh rebellion and a long march—
How malcontents are brought to book 176

CHAPTER VIII.

War is exchanged for commerce—Pellow is sent with the trading
caravan to the coast of Guinea—The route taken by him—
Privations from want of water—How to find it—Wonderful

PAGE

acuteness of the senses displayed by a blind Arab—Lions and
ostriches—How the latter are killed in the desert—Business
being finished on the coast the caravan returns to Morocco—
Displeasure of the Emperor Muley Abdallah at the results of
the journey—He, as usual, slaughters a great many innocent
men—He kills a plotting Marabout or Saint—An expedition
to the River Draa country—A cruel sight—The deaths of
Jerrory and Bendoobash—Treachery of the Emperor—An
easy life again—Hunting and fishing—To Mequinez—War
once more   194

CHAPTER IX.

The truce between England and Morocco broken by the Sallee
men capturing an English ship—A Jewish interpreter burnt
for daring to advise the Emperor—Mr. Pellow meets with an
old schoolfellow in misfortune like himself—The flight of
Muley Abdallah to Tarudant—Another reverse in the fortunes
of war—Muley Ali deposed and Muley Abdallah again Emperor—The fate of a rebellious chief—How the Fez deputation
was treated by Abdallah, and how the blind man spared
utilized his freedom—Our author once more meditates escape
in the confusion of the civil war—A native fortune-teller prophecies fair things for the future—He, at last, makes a burst
for freedom   215

CHAPTER X.

On the road to freedom—At Sallee the fugitive meets with Muley
El Mustadi, afterwards Emperor of Morocco— He is suspected
and arrested, but is permitted to go—Leaves for Mequinez as
a blind, but actually makes for Tedla—Meets a band of conjurers, and, as the result of being in bad company, is robbed
by a rival gang—Falls in with two Spanish quack doctors,
and takes up their trade—He meets an old friend, and practises physic with indifferent success—Fish without fish-hooks
—In peril from wild beasts—Food without lodgings—How a
Moorish highway robber is chowsed—Arrives in Morocco
city, and is succoured by a friend—Sets out for Santa Cruz—
Doctoring on the way   233

CHAPTER XI.

On the road to liberty—Another old friend—An awkward meeting,
but a former enemy is luckily not recognized—Robbed of
everything, Mr. Pellow reaches Tarudant in a woeful plight
—Re-equipped, he arrives at Santa Cruz, and as a measure

of precaution takes up his quarters in a cave, where he meets with strange company—Dreams, and their interpretation—Enters into a new partnership—Takes to duck killing for a livelihood—A new partner of the faint-hearted order—Being again stripped, he "borrows a point of the law" in order to exist—He takes refuge in the Kasbah of Ali Ben-Hamedûsh at the Tensift River—At Willadia he falls in with an old schoolfellow, and, worse luck, meets the mother of Muley Abdallah—Plays the courier, escapes from robbers, and passes the night in a tree, surrounded by wild beasts . . . 260

CHAPTER XII.

Mr. Pellow keeps north—Gets to the Tensift River and again takes shelter in the castle of Ali ben Hammidûh—Back to Saffi—He finds it necessary to try a Cornish hug with a robber on the road—At Willadia, where he meets with English ships—Engages himself as interpreter, when he frustrates a plot of a Moorish merchant to get quit of his obligations—The vessel on which he is on board of is plundered by the knavish officials—The hard way in which ship captains had to transact their business in those days—Mr. Pellow has to keep concealed, as the Moors suspect him—Sails for Sallee—More trouble, which determined the captain to take French leave—As a precaution the Jews and Moors are put under hatches . 289

CHAPTER XIII.

Compelled to anchor off Mamora, fresh troubles make their appearance—Apprehension of an attack from the Moors—Arms are served out; but a fair wind springing up, Mamora is left behind—Distress of an involuntary lady passenger—In passing Cape Spartel, those who had never sailed through the Straits before, pay their footing to those who have—A Jew objects, and what came of his objection—Gibraltar is reached, and the slave, after twenty-three years of captivity, is again a free man among his own countrymen—He is cross-questioned by the officials, and claimed as a Moorish subject by the Emperor's agent—Governor Sabine speaks a bit of his mind—He is well treated, and arrives in the Thames—A painful meeting with William Johnson's sister, and a happy arrival in his native town—The end 313

NOTES 333

INDEX 373

LIST OF ILLUSTRATIONS.

(1) MULEY ABD-ALLAH, EMPEROR OF MOROCCO 1729–1757 (from Troughton's Narrative of the Wreck of the *Inspector* Privateer in 1745) ... ... *Frontispiece*

(2) BRITISH CAPTIVES DRIVEN FROM TANGIER TO MULEY ABD-ALLAH'S CAMP AT BUSCORAN (Bu-Sacran) in the interior of Morocco. 1. Hadj Abd-Akrim, Kaïd, or Governor of Tangier. 2. The British Captives. 3. The City of Mequinez. 4. The Pilot or Guide. 5. Guards who drove the Captives. 6. Tents of the Arabs who supply the town with butter, &c. 7. Sidi Hamria, a saint's tomb (from Troughton). *To face p.* 52

(3) MARAKESCH, OR MOROCCO CITY. *a*, The Kutubia Quarter, in which is situated the Mosque of Sidi Abou Labbas ; *b*, the Atlas Mountains ; *c*, the Garden of Muley Idris ; *d*, a Powder Magazine ; *e*, the Mosque of Ali ben Yusef ; *f*, the Mosque of Abd el Mumen, which, according to some accounts, is the one which possessed the Golden Balls (p. 341); *g*, *h*, the Palace Quarter (from Hosts' "Nachrichten von Marokos und Fes," 1760–1768). *To face p.* 97

(3) AN AUDIENCE OF SIDI MOHAMMED, EMPEROR OF MOROCCO, about the year 1760. *a*, The Emperor ; *b*, five Councillors ; *c*, the Envoy's introducer and attendant ; *d*, the Jewish interpreter ; *e*, a European Envoy with his suite ; *f*, a Courtier ; *g*, Jews bearing gifts, all barefooted (from Host). *To face p.* 135

(4) AZAMOOR IN 1760.　*a*, A saint's tomb; *b*, ferry over the river and the road to Saffi; *c*, the Jewish Quarter or Mellah; *d*, the river Om-er-R'bia; *e*, the road to Sallee (from Host)　...　...　*To face p.* 156

(5) MEQUINEZ IN 1760.　*a, b,* The Palace; *c,* the old Spanish Convent, now abandoned (from Host).

To face p. 185

(6) CHRISTIAN SLAVES AT WORK IN THE CASTLE OF BUSCORAN (BU-SACRAN) NOT FAR FROM MEQUINEZ (1745). 1. The task-masters. 2. The English slaves at hard labour. 3. The manner in which the slaves raised pieces of tabia, weighing ten or twelve tons, " by the purchase of a plank, and then jogging on it, which is fixed at the bottom of the said pieces of tabby wall." 4. The ruins of the remainder of the Castle which the English slaves pulled down. 5. The gate at the entrance of the Castle. 6. The Castle walls (from Troughton) ...　...　*To face p.* 211

(7) SALLEE AND RABAT IN 1760.　In this view Rabat is on the right (*c*) and Sallee on the left side of the picture (*a*), the river Bou-ragrag dividing them. In Rabat, at *b*, there were five cannon, but without carriages or other appurtenances, and lying on the rocks, though sometimes used; at *c* is the town of Rabat proper, though it lies so low that it is not seen over the walls, and cannot therefore be represented in the engraving. The tower, Sma- (or Barge-el) Hassan, is shown at *d*; at *g* is the sea-gate of the town and also the cemetry, the cupolas shown in the view being " kubbas," or tombs of saintly personages, of whom there are a great many in these parts; *f,* a small battery, where a landing is more frequently effected than by passing over the river bar. On the Sallee side (*a*) the entrance to the river is at *e*, where there was a battery of some thirty cannon (from Host)　...　...　*To face p.* 262

(8) SANTA CRUZ, OR AGADIR (from Host)　...　*To face p.* 304

(9) A PIRATE ZEBEK OF SALLEE, 1760 (from Host).

To face p. 335

INTRODUCTION.

THE voyager who sails for North Africa by way of the Spanish Peninsula, is not long before he becomes conscious of the enduring personality of the Moors. At Lisbon even, should he be a philologist, he will find the dialect of the Portuguese boatmen plentifully tinctured with words, phrases, and idioms which may at once be recognized as Arabic. These foreign admixtures grow more numerous as the region once held by the Moorish sovereigns is reached, until in Andalusia there are towns like Tarifa which look more Oriental than European. But it is at Gibraltar and the Strait which separates Spain from Morocco, Christendom from Islam, that the nearness of the true home of the Moors is apparent. Here, is Djebel-Tarik, " the Mountain of Tarik," the spot on which that invader of the country which is still lovingly spoken of as " Andaloss " first set foot. The old Moorish castle forms a prominent object amid the buildings which cover the side of the rock, and the streets are lighted up by the gay costumes of the stately subjects of Muley-El-Hassan from the African side of the narrow gut, which the Scandinavians knew as Norfa's Sound. East and west of Gibraltar the shore is dotted at intervals by tumbling towers, where, within the memory of man, wake-fires blazed for the purpose of warning the country when a Moorish raid was expected; and half the legends which the peasants tell are filled with gruesome memories of the days when the sea between the Pillars of Hercules was scoured by desperate pirates, intent on pillaging the commerce of Christendom and carrying into slavery the hapless crews of the captured vessels.

The two sides of this division between Europe and Africa do not differ widely. If the season when they are sighted is spring, they are equally green with the early herbage, variegated with a hundred flowers, and fragrant with the blossoms of orange, and oleander, and prickly pear. But autumn finds them both alike brown, and bare, and dry. Yet it is scarcely possible to point to any other twelve miles of water which divides two lands more the antipodes of each other, so far as manners and faith and future are concerned. For they intervene between the Cross and the Crescent, between Europe with its progressive culture and Africa with its unadvancing barbarism. In an hour we are back into the middle ages—we seem to have steamed a thousand miles. And all this holds true of "brown Barbary" until the exotic civilization of Algeria is reached in one direction, and the still less native polish of Senegambia in an opposite course. Along the Mediterranean shore of Morocco there are a few posts to which Spain clings tenaciously; but along the Atlantic sea-board Muley-El-Hassan is not offended by the flouting of an infidel flag, until he come to Ifini, on the border of the Empire, where Spain is supposed to have a fishing-station—unless indeed the English trading-post at Cape

Juby is within his bounds. For when there are indemnities
to be paid for outrages, the Sultan denies his responsibility
for the tribesmen thereabouts; but he is apt to play the
King when there are duties in the wind.

As we sail southward along the tawny African *The Sallee*
shore, we pass many a decaying town, the *Rovers.*
white houses of which look like huge cubes of chalk heaped
along the strand. Here for instance are Azila, and
Larache, and Mamora, with little to tempt a merchant to
tarry; and by and by a picturesque collection of white
buildings on either side of a river, over the bar of which
the breakers moan in wearisome monotony, attracts the
eye. A sea-wall with some not very dangerous looking
guns, the minarets of a few mosques, and the great tower
of Sma-Hassan behind, form a scene seemingly more sug-
gestive to the artist than to the historian. Yet this is the
twin town of Rabat-Sallee, which has a long chronicle of
blood and slaughter, and has perhaps been the scene of as
much misery as any spot between Agadir and Algiers.
For Sallee was, during several ages, the capital of those
Moslem pirates who divided with the Tunisians, Tripo-
litines, and Algerines, the evil eminence of doing more
damage to commerce than any other set of sea-robbers at
large. Over that bar has passed in tears and sadness,
hopeless as the entrants into Dante's Inferno, thousands
of Christian * captives, from the period when first this port
conceived the idea of growing wealthy by other means

* In the Barbary States religion is the great division between one
people and another. All who are not Moslems are " Christians " if they
are not Jews, albeit their Christianity is often of the slenderest character. Indeed, as an Arab once told me, the Jews would soon have
everything were it not that they keep their Sunday. But the " Christians " in Morocco regarding all days alike, get just twenty-four hours
ahead of the pan-absorbing Israelites. Hence we hear in Barbary of
Christian clothes, of Christian swindlers, and even of Christian oaths.

than decent toil, until the wrath of Europe and the shoaling up of their harbour no longer permitted of piracy being profitable.   Yet while it lasted, the " Sallee Rovers " bulked more largely in history and romance, and were the cause of more diplomatic missions, correspondence and expense, than it seems possible to believe so despicable a band of ruffians could ever become to maritime powers owning guns enough to pound this den of thieves into its native dust.

Origin of Morocco Piracy.   The stereotyped tale told of the origin of Barbary piracy is that the Moors, driven out of Spain, took revenge upon the Christians by preying on their shipping.   I have long seen good reasons for doubting the universal accuracy of this statement.   The Moriscoes of Spain were for the most part an inland people with little sea-borne commerce, and few ships of any sort, while their Christian compatriots were in possession of a large and powerful fleet.   It is therefore difficult to understand how a race unaccustomed to maritime warfare became so speedily, merely by the stimulus of hatred, the most skilful corsairs of the years succeeding their arrival on the opposite shores of Africa.   Those who fled to what is now Algeria and Tunis might, no doubt, have taken more aptly to their new trade.   For the Turks were there already, and besides having at their disposal a plentiful supply of Greek and Italian apostates, all expert in seafaring wickedness, these Moslems had long been accustomed to traverse the Mediterranean either as " common carriers," or for the more congenial purpose of obeying the mandate of the prophet touching the spoiling of the Infidel.

But no such ready teachers were to be found in Morocco. The truth seems to be that the Sallee men, and their brother pirates in the few other parts of Morocco not in the hands of Spain and Portugal, were taught their trade by European outlaws, the majority of whom were sea-robbers chased from the English coasts, and that they in their turn imparted their knowledge to the latest refugees from Spain. This is clearly shown by a statement of the famous Captain John Smith, of Virginia, who it may be remembered "took a turn," as Dugald Dalgetty would have said, in the Sultan of Morocco's service. This passage,* though of great historical value, seems to have been strangely neglected even by those writers who profess to obtain their information at first hand. For here we learn that the most "ancient pyrats" on the English coast within the threescore years over which Smith's recollection extended, were "one Cellis, who refreshed himself upon the coast of Wales; Clinton and Pursser, being companions who grew famous till Queene Elizabeth of blessed memory hanged them at Wapping; Flemming was as expert and as much sought for as they, yet such a friend to his country, that discovering the Spanish Armada, he voluntarily came to Plimouth, yeelded himselfe freely to my Lord Admirall, and gave him notice of the Spaniards comming; which good warning came so happily and unexpectedly that he had his pardon and good reward." †

The vigilance of the armed merchantmen was, however, so great, that until the peaceful reign of James I. let loose a host of privateers or "men of warre" who had been amply employed in the stormy times of Elizabeth, there were very few rovers at large. They were all good patriots enriching themselves by robbing the Queen's Enemies

* "The Trve Travels, Adventvres and Observations of Captaine Iohn Smith in Europe, Asia, Africke, and America, beginning about the yeere 1593, and continued to the present, 1629 " (1630), pp. 59–60.

† This is an even more picturesque tale than Macaulay's "gallant merchant ship," apart from the fact of the one story being true, and the other only a poet's figment.

along the Spanish Main. But in the early years of the seventeenth century a host of masterless men were left at large without anything to do, or much taste for an honest calling. Then " those that were poor, or had nothing but from hand to mouth, turned Pirats : some because they became slighted of them for whom they had got such wealth ; some for that they could not get their due ; some, that had lived bravely, would not abase themselves to poverty ; some vainly, only to get a name ; others for revenge, covetousnesse, or as ill ; and as they found themselves more and more oppressed, their passions increasing with discontent, made them turne Pirats." Hunted out of the European seas, hosts of these knaves retired to Barbary, and there " turning Turk," entered the service of the Grand Seigneur, who by his deputies, the Dey of Algiers, the Bey of Tunis, and the Bashaw of Tripoli, had taken very kindly to the ancient trade of Piracy.* But several preferred Morocco, where for a time they did famously well. " Ward a poore English sailer, and Dansker a Dutchman, made first here their marts, when the Moores knew scarce how to saile a ship : Bishop was ancient and did little hurt : but Easton got so much as made himselfe a Marquesse in Savoy : and Ward lived like a Bashaw in Barbary : these were the first that taught the Moores to be men of warre." Now and then they came to condign grief if captured by the galleys of the Knights of Malta, of the Pope, the Florentines, and the Genoese, or by the Dutch and English men-of-war, on the outlook for them. But King James was a merciful prince, when his own life was not in peril, and pardoned whole batches of the captured Corsair captains, though " Gennings, Harris,

---

* For a full account of Piracy in the Barbary States other than Morocco, the reader is referred to Mr. Lane-Poole's " Barbary Corsairs " in the " Story of the Nations " series (1890).

Thompson, and divers others," being taken red-handed in Ireland, a coast much in favour with them, were duly executed at Wapping Old Stairs. They were, however, a lazy set of villains, rioting ashore among Jews, Turks, Moors and worse, until their ill-gotten gains were gone, and soon disgusted their Moslem associates. By and by the latter having learned all they could teach, "beganne to command them as slaves" and the worthless rapscallions they were, one and all. In this way, Captain John Smith tells us—and he is speaking of what he knew as well as any of those contemporary with the events described— the Sallateens—as the Sallee folk were called—became so powerful that by the advent of Charles I. they were the terror of "all the Straights," and even of the merchantmen in the Atlantic and in "the narrow seas of England," where their armed vessels were often seen.

This explanation of the origin of the Morocco pirates is confirmed by the fact that, on the Portuguese capturing Mamora, they found * it a perfect kennel of European outlaws—English, French, and Dutch, but few Italian or Spanish—the offscourings of every port, who, like the " squaw men " of the West, and the " Beach Combers " of the Pacific, led a congenial existence among the Barbarians. But when the Sallee Rovers first occupy a prominent plan in history—and they appear very often in the Public Records of the two and a half centuries between the eras of Elizabeth and George IV.—they were to all intents and purposes Moors, though now and then a Renegade Captain is noted as in command.

Sallee had, indeed, soon after the establishment of Muley Ismaïl on the united throne of **The way of the Sallateens.** Morocco, become a sort of Republic, under a Bashaw of the Emperor's appointment, but otherwise to a

* *Note* 40.

large extent self-governing. The Emperor not only shared in their plunder and winked at their inequity, but actually provided the vessels, though it was not until Sallee lost its *quasi-*independence that the Sultan became his own pirate, and took all the profits. Even then he preyed, nominally at least, only on the commerce of the Christian States with which he was at enmity, or had not been bribed to keep at peace. In truth, he was not very particular, disputes continually arising over the unfriendly nations sailing under the flags of the friendly ones, and exhibiting their "passes." But when the Sallateens were most flourishing, there was no pretence of favouring any flag; and at the very time the "rovers" were bringing their prizes into the Bou-ragreg River, there were merchants of all nations living peacefully in the pirate town, and even Consuls (Jews generally and traders always) accredited to the country, and yet powerless or reluctant to interfere. The rise of the twin-town, after the combined attack upon it by Muley Zidan's forces by land and Charles the First of England's fleet on the seaward side, and its elasticity under various subsequent sieges, were due to the wealth which the lucrative trade of the majority of the inhabitants poured into the Corsairs capital. At all events, in the reign of George I., when the hero of this volume made his first involuntary visit to it, Sallee was flourishing, and continued to prosper for many years afterwards.

This port was especially in favour with the pirates, mainly because the others were in the hands of foreign powers. But after Mamora, Azila, and El Arish (Larache) were taken from Portugal, and Tangier was abandoned by England, all of these places, and especially the first, shared in its evil reputation, though the destruction of the mole, the remains of which can still be seen above the surface of the sea at low water, coupled with the proximity of Gibraltar, rendered the latter a less convenient shelter than it would otherwise have been. When it suited the Sultan's purpose, he disowned responsibility for Sallateens, declaring, as he did at a later date in the case of the Riff Pirates, that they were beyond his jurisdiction. At other times, he treated them simply as privateers who paid him well for the privilege of preying with impunity on the Nazarenes. Yet in January, 1745, at a date when England was at peace with Muley Abdallah, the crew of the *Inspector*, a British privateer wrecked in Tangier Bay, were seized and detained for five years in captivity at Mequinez and Fez; the Emperor being evidently of opinion that, as another Moorish monarch remarked on being reproached with breaking a treaty, a Moslem should not, like a Christian, " be the slave of his word." Indeed, had Muley El-Jezîd been able to take Ceuta, which he besieged twice towards the close of last century, his intention was to use it as a port from whence his galleys might sally forth for the purpose of capturing ships passing through the Straits, without much punctilio as to the flags which they flew.

The Moors' capacity for ship-building rarely permitted of vessels much larger than thirty, forty, or at the outside sixty tons being built by themselves, by the renegadoes, or by their Christian slaves; and even when they captured larger craft suited for their purpose, the difficulty of getting them over the bars of the Bou-ragreb and Sebou, rivers which were yearly more and more shoaling up the harbours of Sallee and Mamora, rendered them chary of utilizing such windfalls. Muley Abdallah and his son, Sidi Mohammed, swaggered loudly about their intention of fitting out larger vessels capable of cruising on the high seas. But their efforts never went very far in that direction, for by the time the latter managed to launch a frigate of forty-five guns, with a crew of 330 men, under

the Reis Hadjj Ben Hassan Houet Shivi, the bar was
so bad that the cannon had to be unloaded into barges
before such a heavy draught vessel could enter the port.
Even Tetuan, which was tried as a harbour, was found
too exposed, in spite of the chains across the Martin
River which were jealously maintained far into this
century, for this fleet, which, if we may judge of the
remnants of it which until lately lay rotting in El
Arish—the Garden of the Hesperides—would be nowadays accounted a sorry task for the smallest of gun-boats
to demolish. But these heavily armed rovers, manned by
bold, desperate ruffians skilled in attack and defence,
were formidable foes for the crew of a merchant-ship of
small tonnage and few hands. Generally the Sallateens
managed to get alongside by flying false colours, or by
pretending to be Algerines, then much dreaded, and often
on some pretence or other weakened the doomed ship's
power of resistance by inducing the captain and some of
the crew to come on board their own vessel. Yet when
fighting was necessary, the Moors seldom showed any
lack of courage, boarding the enemy in gallant style after
she had been disabled by the fire of their artillery. Most
frequently they contented themselves with plundering the
ship, and then either scuttling or setting her adrift. But
the crew were invariably carried into port, for they consti-
tuted the most valuable portion of the prize. The daring
of these Sallateens was occasionally remarkable, for not
only did they attack large ships, and make sudden raids
on the farms and villages of the opposite coast, but in
summer they would venture across the Bay of Biscay,
and lie under the shelter of Lundy Island ready to cut out
vessels sailing down the Bristol Channel. Now and then,
however, they met with sore disasters, and not only were
beaten off with loss, but even had the tables turned upon

them ; while cases are on record in which they were tempted
to try issues with a disguised war-sloop, when, in the
words of an old song describing such an encounter—

> " The answer that we gave them,
>   Did sink them in the sea."

It must have been after some such mishap that, with at
view to keep the peace, the governor ordered every man to
put his thumbs in his girdle the moment the painful
theme was discussed in the street. The Chevalier Acton,
commander of a Tuscan war-ship, falling in with five of
Sidi Mohammed's "xebeks" off Cape Spartel, captured,
ran ashore, or dispersed all of them.

Indeed, the ships which the Sultans built when they
took piracy into their own hands were constantly being
lost by the clumsiness of their captains, as the "Reis"
was selected not so much for his seamanship as for his
ability to pay for any damage which the vessel in his
charge might sustain. The result was extreme caution
on his part, and, as the Emperor took all the profit, a
natural reluctance on the part of the Moors to serve as
sailors—a circumstance which led to a decline in the
number of the prizes taken. But this was not always so.
In Muley Ismaïl's reign, the Sultan claimed ten per cent of
the value of the prize : if he took more than this number
of slaves, which he generally did, the pirates were supposed to receive value for them. Hence, in spite of
many of them being armed with no better artillery than
stones, with which the crew were so violently assailed that
they ran below and allowed their vessel to be easily
boarded, the rovers did a brisk trade. Muley Abdallah
reserved the slaves for himself, paying the pirates for
them at a low fixed rate; but Sidi Mohammed, after
depriving Sallee-Rabat of its semi-independency, com-

manded the Corsairs to act for his profit alone. However, looking upon the slaves as a resource of revenue,
he treated them with more humanity than his father or
grandfather.

How the
captives were
treated.

This was, nevertheless, very much a matter
of chance, depending as it did on the whim of
a despot, or the character of the officials to
whose custody they were committed. The latter were
rarely actuated by kindly feelings to the unfortunates.
Embittered by religious fanaticism, or by the memory
of their countrymen driven out of " Andaloos," drowned
in the Straits, or hung at the yard-arm or toiling in
the Christian galleys, they heaped upon the prisoners
every malediction to be raked out of the foul kennel
of Moorish profanity, cursing their burnt fathers and
unveiled mothers to the remotest generation, and too
frequently emphasizing their words by blows. As
the captives defiled through the filthy lanes to the
underground dungeons—still to be seen—in Sallee, they
were hooted by the rabble, pelted by the children, and
spat upon by the women. And from the hour they left
that town, until ten days later, they arrived footsore and
weary in Fez or Mequinez—then the usual residence of the
Sultan—hard fare, black looks, and constant revilings
were there unvarying lot. In the interior they met with
no countrymen in a position to help them ; all were either
slaves like themselves, or apostates who had forsworn
their king and their faith. But even in the coast
towns the merchants, living as they did by sufferance, and
eager to truckle to the authorities, seldom displayed much
pity for their helpless compatriots. For when they might
have been less timorously discreet, they were afraid lest
any familiarity might lead the officers to imagine that the
captives to whom the foreign trader or " tadjir " showed

attention were people of consequence, and therefore likely to fetch a heavier ransom.

In the capital, the life of the white slaves was no better. There, after being inspected by the Emperor, they were set to work, until overtures for their ransom arrived. This system, it ought in justice to the Moors to be remembered, was not long before in vogue all over Europe. For were not sovereigns seized in passing through the territories of rival princes, and shipwrecked mariners treated in like manner, until their freedom could be purchased for a sum of money proportionate to their rank—a state of matters still kept in memory by the phrase, "a king's ransom"? The only difference was that the Moors were a little behind the progress of the age in following this fashion of a bygone period, just as they are at the present day in selling offices when this method of entering the Civil Service has been abandoned in the realms of Christendom. The slavery of the times to which we refer was dismal in the extreme. Compared with the toil to which thousands of English sailors were put, the life of the negroes in the Southern States of America was a pleasure. Muley Ismaïl and his successors had a mania for building. No Moorish sovereign ever inhabiting the same palace or the same rooms as his predecessor, the slaves were for the most part employed in erecting houses, or in preparing the materials for the masons. This consisted in stamping earth mixed with lime, gravel, and water, in order to make the "taib" or concrete, which after being moulded like bricks in boxes, hardens into blocks almost as lasting as stone. The amalgamation is accomplished by a heavy wooden stamper of about twelve or fifteen pounds weight, being worked, as an old slave of Muley Ismaïl has put on record, "from the Break of Day till Stars appear at Night without intermission or standing still." The whish! whish! of this instrument is still, in the interior cities of Morocco, where no rumble of wheels breaks the stillness of these sleepy hives of Drowsihead, the most frequent sound which reaches the ear. Others were engaged in digging out earth, quarrying limestone, and burning it, or in collecting fuel with which to heat the kilns. Among the many buildings which they erected in Muley Abdallah's reign may be mentioned the palace of Dar Debibeg near Fez, and in Muley Ismaïl's an entire "town for the Jews." The eight-span bridge over the Tensift River near the city of Morocco is also said to have been built by the Portuguese captives who survived the defeat of Dom Sebastian at that battle of Alcazar which has been the theme of so many poems and stories, besides the famous play of George Peele.

In those days wheeled carriages, now all but unknown in the interior of Morocco, appear to have been in use; for the slaves were also employed as carters, and went all day with waggons full of building materials, drawn by bulls and horses yoked together—this incongruous team being nothing out of the way in a country where a camel and a mule may be seen drawing a one-stilted plough, and on two occasions I noted a woman and a donkey harnessed to this primitive agricultural implement. The Christians had even to drag the Moslem artillery. The more skilful mechanics were set to make gunpowder, and to cast cannon—an art which died out after Christian slavery ceased—or to help the native artizans to make or repair small arms. Sawing, cutting, cementing, and erecting marble pillars occupied the time of others. The less able-bodied watched the beasts in the fields at night, attended to the horses, or raised water by the cumbersome wheel still in use. Pulling down old buildings with the rudest tools was another labour to which they were commonly put, and so careless were their overseers that it often happened the slaves were killed or hurt by the falling walls. Their tasks were sometimes superintended by the Emperor Ismaïl in person, and if it suited his humour he would dismount and take a turn with the pickaxe, or the mallet. Yet his presence was even less desired than that of the ordinary overseer; for during the time he remained the slaves were not allowed a moment's rest, not even to stand upright to ease their weary backs or to get a drop of water, though the summer sun was so hot as to blister their half-naked bodies.

Sickness, which soon overtook the whites unused to such toil in such a climate, was not considered any plea for relief, and many a poor fellow worked under the stimulus of the stick until he fell down, and was carried off to die. They were beaten on the slightest provocation or out of mere wantonness, and the most insulting epithets hurled at the poor wretches, in any language of which the drivers happened to have picked up a few words. The daily toil over, they were housed in damp underground cellars, or "Matamoras," or in open sheds exposed to the rain or snow, which in winter sometimes falls to a considerable depth in Fez and Mequinez, where ice an inch thick is by no means unknown. Even there they were not always free of annoyance, by the baser order amusing themselves by throwing stones and clods of dirt at them. "Kaffir!" or "Unbeliever," was about the mildest word addressed to them, and as an Arab generally applies this term to his donkey in the interval of whacks, the opprobriousness of the epithet may be imagined.

To sustain a life of such unending toil the captives were fed very sparingly on the worst of food. Sometimes they were allowed a small sum—about 2d.—to board themselves.

Yet as they were not always permitted to go at large in
the town, and had therefore to entrust their marketing
to some Moor, they were usually cheated out of half their
dues. Clothing they had none except a few rags, so that
the most miserable beggar in Mequinez was better fed and
sheltered than the man who might a few days before have
been the master of a stout ship, or a merchant in a considerable way of business. Occasionally, however, their
feet fell in pleasanter places, in so far that the Emperor
soundly bastinadoed a more than ordinarily brutal overseer, and solaced the injured slaves by sending them a
plentiful supply of " Cuscussoo," the favourite Moorish
dish. Yet a few minutes later, the same uncertain-tempered
tyrant would spear a captive whose mode of work displeased him, or order him to fight with the wild animals
in his menagerie.

In very exceptional cases, the slaves enjoyed a life
almost of freedom, being permitted to engage in trade, and
even to keep taverns, where they made so much money
as to be able to buy their freedom. But the common
lot of a white slave in Morocco, if not worse than that
of the captives in Algiers, Tripoli, or Tunis, was no better,
except that they were seldom employed to row in the
galleys, the Emperor not caring to risk keeping them near
the coast. All classes had to endure this misery, though
as a rule most of them were seamen, and often the higher
the position of the slave the worse he was treated, in order
to stimulate his friends to send all the sooner the large
ransom demanded for him. Often after obtaining their
liberty, the captives' constitutions were seriously injured
by their treatment in Barbary, though, judging from the
pious titles of the narratives which they wrote on their
return, and the religious reflections after the manner of
Robinson Crusoe on his island, or of Master Pellow at the

outset of his story, their moral fibre was considerably improved by the chastening they had endured. But in all my reading of these quaint little volumes, I cannot remember more than one instance in which a captive's physique was benefited by his travail among the infidels. This exception was that of Sir Jeffrey Hudson, the peppery dwarf of Charles I., who went into captivity eighteen inches high, and emerged therefrom three feet and a quarter, a result which the little man attributed to the hard work he had to perform.

There have, however, been instances in which the slaves utilized the experience they gained for the mutual benefit of themselves and their relations. A romantic instance of this is commemorated by a huge tenement in the Canongate of Edinburgh, still known as "Morocco Land." Though now inhabited by the poorest people, it bears like many houses in that street the traces of former grandeur. Over the alley passing under it is a Latin legend :—

"MISERERE MEI, DOMINE : A PECCATO, PROBO, DEBITO ET MORTE SUBITA. LIBERA ME 1.6.18 "—

and from a recess above the second floor projects the effigy of a Moor, a black naked man, with a turban and necklace of beads. This was evidently the notion entertained by the Scottish artist of 1618 regarding an African potentate belonging to the same race as Othello, who even yet, with a realism to which ethnology lends no countenance, is represented by a negroised personage. The tradition attaching to this building is, that early in the reign of James I., a Scottish girl having been captured by a Sallee Rover, became a favourite with the then Emperor of Morocco. Desirous of utilizing her influence for the benefit of her brother, she sent for him, and he, proving

successful in his commercial dealings, returned home, and
erected this mansion, on the façade of which he set up the
effigy of his imperial brother-in-law and benefactor. This
is one legend. But there are several others, and possibly
the following alternative one is quite as picturesque, and
perhaps not less historical. It is to the effect that soon after
the accession of Charles I., the house of the Lord Provost
—or chief magistrate—was set on fire by a mob led
by Andrew Gray, the scapegrace cadet of a noble
family, who, in spite of all the influence brought to bear
upon the judges, was condemned to be hanged. But
before the day appointed for his execution arrived, the
culprit managed to escape, and was forgotten, until, many
years subsequently, a Barbary pirate appeared in the
Frith of Forth, and demanded an enormous ransom from
the city. At that hour the town was so depopulated by
the plague that there were not sixty able-bodied men
capable of resisting the fierce Corsairs. The stricken
citizens had perforce, therefore, to agree to their terms.
But the Provost was unable to send his son as a hostage
for the fulfilment of the contract, for his only child was
a daughter, and she was dying of the epidemic. On
hearing this the pirate captain declared that he had an
elixir which would cure her, and that if he failed, the city
should get quit of the promised ransom. The lady was
cured, and then the pirate-physician revealed his identity.
He was the fugitive Andrew Gray, who, entering the
service of the Emperor of Morocco, had returned on board
this pirate ship determined to take vengeance on the city
which had so despitefully used him. But love was then
as now " the lord of all," and so the Sallee Reis abjured
roving, married the Provost's daughter, and died a sober
citizen in the town where he had begun life so untowardly.
He it was, according to this version, who fixed the

Emperor's bust on the house to which he brought his bride, and where in his piratical days he cured her of the plague. This was in 1645, the year in which Muley El-Valid, the most clement of the El-hhoseini dynasty, died, and his brother Muley Ahmed-Sceikh, last of the sons of Muley Zidan, began his indolent reign. History, very fragmentary so far as the Morocco of those times is concerned, has preserved no trace of this repentant renegade. But, curiously enough, Sir Daniel Wilson, the eminent archæologist, tells us that though the existing title-deeds of Morocco Land do not extend further back than 1731, the owner at that date was one John Gray, who might therefore have been a descendant of the Sallee Rover and the Provost's daughter.

How far this pretty tale is true cannot now be known for certain. But except that it is doubtful whether in 1645 the Sultan of Morocco had any vessels large enough to venture as far as Scotland, there is nothing in either variant not in accordance with actual incidents in the romantic chronicles of Moroquin slavery. The mother of Muley Abdallah—the astute Lalla Yoneta or Khoneta—is said to have been an English captive, and among the many other wives of Muley Ismaïl were ladies of Spanish, English, Greek, and other European nationalities. Thus the mother of Muley El-Valid was a Spaniard, and that of Muley es Shereef—often mentioned in Pellow's narrative— " a Christian " until she " turned Moor." Early in last century a Mrs. Shaw, an Irishwoman, was a temporary inmate of his harem, but in 1727 she was seen in Mequinez in rags, the wife of a Spanish renegado, and so far lost to civilization as to have forgotten her native tongue in the course of the nine years she had been in captivity. Muley Ismaïl had even the effrontery to demand in marriage the Mdlle. de Blois, afterwards Princess de

Conti, daughter of Louis XIV. of France and Mademoiselle de la Vallière, an incident which forced the wits of Versailles into verse, of which J. B. Rousseau's lines are perhaps not the worst :—

> " Votre beauté, grand princesse,
>   Porte les traits dont elle blesse,
>   Jusques aux plus sauvages lieux ;
>   L'Afrique avec vous capitule
>   Et les conquêtes de vos yeux
>   Vont plus loin que celles d'Hercule."

One of the first wives wed by Sidi Mohammed was Lalla Seersceta, or Zazet, daughter of an Irish or—as other legends affirm—a Hessian renegade; and one of his last was Lalla Douvia, a member of the Genoese family of Francischini. But though the first-named lady was the mother of Muley El-Jezîd, the present Sultan being descended not from that sovereign, but from his brother, Muley Hisciam (the son of another wife), cannot, as often said, have "Irish blood in his veins." There is, no doubt, a tale told how the widow of an Irish sergeant of artillery who had been employed by the father or grandfather of Muley El-Hassan, finding favour in the Sultan's eyes, and being a "lone woman," accepted his Majesty's offer, and so rose into lofty rank as the mother of the future Emperor. But except as a confused version of Sidi Mohammed's matrimonial venture, I cannot find any basis for this bit of Hibernian romance. Again, some of the captives now and then managed to obtain considerable influence over the Sultan. Thus, Muley Ismaïl's doctor was a Spanish slave, and the " Maestro Juan," who exercised such power that he was denied almost nothing, seems to have been a Catalonian captive, noted for his sincerity, discretion, and good works. The Spanish prisoners, however, like the Portuguese, though allowed a chaplain and a hospital in Mequinez, were never regarded with the same goodwill as those belonging to other nationalities. Abdallah, Pellow's last master, would seldom permit them to be ransomed, in revenge for the hardships inflicted upon the Moorish captives in the galleys of Cadiz and Lisbon, and on the Moriscoes when they were driven out of the Peninsula. As the English did not then enslave their captives, the Emperor treated our people rather better, though none of them were quite pampered either by him or by his successor. Yet Muley El-Jezîd, the "Red Sultan," amidst all his truculence, bestowed marked favours on the countrymen of his mother, albeit that lady received little filial affection at his hands.

The Moors had, however, no great liking for Christians simply as slaves, though Muley Ismaïl, for ostentation's sake, kept great numbers about him. Negroes were in every respect better servants— unless the captive happened to be a skilled artificer—and made no attempt to escape. This, it is needless to add, the captured Christians never ceased to regard as a possibility. Ransom was therefore what they were detained in the hope of bringing. The wealthier only could usually arrange for this being sent from home. The poorer ones, if Roman Catholics, looked to the Fathers of Our Lady of Mercy, or to the Trinitarian, or Mercenarian, or Redemptionist Fathers, orders specially charged with the collection of money for the ransom of "Christians among the infidels," and to undertake the weary, and oftentimes dangerous, journeys demanded by their benevolent missions. The English bondmen lived in hope of the king sending, as he usually did, a periodical embassy for the purpose of obtaining the freedom of his enslaved subjects. If this failed, there were pious benefactions like that which Thomas Betton left in trust with the Ironmongers' Company for the express purpose of redeeming those so

Ransom or Escape.

unfortunate as to experience the fate which had been his.
At every church door also there were collections for the
manumission of poor sea-faring folk who had been "taken"
by Algerines or Salleteenes, so that with patience there
was always a chance of the slave seeing his native land
again. But as the experience of many of them proved,
by and by meant an indefinite number of years. Even
when the Sultan was willing to free them there were endless obstacles in the way, and it is feared that not
unfrequently the "Christian merchants" and the Jews,
who somehow or other managed to squeeze a profit out of
the Nazarenes' toil, did something to retard their ransom;
for as the Sultan did not care to be paid for his prisoners
in money, but in ammunition, arms, and the like, the
traders in the coast towns found a less lucrative customer
in him than they would otherwise have done. Nor were
the apostates very fond of seeing their countrymen who
had been more steadfast in the faith receiving the reward
of their endurance. Hence, dealing as the agents did with
a shifty despot, they had sometimes to return without
accomplishing their errand. Even when they succeeded,
the average cost was between two and three hundred
dollars for the purchase of each captive, and when
Moorish prisoners were accepted in exchange it was seldom
that the rate was lower than ten of the Faithful for one of
the Unbelievers; and when manuscripts left in Spain were,
as in one instance, accepted in barter, the ratio was fixed
in a manner quite as disproportionate.

To escape was not so easy. The captives were closely
watched, and treachery among their own number was constantly to be dreaded; for just as misfortune brings out
the heroic in the humblest of souls, so does it develop the
baseness of the worser sort. All kinds of expedients were
adopted to enable the runaways to get a start before they

were missed, or to avoid pursuit when they were on the road. In Algiers it was comparatively easy to make a burst for freedom; for as that city is on the sea-shore boats could be seized, and ship captains found ready to run the risk of concealing the white slaves determined to be free. But in Fez or Mequinez or Marrakesch * a long journey through hostile tribes and a roadless country had to be undertaken, and after the Europeans had abandoned Tangier, Azila, Larache, Mamora, Mazagan, Saffi, and Agadir, it was even more dangerous for the captive to arrive at the sea in the hope of being able to make the European coast. However, Christian slaves were numerous, and so it occasionally happened that the runaway managed not to attract attention. But if caught, the bastinado was about the mildest punishment he could expect. In Muley Ismaïl's day he would most likely have been tortured, or speared, and his captors been compelled with cruel irony to pay the Sultan for the loss he had sustained by the death of so presumptively valuable a piece of property.

Comparatively few, therefore, had either a chance to undertake the risk of this venture, or the courage to face the fate which would certainly await them if they failed.

There was, however, a last expedient to escape the misery of daily toil, and this **Renegadoes.** many a faint heart adopted at an early stage of his captivity. They "turned Moor." In other words they became Apostates, or, as the Spaniards call them, Renegadoes or Renegades, by professing, in name at least, the Mohammedan faith. Then, though it did not always ensue that they were free to follow their own inclinations so long as they did not leave the country, they usually received a remission of much of their toil, since it was accounted infamous not to treat the "convert" as a being very much

* The Moorish name for Morocco city.

superior to his Christian brethren. The number of these
renegades was at one time very great. In 1690, it was
estimated that very few of the 2,000 people captured at the
surrender of Mamora had not abjured their faith, and that
only 400 out of the 1,800 enslaved at the fall of Larache
were "not then Moors."

And no doubt, to loose-living sailors, there was an often
irresistible temptation to take this course. The love of a
swarthy lass, the desire for an easier life, the yearning to
take vengeance on the task-masters who had so cruelly
treated them when protest was unavailing, and finally
the belief that by an outward show of Mohammedanism
their opportunities for escape would be greater, were among
the mixed motives which instigated this step. Nevertheless, as Pellow's experience shows, even the renegade did
not always find his exodus from the house of bondage so
easy as he had expected. The women almost invariably
adopted the faith of their captors. Then they disappeared
into the harems, and were seen of christened men no more.
Their lot, always a miserable one, was not lightened by the
hope of ransom; for, as subjects of the Sultan—as all
renegades were regarded — they were excluded from the
bounty of the "redemptors," and from their secluded
position, escape, if ever they had any care to return in
dishonour to their native land, was all but impossible.
The captives were, however, not usually importuned to
change their religion, unless it happened that they fell into
the hands of bigots; for as there was an implied contract
that they were to be free, every Christian "turned Moor"
meant simply one slave less to his Moslem master. Nor
were they much esteemed, or trusted more than the majority
of them deserved, for the sincerity of people who so readily
turned their religious coat at the bidding of self-interest
was naturally suspected. A large number of them were,

in truth, unmitigated rascals of no creed, and ready to play into the hands of the Moors or of the Christians alike, and to betray both as seemed to promise most profit for themselves. Hence an "Oodali" or Christian pervert was —and is to this day—regarded by the Moors as only a trifle better than an "Aselami" or turncoat Jew, who is considered as having reached about the lowest depth to which human nature can descend. Yet Israelitish regenades are frequent, the motive at work in their nominal conversion being almost always a desire to escape the disabilities of the race, or a hope of gaining something thereby. In the early days of the Arab invasion of Morocco most of the little Atlas tribes of Jews abandoned their faith, and the late Grand Vizier, Sid Mohammed Ben Araby, uncle of the Emperor by marriage, was the chief of one of these supposed renegade communities, a rumour to which his markedly Hebraic features lent ample countenance.

The renegadoes got wives, but it was seldom that they were permitted, like Haidee's corsair father, to wed

"... a Moorish maid from Fez,
Where all is Eden or a wilderness."

Most frequently they had to content themselves with negresses, women of low degree, or the daughters of other renegades, and thus to become a class by themselves. Even their children were despised. Muley Ismaïl actually ordered an investigation to be made, so that the offspring of slaves and renegades might either be taxed or reduced to the condition of their forefathers. In Fez and Mequinez there are still swarms of people descended from European ancestors, and easily distinguished by their fair complexion, and not infrequently fair hair. Agoory, a town where Pellow lived for many years, is almost entirely peopled by them. Muley Ismaïl, after a renegade had attempted his assassination, determined to have about him as few of the *Mala Casta* (to use the Spanish name for them) as possible. Accordingly, he transported about 1,500 of them to the distant province of Draa, which, on that account, was long known as the Land of the Apostates—and in the chief town of that region their descendants live to this day, little, if anything, distinguishable from the natives around them.

Still, one or two of greater cunning, ability, or knavery, managed to attain considerable positions in the country. Thus several of the vilest, unable to return with safety to their own countries, were captains of pirate vessels. As late as 1780, "Omar," a Scotchman, was "Reis" of a "zebck" of sixteen guns and 124 men; and early in last century a Monsieur Pillet, a former French merchant and a friend of Pellow's, was for twelve months governor of Sallee. "One Carr," a renegade, was in 1727 Kaïd of the Jews, and had been governor "on the frontiers of Guinea," though he preferred offices less apt to incur malice; while it is scarcely necessary to recall the romantic tale of the Duke of Ripperda, who, to take vengeance on Spain, of which he had been Prime Minister, crossed the Straits, and as the Grand Vizier of Muley Abdallah did his best to serve his adopted country, and finally, after having been successively Protestant, Roman Catholic, and Mohammedan, passed the closing years of his life in trying to persuade the Moors of Tetuan that he was the last of the Prophets.

The little esteem in which these apostates were held is shown by the fact that Christians who had made no pretence of adopting Islam were readily employed by the Sultans. Thus, among the principal architects and military engineers in the service of Sidi Mohammed and his successors, were Cornut, a Frenchman; Petrobelli, a Triestan;

de Pietrasanta, a Tuscan ; and Chiappe, a Genoese. As a
rule the renegades were employed as soldiers, kept at
work far from the coast, or quartered in distant " kasbahs "
until they got knocked on the head by the plundered
country people. In Muley El-Jezid's reign Mogador was
garrisoned by 250 French turncoats—wrecked seamen who
had apostatized to save their lives—commanded by Boisselin, the son of a Parisian hatter, who had voluntarily
chosen the faith and service of the Sultan, and it would
appear that Pellow and others were raised to considerable
posts in the army. These voluntary apostates were, however, generally scoundrels who had left their country for their
country's good, escaped convicts from the Spanish fortresses
on the coast, or individuals who found in the license of a
semi-lawless land a life more agreeable than that to which
they would have had to submit in Europe. They therefore
seldom attempted to leave. But the captives generally
cherished secret longings in that direction.

Pellow's Narrative. If they managed to accomplish this aim,
their home-coming was an event too rare not
to excite much attention, and though " interviewing " was
then uninvented, some particulars about them usually
found their way into the news sheets, and not infrequently
the manumitted bondman was presented to the king, in
the hope of obtaining through his Majesty's bounty a
pecuniary solace for the hardships he had undergone. As
a means of " raising the wind," the escaped seaman sometimes, with the aid of the local schoolmaster, or other
literary character, tried to write an account of his adventures, which he hawked about the country, or disposed of
by subscription. I have collected upwards of a score of
these quaintly written, badly printed, dog-eared, narrow-
margined narratives, and possess a copy of one in Dutch
which is believed to be unique, as it is unknown to any of

3

the bibliographers of Batavian literature. How far these narratives were actually the work of the ostensible writers, it is not now easy to ascertain. Nor does it matter. They had assistance, no doubt. The bits of fine writing, the ponderous periods, and the occasional scraps of Latinity, bespeak the parson; while the "padding" out of the slim volume with unacknowledged extracts from other authors, cheek-by-jowl with moral reflections, smacks of the literary gentleman who lodged at "the thief-catcher's in Lewkner's Lane, and wrote against the impiety of Mr. Rowe's plays." For in those days, years after Defoe had penned his deathless classic, Grub Street was very busy with the Sallee rovers and Barbary slavery, as Robert Chetwood's "Adventures of Captain Boyle," and the "Voyages of William Owen Gwin Vaughan" abundantly testify. Such help was necessary, for, with few exceptions, the Barbary bondmen were "no scholars." Even when they could write, many of them had almost forgotten their mother tongue, and the fact that Pellow still spoke English may have been due to his better early education, and to his continually conversing with other English captives either in the interior or in the coast towns.

Pellow's little-known work is perhaps the most valuable of these personal narratives. For not only did he travel further than most of his fellows in misfortune, but he lived longer in Morocco. At first, I was a little suspicious of its authenticity, mainly from the fact that several of the pages were verbatim, and not always acknowledged, extracts from Windus' "Journey to Mequinez." But it was soon evident that these interpolations had been sandwiched into Pellow's account by the original editor in order to pad out the book, for they were lugged in without any regard to the sequence by a person ignorant of Morocco, and too illiterate even to put his literary loot into his own words. Much the same extracts appear in Troughton's account of the wreck of the *Inspector*, and to some extent also in Ockley's work, and in the English edition of Chenier's history. We may therefore presume that in an age of no copyright, and consequently of loose morality, Windus' oft-pirated volume seems to have been regarded as a free warren for the first poacher who passed that way.

The essential truthfulness of the book was however easily demonstrable. Rivers, towns, and other localities were mentioned which at the time were not to be found on any map and in no work; while the phonetic spelling—though not more phonetic than some by more scholarly travellers of a later period—showed that the author could not have consulted "Authorities," otherwise he would have adopted the usual orthography. Events are noted and men mentioned who, though now familiar, were at the date of his writing strangers to European fame, and indeed were not celebrated in print for years subsequently. Here and there, as I have shown in the appended notes, Pellow makes blunders when, had he been inventing a history, he would have insured accuracy by pillaging from early accessible books capable of supplying the necessary information.

To this may be added that the Pellow family are still numerous in and about Penryn, and that the people mentioned in the course of the narrative have enabled us to check the statements made by him. Colonel James, who wrote a description of the Gibraltar Straits, saw the MS. of the book, and finally, if further proof were necessary that Thomas Pellow was a real personage, this is supplied in a manner which admits of no possible cavil. In the course of his narrative he casually notes that "Captain Russel" had arrived in Morocco, but vouchsafes no other information regarding him. But in turning to Braithwaite's account of Mr Russel's embassy, we find a

confirmatory description of Pellow—or Pilleau, as he spells
the name — under date Nov. 27, 1727: "To-day were
visited [in Mequinez] by one Pilleau, a young fellow of
good family in Cornwal but now turned Moor. He was
taken very young with Captain Pilleau his Uncle, and being
a handsome boy he was given by Muley Ismael to one of
his sons. The Christian captives gave this young man a
wonderful character, saying he endured enough to have
killed seven men, before his master could make him turn.
Pilleau being taken very young spoke the Arabick language
as well as the Moors, and having traversed this vast country
even to the frontier of Guinea, was capable of giving a very
good account of it. He is at present a soldier, as all the
renegadoes are, who have no particular trade or calling;
but their allowance of pay and corn is so small that they
are in a starving condition, being obliged to rob and plunder for the greatest part of their subsistence; for which
they were often killed when taken." We also find from
other allusions that he frequently acted as interpreter for
the Embassy.

Apart, however, from its interest as a tale of strange
adventures, Pellow's narrative, written thirteen years
subsequent to the date of this interview, is valuable as a
geographical document, though, strangely enough, it has
been neglected by Renou and other commentators on the
topography of Morocco, and does not find a place in any of
the imperfect bibliographies of Moroquin literature. Yet
Pellow visited many parts of the country for the first time,
and several which not improbably have not been seen by
any other European traveller. He was, moreover, a soldier
under Muley Ismaïl, Muley Dehèbhi, Muley Abdelmalek, and
Muley Abdallah, and was an eye-witness to most of the
sanguinary episodes of their reigns. His tale appears to
have been compiled by the aid of notes of some kind

though in not a few instances his memory was too implicitly relied upon for distances, dates, and the names of places. This he confesses, when it would have been easy enough for a less conscientious author to have invented what he had forgotten. For as Sir John Maundevile puts it, "thinges passed out of long tyme from a Mannes mynde or from his syght, turnen sone into forzetynge."

The book, of which two editions were " Printed by R. Goadby, and sold by W. Owen, Bookseller at Temple Bar, London," was issued without date, in 1740, under the following prolix title :—" The History of the Long Captivity and Adventures of Thomas Pellow, in South-Barbary. Giving an Account of his being taken by two Sallee Rovers, and carry'd a Slave to Mequinez, at Eleven Years of Age: His various Adventures in that Country for the Space of Twenty-three Years: Escape, and Return Home. In which is introduced, a particular Account of the Manners and Customs of the Moors ; the astonishing Tyranny and Cruelty of their Emperors, and a Relation of all those great Revolutions and Bloody Wars which happen'd in the Kingdoms of Fez and Morocco, between the Years 1720 and 1736. Together with a Description of the Cities, Towns, and Public Buildings in those Kingdoms; Miseries of the Christian Slaves; and many other Curious Particulars. Written by Himself." This anachronistic periphrasis we have somewhat abridged. But with the exception of the omission of some of the passages stolen from other authors, the body of this volume is a full reprint of the mariner's curious tale. Even the illiterate spelling of the names has not been altered, for the author evidently wrote them without much idea of Arabic orthography ; so that any attempt to modernize them might prevent the less patent ones from being deciphered. The notes, however, which I have appended will elucidate the more obscure allusions. Altogether, the book may be treated as a fairly accurate picture of Morocco between 1715 and 1738, in addition to being an account of twenty-three years' unique experience in a country still only partially known, and in those days even less familiar to Europe. I am the more confirmed in this opinion by the fact that my accomplished young friend, Mr. Budgett-Meakin, of Tangier, who printed the greater part in the "Times of Morocco," and to whom I am indebted for some of the modern names and vernacular Arabic, has, in common with other English residents, arrived at the same conclusion regarding its authenticity, though until now its importance in the history of Moroquin geography has not been recognized.

The Suppression of Slavery in Morocco. But of "all good things there cometh an end." And thus in the fulness of time a traffic so lucrative as that of the capture and enslavement of Christians began to draw to a close. Europe was getting stronger and Morocco weaker. All of the Barbary States had been feeling the heavy hand of the Nazarenes, and Morocco was not long to escape. In 1791, England framed a treaty confirming one of a previous date which gave our merchants much greater liberty than they had hitherto enjoyed, and permitted any renegade to return to his old faith so long as he had not appeared on three separate days before the governor of a city or province and the English Consul, declaring each time his resolution to remain a Mussulman. Prisoners, were, however, still "taken" and still ransomed as of old. But in 1800 Muley Suliman agreed with Spain that there should be a reciprocal interchange of captives, and similar contracts were soon afterwards entered into with other powers. Then, in 1817, Suliman agreed to disarm his war vessels, and formally put an end to the system which had so long prevailed, a course to which he was the more readily persuaded by hearing of the trouble which had befallen Tripoli, Tunis, and Algiers, by the growing strength of the British in the vicinity of Gibraltar, and lastly by the difficulty found in sheltering his pirate fleets in their old haunts, owing to the shoaling up of the river mouths.

Still, though piracy and slavery were no longer officially recognized, they did not entirely cease. They were too profitable. Along the wild Riff shore, where the inhabitants scarcely recognize the authority of the Sultan, it was perilous for a merchant ship to lie becalmed, especially in the vicinity of the village of Beni-boogaffer, near Cape "Tres Forcas" (Ras ed Dir), about fifteen miles to the westward of the Spanish presidio of Melilla. For suddenly the natives launched their "kareebs," hidden in nooks or buried under sand, and bore down upon the vessel, firing volleys to frighten the doomed crew, who, if they did not escape in their boats, were certain to be enslaved and their ship pillaged and burnt. But though compelled to labour in the fields, on a scanty allowance of poor food, they were not actually ill-treated unless they offered resistance—which was difficult, as the "kareebs" were each manned by thirty or forty men all armed with long guns, pistols, and daggers.

This went on up to the year 1856, when Sir John Drummond-Hay succeeded in rescuing some prisoners, and exacting a promise that similar conduct should not occur again. This compact was kept; for the capture of a Spanish vessel in 1889 was really not an act of piracy, but an exercise of zeal on the part of the tribesmen desirous of punishing a ship's crew engaged in contraband trade. Along the Sûs coast, and further south, every vessel wrecked there was looked upon by the wild Arabs as a lawful prize, and though the Sultan used means to rescue the crew, he

invariably disclaimed responsibility for these outrages.   In
this way Saugnier, Riley, Adams, Puddock, Cochelet, and
other seamen who wrote narratives of their adventures,
were enslaved.   A Spanish subject of British descent—Mr.
James Butler, generally known as Butler-Abrines—having
in 1868 landed on this coast, at a spot only five days'
journey by land south of Mogador, was, with two friends,
seized by the Sheik Habïb ben Baruk, and held until the
Spanish Government redeemed them, after seven years'
captivity, for the sum of £5,400.   Señor Butler died only
four years ago.   M. Camille Douls, a young French traveller,
was the latest victim of these brigands, who treated him
with the greatest cruelty during his detention in 1887.
But though the Sultan affected to disarm his vessels, he
did not altogether lay them up in ordinary.   As late as
1829 he captured the ships of Powers with which he had
not formed treaties, under a peculiarly Moorish convention
which took for granted that they who were not with him
were against him.   In that year when Sir Arthur Brooke
was at Tangier, he noticed the departure of two Moorish
brigs "in the hope of pouncing upon some hapless Bremen
or Hamburg merchantmen," and mentions that Sweden
and other States, to save themselves the expense of maintaining costly squadrons in the Mediterranean, actually
paid Muley Abd-er-Rahman good round sums by way of
propitiation.

Their escapades nevertheless cost His Shereefian Majesty
rather dearly.   For in 1828 the English established a
blockade of the Morocco coast in retaliation for some
damage done by his corsairs, and in 1829 the capture of
an Austrian ship led to the bombardment of the ports of
Tetuan, Azila, and Rabat-Sallee, while there were constant
bickerings with Spain over the piratical proceedings of the
Riff men already mentioned.   These difficulties, coupled

with a variety of other "outrages" more or less well founded, culminated in the Spanish war of 1859–60, which taught the Moors a well-remembered lesson.

The truth seems to have been that the Sultans of Morocco, like their brethren in Tunis, Tripoli, and Algiers, yielded only to the *force majeure;* and it is now known that before the French occupation of the last-named city demonstrated the hopelessness of any return of the good old days, secret embassies, with the object of establishing an anti-Christian league, were passing backwards and forwards among these pirate-powers of Islam. But in time, piracy was relegated to the traditions of Morocco, though the engrained legend that the Unbeliever was the lawful prey of the Faithful died hard along the wilder shores of Barbary. For apart from the long-continued robberies by the Riffians, and the plunder and enslavement of shipwrecked mariners on the coast of Sûs, and the eastern littoral of Tunis, which continued until a very late date,* a spot so near Tangier as Cape Spartel, where there is now a lighthouse, was a dangerous locality only sixty years ago. Indeed, it was then and for a long time subsequently perilous to wander far out of sight of the military escort still—*pro forma*—sent with travellers, in case some tribesmen should be lurking in the vicinity. Sir Arthur Brooke, writing in 1831, remarks that "the country Moors on all parts of the coast are constantly on the look-out for Christians, and instantly make prisoners of all who have either landed accidentally or have been

* In 1832, Sir Grenville Temple's yacht was twice pursued by Greek and Turkish pirates hovering off the corsair-infested shores of Tunis. But in 1889 I wandered unmolested among the Arab villages in the date-covered oasis of Gabes, where, until the marauders were awed by the French Army of Occupation, any traveller not well guarded would assuredly, if not murdered, have been stripped to the skin. To pass from Tripoli along the shores of the Lesser Syrtis, by Djerba, "the Isle of the Lotos-Eaters," was perilous even for small bodies of troops, the Bedouins being bold to recklessness.

shipwrecked. Parties that are occasionally formed, as
ours was, to visit Cape Spartel, are even subject to this :
and in one recent instance the lady of the English Vice-
Consul, who had strolled to a short distance out of sight
of the guard that attended her, was on the point of being
made a prisoner of by a body of natives who surrounded her
and her party, thinking they were alone, until undeceived
by the timely appearance of the escort."   A boat's crew
who had landed the year before, narrowly escaped being
marched to Fez, and were finally ransomed by the British
Consul in Tangier; and still nearer our own time, the
Highland Lad transport having been becalmed off Cape
Spartel, an officer who went ashore, and incautiously proceeded a little way inland, was surrounded and carried off,
while his companions managed to reach their vessel under
the fire of their pursuers.   In spite of all the efforts of the
British Consul-General nothing more was ever heard of
him, so that the chances are he was murdered by his
merciless captors.

Changes
in Morocco
since
Pellow's time.   All this is, however, very ancient history.
The Moors no longer enslave the whites, and in
most parts of Western Morocco the Christian
can travel without any danger of being held to ransom, or
even of receiving worse treatment than a little rudeness
from a boor or a little polite insolence from a Bashaw.
Not a year passes without Fez, Mequinez, Morocco, and
Wazan in the interior being visited by Europeans without
the slightest mishap befalling them. No one now dreams of
travelling in disguise, unless indeed he is anxious to excite
the suspicion of the Moors that his proceedings are under-
hand, or that he is afraid of them, when—not improbably
—the traveller will be taken at his own valuation. As for
any one journeying to Morocco city " disguised as a Jew,"
this would be courting insult, as a Christian is far more

esteemed than a Hebrew; while the story about seeing Christian ears nailed to a post—which a recent tourist who went so " disguised " had the effrontery to declare he did— is so absurd, that we can only conclude that his power of distinguishing the ears of different nationalities must have been as powerful as was his capacity for being hoaxed, or of trying to hoax others. For never in the memory of man were such outrages committed, and to-day the main fear of the town Moors — unless a half-crazy Dervish cursing the Infidel dog be excepted—is lest they should in the remotest manner incur the vengeance of the Christian envoys at Tangier by molesting their fellow-countrymen. The Sultan is no longer aggressive, though as reactionary and hard to move in the paths of progress as ever. But so far from wishing to annoy the Nazarene, his ever-present dread is lest he should in any way embroil himself with these peppery folk, and, as a consequence, is sadly imposed upon by the host of petty consular officials who, though paid nothing, manage to make a lucrative trade out of indemnities for injuries which were never inflicted, and by the sale of " protections " to knaves who buy them only to oppress others less fortunate.

The days of the Sallee Rovers are also over, and the sole representative of the Moorish navy is now the *El Hassani*, an English freight steamer, manned by a foreign crew— though, as there has been a difficulty over the payment for the vessel, at the hour of writing even this craft is doubtfully the property of the monarch after whom it is named. The old pirate town seems given over to shoemaking and fanaticism. Europeans are not permitted to live either in it or in Azamoor, and an unknown Christian in exploring its dirty alleys is apt to get stones and bad language hurled at him with an emphasis which recalls the period when to " swear like a Barbary Pirate " was a proverb among seamen. A few rotting hulks recall the palmy days of piracy, and anecdotes of the good old times form the staple of that languid conversation which goes on as the lazy citizens squat on their heels under the shade of the sea wall. The old Bashaw—who has now made his peace with Allah — just remembered seeing as a boy the last gang of Christian slaves marched through Rabat; and Abdul ben Reis—Abdul, son of the Captain—still recalls some of the joyous tales with which his father, the rover chief, entertained the family circle—years and years ago. In these degenerate times it pays better to save the ship-wrecked mariner than to enslave him, so that dozens of stalwart fellows who when the century was young would have been doing a brave business on the high seas, point with honest pride to the medals they have won in rescuing " Roumi " * from the waves.

With Christian slavery departed also the chief motive for renegadoism. Very few European Apostates now exist in Morocco, and without a single exception, of which I am aware, the hundred or so who are scattered over the country are generally of such seamy antecedents as to justify the Scotch characterization of a worthless scamp as a " runni-gate." Most of them are either " forcats " escaped from the Spanish convict stations at Ceuta and elsewhere on the Morocco coast, deserters from the French army, or levanted criminals from Algeria and Spain. They are usually employed in various subordinate positions in the army, and the military band which discourses curious versions of familiar tunes when the Prince of True Believers appears in public includes numbers of these individuals. I know of no British renegade—the last and

---

* " Roumi," or Romans, is the name applied to Christians by the Berbers or aborigines of the Barbary States. The Arabs more generally term them " Nasrani," or Nazarenes.

the most respectable of the order, a Scotchman, who lived at Rabat, much esteemed for his intelligence and honourable conduct, having died two years ago. Were the history of these turncoats fully known, the story of their lives would be a curious chapter in the annals of human nature. One of the most romantic of these tales was that of an old white-bearded man who, when the French Military Commission first entered Fez in 1877, was seen silently and sad-eyed, supported by two attendants, contemplating a uniform with which in days gone by he was very familiar. This aged renegade was known as Abd-er-Rhaman; but his christened name was Count Joseph de Saulty, formerly a lieutenant of engineers in the Army of Algeria. In a weak moment he eloped with his commandant's wife, and remained in Tunis until she died. Then becoming painfully conscious of the grave position in which he was placed as a deserter from the colours, he passed into Morocco, changed his faith, and as a military adviser of the then Sultan, whose name he took, rose high in the imperial favour, and had his advice been listened to might have saved Morocco from the disaster of Isly. He died in 1881, and is buried at the gates of Fez in the cemetery of Sidi Bou Bekkr el Arbi, though so thoroughly did he put the past behind him, that his son, now occupying a high position in the Court, is entirely ignorant of any language except Arabic. Another renegade of note was the English officer still remembered as "Ingliz Bashaw," under whom Muley El-Hassan, the present Sultan, learned the art of war, and who was the first individual to impart anything like discipline to the Moroquin army. Why he came to Morocco is not known, and so jealously was his identity —like that of the Count de Saulty—kept dark, that in a recent work by the Viscount de la Martinière his real name is declared to be unknown. At this date there can be no reason for concealing that it was Graham; and I have been told by those who have every reason to know that, like so many others who incur the jealousy of the Moorish dignitaries, he died of poison.

The majority of the Apostates are, however, the vilest of rapscallions, in whom no trust is to be reposed, and who, if despised by the Moors, quite deserve the low esteem in which they are held. Yet even they are happily getting fewer, since by a recent treaty between Spain and Morocco all refugees from justice are to be mutually surrendered.

Otherwise, Morocco is much as it always was. Justice is, as of old, bought and sold. Roads there are none, except the rutty paths which droves of mules, and donkeys, and horses, and camels have worn in the course of ages. Oppression is the rule: fair play the exception, and the dungeons so horrible, that the first object of a governor is to immure in one of them some man wealthy enough to buy freely the privilege of getting out of this dreadful den. But though Maghreb Al Aksa—the "Furthest West"—has been styled "Un Empire qui croule," its stability is in its weakness. For being always supposed on the eve of dissolution, the jealousy of the powers who wish to share in the scramble, but are not yet prepared for the war which would usher in that moral spectacle, renders the ever tottering throne of Muley El-Hassan rather safer than some which seem firmer "based upon a people's will." And so, we venture to think, the Emir-al-Mumenin will be wagging his beard in the sweet gardens of Fez, or Mequinez, or Marrakesch, long after many a crown has rolled in the dust of the Land of the Nazarenes.

THE HISTORY

OF THE

LONG CAPTIVITY AND ADVENTURES

OF

THOMAS PELLOW.

———•◦•———

CHAPTER I.

The Author; youth and schooling—He goes to sea—Is captured by
the Sallee rovers and wrecked on the bar of the Bouragreb River
between Sallee and Rabat—Escapes drowning only to become a
slave—Is sent to Mequinez with the rest of his shipmates—They
are attacked by the mob—They are taken before the Emperor
Muley Ismaïl—The author becomes the slave of Muley Spha, the
Emperor's son—He is beaten in order to force him to change his
religion—He "turns Moor," and is made an officer of the Emperor
—He has a perilous adventure with the latter—His uncle dies—
The cruelties of the Emperor—The terrible punishments inflicted
by him—The dreadful death of Larbe Shott, whose ghost appeared
unto Muley Ismaïl.

HE exceeding love and great compassion
of God towards mankind in general,
shows us how good, gracious, and
merciful He is to all who love, fear,
and steadfastly believe in Him, and
His Son Jesus Christ, our Lord; and
how, of His great providence, He (contrary to all human

imagination, and even our own expectations) bringeth the prisoner out oi captivity, as He hath, of His infinite mercy (in His own appointed time), delivered me, His poor unworthy servant, out of the hands of cruel and bloodthirsty men, after a long and grievous slavery, for the space of almost twenty-three years, in South Barbary, bringing me by the right way to the city where I dwelt, thereby delivering me from my prison and chains, and probably from ever-lasting death. For ever and ever blessed be His most holy name. Amen.

In the eleventh year of my age, the second of the reign of our late Sovereign Lord King George the First, and of our Lord Christ 1715, I being at the Latin School in Penryn, in the county of Cornwall, and John Pellow, my uncle, being about to proceed on a voyage from Falmouth to Fowey, and thence for Genoa with pilchards, in the good ship *Francis*, Valentine Enes (then of Penryn), merchant, the owner; and I by no means liking my so early rising, and (as I then thought) most severe discipline of the school, so far insinuated myself into my uncle's favour as to get his promise to obtain the consent of my parents for me to go along with him; and which indeed he did, though not without much difficulty, they urging the hardships which probably I might, in my so tender years, undergo thereby, and their ominous fears of our falling into the hands of the Moors, who were then at open war with us, and had, as they saw by the newspapers, very lately taken some of our ships; so that it was with the greatest reluctance and regret that I obtained their consent, which at last I did, and was soon rigged in my sailor's dress; and after taking (as it proved) my so long, long farewell of my friends, our ship sailed from Falmouth to Fowey, where in a few days we completed our cargo; and as soon as all other our necessary business was dispatched, we set sail for our

desired port. Of which our voyage it cannot be expected
I should give any particular account, as I had never been
at sea before, and was entirely unacquainted with the
method of keeping a journal; but I well remember that
I soon began to repent of my rash undertaking, and
heartily wished myself back again, though even to be
again sent to the Latin school, my uncle keeping me so
close to my book that I had very little or no time allowed
me for play; and which, if I at any time presumed to .
borrow, I failed not of a most sure payment by the cat
of nine tails ; so that by the time we got to Genoa I thought
I had enough of the sea, being every day, during our voyage
out, obliged (over and above my book-learning) to go up to
the main-top mast-head, even in all weather.

All which (though very irksome to me then) I now most
gratefully acknowledge, and plainly see, was only intended
for my good ; and had not our sad misfortune of falling
into the hands of the Infidels, and our long unhappy
slavery prevented it, my uncle would have certainly made
me a complete sailor, as he himself was, by those who knew
him, allowed to be ; but what God thinks proper should be,
no human power can prevent.

And now, indeed, the unhappy part of my life draws
near. For having made our voyage, our cargoes out and
in, and by God's providence bound home, we were off Cape
Finisterre very unhappily surprised by two Sallee rovers,
and, together with Captain Foster, of Topsham (after such
small resistance as we could both make), taken and carried
prisoners on board of the infidels, as was also the next day
Captain Ferris of London, in a ship of much greater
strength, having twenty men, eight swivel and eight
carriage guns, though they behaved in the bravest
manner, fighting ten hours, and with a noble resolution,
putting the Moors off, after boarding them three times,

4

and killing many of them; but being overpowered by a superior force they were also obliged to submit, and to become our comrades.

It is impossible for me to describe the agony I was then in, being separated from my uncle; he being, together with Briant Clarke, John Crimes, and John Dunnal (three of our unhappy men) confined on board one of the Sallee-teens, commanded by Ali Hacam; and myself, with Lewis Davies, George Barnicoat, and Thomas Goodman, the other three (our whole number consisting but of eight persons) on board of the other, commanded by Elhash Abdrahaman Medune,* the Admiral of Sallee, where we were closely confined, and treated after a barbarous manner during the space of one whole month, which the infidels passed in looking sharp out after other prey, and in examining into the value of our cargoes, according to our several invoices and bills of lading, the prizes being sent to Sallee for better security, and to leave them at more liberty to encounter others during the time of their cruize; but seeing no likelihood of any more prizes, and their provision growing short, they followed the prizes, and found them safe at anchor on the outside of the bar of Sallee; when, on a signal from the shore of there being water enough on the bar to carry them over, the prizes were ordered to weigh, and got all well in, the Salleetens casting anchor without till the next day; when, about noon, the infidels being in their jollity, were all on the sudden in an extreme hurry on their discovery of a sail standing right in from sea upon them, they crying out, in great confusion, " Garnoe ! Garnoe !" meaning thereby Captain Delgardenoor,† who they knew then commanded a British man of war of 20 guns on that station; and as they feared so it proved, for it was Garnoe indeed; but,

* El Hadjj Abd-er-Rahman Medune.   † *Note* 1.

alas! too late for our assistance. Medune weighing his anchor, and Ali Hacam slipping his cable, they ran both aground on the bar, Delgardenoor following so near them as in safety he might, some of his shot flying about them, and some of them far beyond them, insomuch that they were both, through means thereof, and a great sea, soon beat to pieces; and almost every one that could swim swimming for his life; but, for my part, I could swim but very little, and which, had I attempted, the merciless sea must soon have overwhelmed me; so I cried to Lewis Davies, who I knew could swim very well, for assistance, though from him I could get none, he saying (and very truly) "that all his strength was highly necessary towards his own preservation; and that should he take me on his back, it would in all likelihood loose both our lives; whereas by his throwing himself into the sea disentangled, and I getting on the mast (which was cut down), it might be a means of preserving both of us;" and which, through the wonderful and ready help of Almighty God assisting (He having ordained us for larger and more grievous trials and sufferings), accordingly happened: Davies committing himself to the waves, and I myself to the mast, from which I was taken by some people in a boat from the shore. As for the Moors, they were under no apprehension of danger from the sea, leaping into it and swimming to shore like so many dogs.

It may easily be imagined what sad terror and apprehension I was under in so dangerous a situation; for though I could see nothing else by being delivered from death than the more grievous torments in my becoming a slave, &c., yet did I endeavour all in my power to avoid it, and save myself.

Being now all safely landed, we are in a very low and feeble condition conducted to two separate prisons; myself,

Lewis Davies, M. Goodman, and Briant Clark, with divers
others of Ferris's men, in all twenty-six, to New Sallee,*
and my uncle, John Dunnal, Thomas Cremer, and George
Barnecoat, with seventeen Frenchmen taken in other
ships, and the rest of Foster's and Ferris's men, twenty-
six more, to old Sallee, and for three days closely shut up
there, and our allowance by the Moors nothing but
bread and water, though I must thankfully own that we
met with some better refreshment through the goodness of
some French and Irish merchants residing there, which
was to us in our so weak and disconsolate condition of very
great service.

On the fourth day we were all, in number fifty-two,
taken out thence and sent prisoners to Mequinez; some
being put on mules, some on asses, and some on horses;
on one of which my uncle and I were mounted together.
We travelled the first day to Lorshia, being obliged in our
way hither to pass through the woods of Sallee, which were
plentifully stored with most stately timber trees, of oaks,
and vast quantities of wild hogs, lions, tigers, and many
other dangerous creatures.   The second day to the River
Teffifilla, though by some called Teliffla, in the province
of Wolelsager; the third to Darmulsultan; and the fourth
about sunrising (it being about three miles' travel into
Mequinez), all the way lodging in tents, as being in that
part of the country the only habitations, and which are at
the discretion of the people removed from one place to
another.   At our arrival to the city, or rather indeed
a mile before we reached it, we were commanded to get
off our beasts and to take to our English shoes (that is to
say, as many of us as had any), and to put on yellow
pumps which were brought to us † by the Moors for that
purpose; and at our entrance into the city we were met

---

* *Note* 1.   † *Note* 2.

and surrounded by vast crowds of them, offering us the most vile insults, and they could scarce be restrained from knocking us on the head; and which I verily believe they would certainly have done had not the Emperor's guards interposed; though even they could not, or at least would not, hinder them from pulling our hair, and giving us many severe boxes, calling us "Caffer Billa Oarosole,"* which signified in English that we were "Hereticks," and knew neither God nor Mahomet.

About eight o'clock we all got to the Emperor's palace; where, before we entered, we were first obliged to take off our pumps, passing barefoot in at a gate called "Bednam Sorelelg," or the "Renegado's Gate,"† a Renegado Spaniard being its keeper; and thence through two other gates, viz. "Bebliashey, Benauma," or, as by others called, "Bebfeelello" and "Bebaurbashyoub,"‡ which brought us into "Dareb Bastion" where Muly Smine,§ or Ishmael, the old Emperor, was, who received us from the hands of the Salleeteens, giving Ali Hacam, in exchange for every one of us, fifty ducats; but out of this was paid back again one-third, and a tenth as a customary tribute; and Medune, the Admiral, for not fighting Delgardenoor, had the very extraordinary favour bestowed upon him of losing his head.

And now are we ordered to be separated as follows, viz. myself, Richard Ferris, James Waller, Thomas Newgent, and three other boys taken in a French ship, sent to the Kubbahhiatin,‖ or place where the tailors work, and the armoury is kept, and where we were directly employed in cleaning the arms. All the fore-mast men, save two, who

---

* *Kafir b-Illah was rasool* in better Maghrebin Arabic.

† The Apostates' Gate, *Bab-Mancoor el álj.*

‡ Bab-liashey, Benauma, or Bab-seelello and Bab-aur-bashyoub, seems the proper spelling.

§ *Note* 27. The Dareb-Bastion seems, Mr. Meakin thinks, the Dar el-Bastyoon,   ‖ *Note* 2.

were wounded, were put to hard labour; and the captains, with the two wounded men, to the Spanish convent; whence, after some short exemption, they were put to hard labour also; and, after some little time, again exempted, and sent to the house of one Mr. Ben Hattar,* a Jew, in a place called the Judaiary [or Mella], he having procured this of the Emperor; and, as everything relating to our affairs passed through the hands of him and his agents, it was, no doubt, very much to his advantage.

After some time, I was taken out of the armoury, and given by the Emperor to Muley Spha, one of his favourite sons (a sad villain), born of his wife Alloabenabiz,† by whom he had in all ten children, viz., seven sons and three daughters. My business now, for some time, was to run from morning to night after his horse's heels; during which he often prompted me to turn Moor, and told me, if I would, I should have a very fine horse to ride on, and I should live like one of his best esteemed friends. To which I used to reply, that as that was the only command wherein I could not readily gratify him, I humbly hoped that he would be pleased, of his great goodness, to suspend all future thoughts that way, for that I was thoroughly resolved not to renounce my Christian faith, be the consequence what it would. Then said he, in a most furious and haughty manner, "Prepare yourself for such torture as shall be inflicted on you, and the nature of your obstinacy deserves." When I humbly entreating him, on my knees, not to let loose his rage on a poor, helpless, innocent creature; he, without making any further reply, committed me prisoner to one of his own rooms, keeping me there several months in irons, and every day most severely bastinading me, and furiously screaming in the Moorish language, "Shehed, Shehed! Cunmoora, Cunmoora!"

---

* Hyatn.   † Lalla ben Abiz.

in English, "Turn Moor! turn Moor!"* by holding up
your finger. Of which cruelty my uncle hearing, he came
one day, and with him one John Phillips, to see if it might
be in their power to give me any relief; and which indeed
was not, although they very heartily endeavoured it,
gaining nothing by their so very kind and Christian-like
intention, but many severe blows on themselves, and on
me a more frequent repetition of them than before.

And now is my accursed master still more and more
enraged, and my tortures daily increasing; insomuch,
that had not my uncle, and some other good Christians
through his means, notwithstanding his so late ill usage
and repulse (even to the extreme hazard of their lives),
privately conveyed me some few refreshments, I must have
inevitably perished, my prison allowance being nothing
but bread and water; so that I was, through my severe
scourging, and such hard fare, every day in expectation of
its being my last; and happy, no doubt, had I been, had
it so happened: I should certainly then have dy'd a martyr,
and probably thereby gained a glorious crown in the
kingdom of heaven; but the Almighty did not then see it
fit. My tortures were now exceedingly increased, burning
my flesh off my bones by fire; which the tyrant did, by
frequent repetitions, after a most cruel manner; insomuch,
that through my so very acute pains, I was at last constrained to submit, calling upon God to forgive me, who
knows that I never gave the consent of the heart, though
I seemingly yielded, by holding up my finger; and that I
always abominated them, and their accursed principle of
Mahometism, my only trust and confidence being firmly
fixed on Him, and in the all-sufficient merits of His only
Son Jesus Christ, my Saviour.

* "Testify! Testify!" This is in the *Lingua franca*, not in pure
Arabic.

I was kept forty days longer in prison, on my refusing to put on the Moorish habit; but I at length reflected, that to refuse this any longer was a very foolish obstinacy, since it was a thing indifferent in its own nature, seeing I had already been compelled to give my assent to Mahometism. Therefore, rather than undergo fresh torments, I also complied with it, appearing like a Mahometan; and I make no doubt but some ill-natured people think me so even to this day. I pray God to forgive them, and that it may never be their mishap to undergo the like trials; and which, if it should, that they may maintain their Christian faith no worse than I did mine.

I was now delivered once more from my prison and chains; and, at the command of the Emperor, put to school, to learn the Moorish language, and to write Arabick; and in the latter I should have certainly been a tolerable proficient, had not my master's insolence, and violent death by the Emperor's orders, prevented it; for after being with him about three months, during which he had often called me Christian dog, and most severely beat me, it coming to the Emperor's ears, he was by his order instantly despatched, by tossing him up, and so breaking his neck.

After this, I was put no more to school to learn the language, but immediately into the hands of Emhamenet Sageer, whose business was to train up and instruct youth how they should speak and behave before the Emperor, and in the war; he having for such purposes under his care about six hundred boys; and with whom I had not been above a fortnight, before I had the charge of eighty of them committed to me, I being made their Alcayde,* or captain, to see they kept clean the walks (during all intervals from exercise) in the Emperor's garden, where

* Al Kaïd.

he and his favourite Queen Hellema Hazzezas (in English the beloved) were used to walk. In this station I had not been but a very little time, when the Queen coming one day into the walks, before I had the power to hide myself in a little house set there for that purpose (and which, at her approach, we were commanded always to do), happened to see me, and the next day begged me of the Emperor, which he readily granting, ordered us immediately out one by one, till she should see the same person; and after the first, second, and third were presented, and turned back again, he ordered their captain to appear, when I instantly appeared, and the Queen saying I was the same she would have, I was forthwith given her, and by her again to her favourite son Muly Zidan, a youth of about eight years of age, and then resident with his mother in the palace of Sherrers; where she, with thirty-eight of the Emperor's concubines, and several eunuchs, were closely shut up, and to which I was made chief porter of the innermost door, that is to say, of the door next without that of the entrance into the galleries leading to the several apartments, and where none could gain admittance, but through me; as indeed none were to be admitted, the Emperor only excepted, nor him neither, in case he should offer to come, without giving notice, at an unseasonable hour; as once indeed he did, and though he had gained admittance in at the several outer doors, yet was he by me denied; for how could I tell it was him, when he was on the one side, and I on the other, of a thick door close shut; and allowing, as by his being let in at the several outer doors, and his usual way of knocking, I might have very little reason to doubt it, and which might likewise have induced me to open it, yet, what did that signify to me, when I had positive orders before (as no doubt had all the rest) to admit none after such an hour, without being before advised of it, and of some certain signs to be given accordingly on the outside of the door; and further, my orders were, that in case any one should attempt to enter at such an unseasonable hour, and not immediately depart after his first and second knocking, and denials of entrance, but should presume to knock a third time without giving the signs as aforesaid, I should then fire through the door—as indeed I had now an occasion to do.

The Emperor being admitted, as aforementioned, in at the several outer doors, and knocking at mine, I demanded aloud, "Who was there?" to which I was answered, "Muly Smine"; and which, indeed, by his voice and usual way of knocking, I was pretty well assured it was. However, I told him that I very much doubted it; for that I had never known His Excellency to come at such an unseasonable hour, without my being pre-advised thereof; and which, as I then was not, he should at his peril be gone, or I would present him with half a dozen bullets through the door, which he prayed me not to do, for that it was actually himself, and that if I would not let him in, he would certainly chop off my head the next day, knocking again louder than before; but, on the contrary, if I would admit him, he would give me such a fine horse (calling him by his name), with all the rich furniture belonging to him, and would make me a great man. I told him I would not do it if he would give me all the horses and furniture in the empire; for that as I was entrusted and commanded by the renowned Muly Smine or Ishmael, the most glorious Emperor in the world, to keep that post inviolable against all impostors and intruders whomsoever, and as I had but too much reason to believe him such, I would not on any terms open the door, be the consequence what it would, being thoroughly resolved not to betray my trust; therefore it was in vain for him any

longer to persist. When he changing his note from rewards
to threats, and knocking again, I fired all the bullets which
I had ready by me in a blunderbuss, quite through the
door, which indeed (he keeping himself close on one side,
as I before imagined) could in nowise hurt him; and on
his seeing my so resolute resistance, and no likelihood of
his admittance, he returned as he came, highly threatening me for keeping him out, and as much commending
those at the several outer doors for their so readily letting
him in, assuring us that we should on neither side lose our
reward; and indeed we did not, being very early in the
morning all ordered out, and all those who gave him admittance had some their heads cut off, others cruelly used;
and myself, after being highly commended for my fidelity,
rewarded with a much finer horse than that he offered to
give me in case I would betray my trust.

This palace of Sherrers is a very large spacious building
(as indeed are all the Emperor's houses), and certainly
prodigious strong, the walls twelve feet thick, and five
stories high, built only of fine earth and hot lime, mixed
and well incorporated by a vast number of slaves kept
for that purpose; for it is thrown, as I may say,
into a mould, being first boarded up on each side, so
that being very well rammed together, it becomes, in a
very little time, harder and more durable than stone.* It
is covered on the top with blue tiles, ceiled in the inside,
and finely painted, and hath in it several hundred separate
apartments for his concubines and eunuchs, besides those
set apart for his favourite queen and her retinue. All his
other wives (in number no less than four thousand) being
closely shut up in several other sumptuous houses allotted
for them; though all, as I may say adjacent, and all
within the same enclosure.†

* Tabia. † *Note 3.*

My lodging was between the inner door before mentioned and that of the entrance into the galleries, leading to the several apartments; my companions six boys, and two young lions about half grown, being reared up there from whelps; but becoming unruly, their removal was desired, and complied with.

Now am I, after my hard keeping, again become in pretty good plight, being allowed very good eatables, as beef, mutton, and cuscassoo (of the nature of which I shall speak by and by), I having in a manner now nothing else to do than to eat my meat, and be careful of my young master's and the Queen's motions, and especially those of the latter, who I found was about to cut me out some new work; so that I was obliged to walk like one walking on the brink of a dangerous precipice, whence, should he happen to make but the least wry step, he is sure to tumble down and break his neck. The Queen, in short, being extremely amorous, and the Emperor no less jealous of her, which really made my condition very dangerous, and might through some unforeseen accident (let my behaviour be never so innocent), happen to prove of very bad consequence to me, therefore I thought it highly prudent to keep a very strict guard upon all my actions.

I now was strictly charged by the Emperor, on pain of losing my life, to visit my uncle every day, he saying to me, in a loud and vehement tone, " Cossam billa illamattim Shea Culsbah Occulashea bus ede Ameck Woolastan cuttarossick," * that is, " If you don't go every day, morning and evening, to kiss your uncle's hand, by Allah I'll cut your head off. For if he were a brute," says he, " you are by nature obliged so to do."

This, any one may suppose, as being the only command

* Properly, *Ela matimshiski kal chah wa kal ás hiya ámak thoosla ydu nnquatálik rasek.*

my present inclinations could be best gratified with, did not at all terrify me, and therefore I forthwith most cheerfully put it in practice; but, alas! that pleasure was of a very short duration, he being, poor man, in a few weeks after taken off by a violent flux, as were a little before him Briant Clark, Thomas Crimes, and John Dunnal, three of our unhappy men; and I shall never forget my uncle's tender behaviour at the interment of the latter, where I and a great many other Englishmen happened to be. The corpse being brought to the grave, and no particular person appointed to read the Christian ceremony of burial, my uncle took it upon him, but indeed he was not able (through the abundance of tears flowing) to go through it, his speech being thereby to that degree obstructed, that he could only now and then utter a word imperfectly; insomuch, that he was obliged to deliver over the book to another; and never did I see such a mournful meeting, every one catching the contagion, and all standing for a considerable time in a dead silence, quite overwhelmed with grief.

I am now to expect no further comfort by way of my poor uncle; and though, indeed, I might not probably stand in so much need of him as formerly I had done, yet was it the sorest affliction I ever met with, and I could never put the remembrance of him out of my thoughts.

Now it is my chief business and greatest concern to study how to oblige the Emperor, his dear Hellema, and my young master; but the latter I confess I did not mind, though he was by nature cruel enough, and I had seen him, even in the seventeenth year of his age, kill his favourite black with his own hand, by stabbing him into the belly with a knife, and only for coming very accidentally where he was feeding a pair of pigeons, and their flying away for a few minutes. Yet, I say, I did not much mind him, as having much higher objects to observe, the Queen being in a particular manner kind, and often recommending me to the Emperor's good liking as a careful and diligent servant, as indeed I really was, so far as I thought might be consistent with my advantage and safety. But I thinking this service very precarious, and that I was every moment exposed, and in danger of her poison, or his sword, I humbly intreated her to desire the Emperor to find out for me some other employment, wherein I might be less suspected, and not altogether out of the way of obliging her; which she readily complied with, I being directly ordered by the Emperor to quit this dangerous office, and to wait on him at his palace for such future commands as should be by him enjoined me. A sudden and pleasing alteration indeed; and though my new business might be attended with more masculine exercises, yet was I well satisfied that it could not be with more danger and uneasiness, of which I was very soon confirmed, I being strictly charged to be observant of the Emperor's commands only, and to wait on him on all occasions; and when he pleased to ride out, I was generally mounted on the fine horse he gave me for my fidelity in maintaining my post at the door, always carrying at my girdle a club of about three feet long, of Brazil wood, with which he used, on any slight occasion, to knock his people on the head, as I had several times the pleasure of beholding. For, in short (although I did not know how soon it might have been my own fate), I did not care how soon they were all dead; and indeed he was of so fickle, cruel, and sanguine a nature, that none could be even for one hour secure of life. He had many despatched, by having their heads cut off, or by being strangled, others by tossing, for which he had several very dexterous executioners always ready at hand; but scarce

would he on those occasions afford a verbal command, he
thinking that too mean, and his words of more value than
the life of the best of them, generally giving it by signs or
motions of his head and hand; as, for instance, when
he would have any person's head cut off, by drawing or
shrinking his own as close as he could to his shoulders,
and then with a very quick or sudden motion extending
it; and when he would have any strangled, by the quick
turn of his arm-wrist, his eye being fixed on the victims.
The punishment of "tossing" is a very particular one,
and peculiar to the Moors.

The person whom the Emperor orders to be thus
punished, is seized upon by three or four strong negroes,
who, taking hold of his hams, throw him up with all their
strength, and at the same time turning him round, pitch
him down head foremost; at which they are so dexterous
by long use, that they can either break his neck the first
toss, dislocate his shoulder, or let him fall with less hurt.
They continue doing this as often as the Emperor has
ordered, so that many times they are killed upon the
spot; sometimes they come off with only being severely
bruised; and the person that is tossed must not stir a
limb, if he is able, while the Emperor is in sight, under
penalty of being tossed again, but is forced to lie as if he
was dead; which, if he should really be, nobody dares
bury the body till the Emperor has given orders for it.*

The Emperor's wrath is terrible, which the Christians
have often felt. One day passing by a high wall on which
they were at work, and being affronted that they did not
keep time in their strokes, as he expects they should, he
made his guards go up and throw them all off the wall,
breaking their legs and arms, knocking them on the head
in a miserable manner. Another time he ordered them

* *Note 4.*

to bury a man alive, and beat him down along with the mortar in the wall.

Nor is the Emperor less cruel to the Moors, whem he'll frequently command to be burnt, crucified, sawed in two, or dragged at a mule's tail through the streets, till they are torn all to pieces.

The most favourable death to die is by his hand, for then they only lose their heads, have their brains knocked out, or are run through the body, for which purpose he always has his lances ready, and is very dexterous at using them, seldom letting his hand go out for want of practice.

In the year 1721, during the time that Commodore Stewart was in Morocco as ambassador from England, the Emperor despatched, in the most cruel manner, Larbe Shott,* a man of one of the best families in Barbary, being descended from the old Andalusian Moors, and deserved the esteem both of his own countrymen and of us, with whom he had lived till the time of his imprisonment; for he had been a considerable time in Gibraltar, as a pledge from the Bashaw to an English merchant, for the payment of money due for goods he had supplied the Bashaw with. Part of the crime laid to his charge was for going out of his country, and living in Christendom a considerable time, without the Emperor's knowledge, and having been friendly himself with Christian women, and often been in liquor. He was also accused of being an unbeliever, and one of those who have invited the Spaniards to invade Barbary.

These things being insinuated to the Emperor, after the usual manner of that court (where everybody has it in their power to do harm, but few to do good), brought this poor man to his end; for early one morning he was

* El Arbi Shat.

carried before the Emperor, who (not allowing him any other trial, but giving way to his accusers, who said, "He was an unbeliever, and not fit to live") commanded him to be sawed in two; upon which he was immediately carried to the place of execution, which is at one of the gates of the town, and there tied between two boards and sawed in two, beginning at the head and going downwards, till his body fell asunder, which must have remained to have been eaten by the dogs, if the Emperor had not pardoned him;—an extravagant custom, to pardon a man after he is dead; but unless he does so, nobody dares bury the body.

It was reported the next day after, that the Emperor dreamt Shott had appeared to him, and asked him, "What he had done to deserve such usage?" telling him, "There would be a time when God would judge between them both;" which gave the Emperor so much concern, that he sent to the place of his execution for some of the dust his blood was spilt on, with which he rubbed himself all over as an atonement for his crime.*

* *Note 5.*

CHAPTER II.

Mr. Pellow is better housed and higher in favour—He dines more
frequently off cuscassoo—How this dish is prepared—The misery
of the slaves—The arrival of Commodore Stewart to ransom the
English captives—The author, being excluded from the provisions
of the treaty, is left behind—Cruelties of the Emperor—His
character and the subservience paid him—The danger of anticipating a remark—The drilling of marksmen—He gets married—
How weddings are conducted in Morocco—He sets out on a
military expedition—Curious advice from a Moslem—The march
—At Sharroot—Kill hundreds of wild boars—He takes command
of the castle (or Kasbah) of Tannonah—His lazy life during
six years—He marches to Morocco city—Expedition into the
mountains.

MY lodging was now on the inside of the entrance into
the palace yard, where were several sheds set up
against the walls like pent-houses, though closer and well
tiled overhead, very long and only just wide enough for
one man to lie at length; and here, I say, I lodged, together
with the Emperor's guards, so that I was always ready at
hand even at a minute's warning, and whence I dared
not to stir but at his approach or command, we having at
the appointed times our meat brought us; and for our
dinner we seldom failed of the Moors' favourite dish, cuscassoo, of which I just now promised to give a further
account, I being really so far of the Moors' opinion as that
I cannot but in every respect allow it truly deserving of
their so very high esteem and commendation, for it is
actually very good, grateful and nourishing, and is prepared

after the following manner : first, they put fine flour into
a large wooden bowl, then they pour thereon a small
quantity of water, and keep continually shaking the bowl,
till the water is drank up ; then they pour on more, and
so continue to shake the bowl, till all the flour is come
into small pellets of about the bigness of Nutmegs ; then
they are put out of the bowl into another utensil like a
cullender, which is made use of for straining the water off
pease, beans, or anything else of the like nature, which,
being put over the steam of a boiling pot or furnace,
wherein are fowls and other meat boiling, in the nature *of*
a cover, and another cover on the top of that. By the
time the meat is well boiled, so are the shot or pellets
(though indeed they call it baking), when they pour them
out into a dish, adding thereto good store of butter, some
salt, spices, and saffron, and then serve up the meat upon
it. This, I say, is excellent eating, and is no doubt used
by some in England and other countries as a regalio ; and
was I of ability sufficient, I should often regale myself
with it. At their meals they never made use of knives,
forks, or spoons, every one putting in his right hand
instead of a fork, and his first two fingers thereof extended
instead of a spoon, all seating themselves in a ring on the
floor, and the meat in the middle ; and in case any one,
though unconcerned in this mess, passed by whilst they
were at it, and did not put in his fingers and eat with
them, he was accounted a very unmannerly fellow, all the
company calling him " Caultsnab," which was as much as
to say, without breeding or manners, though indeed they
were not often guilty of this ill-manners. For my part, I
could readily have excused them if they had.

This cuscassoo of the Emperor's, as being to feed about
nine hundred men, was brought out into the court in a
cart upon wheels ; when, dividing ourselves into several

companies of about seventy or eighty in a company, we
had all our messes served out from the cart in large bowls,
and set in the middle of us on the floor as before mentioned, sitting as close round it as possible we could.
Though I cannot say we had fowls, yet we did not want,
in lieu thereof, for good store of beef and mutton, and
which, instead of decently cutting, we with our hands
hauled to pieces, two pulling one against another; and
any one first taking hold on a piece of meat, and another,
his next neighbour, not taking speedy hold also on the
same piece, it was accounted brutish. For as they are
allowed at their meals the use only of their right hands,
therefore if a man is not so assisted by his neighbour,
whereby he may the easier separate it, it is reckoned the
greatest injury that can be offered them; and it is really a
very dangerous way of eating, especially when people are very
hungry, therefore they are generally attended, during that
time, by several persons with clubs in their hands, in case
any should by chance swallow a piece too large for their
gullets, and it should stick therein—which, through their
greediness, often happened—and then one of those attendants gave the party a very hearty blow with his cudgel in
the neck, by which means it was generally discharged either
up or down, and, in case it was not, then they repeated
the blow till it was. This did I often see, and have been
as often diverted with it.

About this time came Commodore Stewart, ambassador
to Mequinez, with full powers from his royal master to
treat with the Emperor for the so long desired redemption
of the poor English captives.

Here it will not be amiss to describe the exceeding
weight of misery which our fellow-countrymen undergo
who are so unhappy as to be made slaves in Morocco.

The severest labour and hardships inflicted on male-

factors in Europe are lenity and indulgence, compared to
what many worthy persons undergo in this modern Egypt;
even slavery at Tunis or Algiers is a state of repose and
felicity to that in the Morocco dominions. At daybreak
the guardians of the several dungeons, where the Christian
slaves are shut up at night, rouse them with curses and
blows to their work, which here is not repairing or rigging
of ships, but more laborious, as it consists in providing
materials for the Emperor's extravagant buildings,
stamping earth mixed with lime and water, in a wooden
box near three yards long and three feet deep, and of the
intended breadth of the wall. Their instrument for this
is a heavy wooden stamper. Others prepare and mix the
earth, or dig in quarries for lime stones; others burn
them. Some are employed to carry large baskets of earth;
some drive waggons drawn by six bulls and two horses;
and, after the toil of the day, these miserable carters
watch their cattle in the field at night, and in all weathers,
as their life must answer for any accident. The task of
many is to saw, cut, cement, and erect marble pillars, and
of such who are found qualified, to make gunpowder and
small arms; yet does not their skill procure them any
better treatment than those who, having only the use of
their limbs without any ingenuity, are set to the coarsest
works, as tending horses, sweeping stables, carrying
burthens, grinding with hand-mills. Some have also in
charge to manage the water-works, and inspect the aqueducts. In all these so different departments the ignorant
and artist are upon a level, very few instances excepted.
They have all their respective guardians, taskmasters, and
drivers, who immediately punish the least stop or inad-
vertency, and often will not allow the poor creatures time
to eat their bread, but, like Nehemiah's men, they must
work with one hand, whilst they put their coarse morsel

of bread into their mouths with the other. After such a wearisome day, it frequently happens they are hurried away to some filthy work in the night-time, with this call in Spanish, "Vamos a travacho cornutos," *i.e.*, "Out to work, you cuckolds," an appellation of the bitterest reproach among the Moors, except "Thou son of a Christian." But a circumstance more affecting than all these rigours is that men, created in the image of God, have been harnessed in carts with mules and asses. Their lodgings in the night are subterraneous dungeons, round, and about five fathoms diameter, and three deep, going down by a ladder of ropes, which is afterwards drawn up, and an iron grate fastened in the mouth; and here they lay upon mats. Neither has their fare anything more comfortable in it, consisting only of a small platter of black barleymeal, with a pittance of oil per day. This scantiness has put several upon hazarding a leap from very high walls only to get a few wild onions that grow in the Moors' burying-place. The slaves usual habit is a long coarse woollen coat with a hood, which serves for a cap, shirt, coat, and breeches, and four pair of pumps for a year and a half, though lime and mortar, and their daily hard work, wears them off their feet in half the time. It is moderately computed that many Christian slaves have been suddenly killed by Muley Ishmael and other emperors merely out of wantonness, and sometimes finding fault with their dispatch, or manner of working, of which they could have no competent idea. If it be accounted an honour to be the sovereign's slave, like some others, it is very burthensome, for they are not only harder worked when in health than those of private persons, but much more neglected in sickness—though of the care bestowed on the latter, it may with great propriety be said that the remedy* is worse than

* *Note 6.*

the disease. The only alleviation is, that the slaves are allowed to make brandy, and the Jews are taxed with the materials. This is owing to a notion infused into the emperors, that the Europeans would lose all their ingenuity and vigour without now and then a draught of that inspiring liquor. May that notion ever obtain there! But experience shows us that the frequent use of spirituous liquors both enervates and stupefies. The Moors are extremely cautious and artful in purchasing slaves, and, besides inveigling questions and cajolings, have many methods and tokens to judge what ransom a slave will yield, and accordingly will readily give some hundred pounds where all promising appearances occur; but where the greater ransom is expected the usage is the worst. These exasperating sufferings have often prompted the slaves to make some efforts for liberty, but they have mostly terminated in miscarriages. Once a large dungeon was undermined, and great numbers in a fair way to escape, but a Dutchman, breaking his leg by a fall, and crying out with the anguish, they were retaken, and put to a torturing death for an example.

Commodore Stewart was conducted to Mequinez from Tetuan by Hamet Ben Ally,* one of the Emperor's Bashaws; in which embassy, the Commodore being a very able, well-accomplished, courteous, and indefatigable gentleman, notwithstanding his often meeting with very great insults and manifest dangers, managed his point so well, that in six weeks, or thereabouts, he procured the enlargement of all the English slaves (those under my unhappy circumstances only excepted), in number three hundred and one,† releasing them from their long servitude

---

* Hamet ben Ali ben Abdallah.

† The actual number freed was 296. Of the 1,100 European slaves at Mequinez, 300 were English, "not including nineteen who had turned Moor."

and chains, and conducting them to Tetuan, where he
found shipping ready to transport them to their so long
desired homes, there being then more than six years
expired since they were first made prisoners, that is to
say, those taken with poor unhappy me, who you may
imagine could not be allowed to go with them, though I
most humbly intreated it by all the means I could devise,
all my solicitations being in vain, so that I was obliged
to content myself to effect my deliverance by private
escape when opportunity offered ; to which end the
ambassador gave me very friendly advice, together with
many other marks of his favour.

I might here fill up a great deal by way of the several
occurrences relating to the ambassador's entrance, behaviour, usage, and return to Teutan, and,* in short, many
other passages of moment, and which I very particularly
remember; but as I am informed there is a book of it
already printed, I shall not go about in anywise to interfere with it; Commodore Stewart being a gentleman of
so much good observance, that mine might only prove to
be a recital of it, or at least a dull tautology of the same
things ; though I cannot again help saying, and which, no
doubt, in that report is omitted, that he in every point
behaved in so polite, most Christian-like, and majestic a
manner, as not to derogate from, or lessen the trust
reposed in him by his royal master, whose person and
dignity he was to represent, and which I heartily wish
had been so well performed by a certain gentleman† sent
to Mequinez on the same errand about four years before
him ; then had it in all likelihood prevented many aching
hearts, and my poor uncle, with many other poor Christian
slaves (who during that interval died there), had probably
been still alive.

> * *Note 5.*   † Admiral Delaval.

I being now become, as I have already said, one of the Emperor's attendants, and always ready in obedience to his commands, in receiving him bare-headed and bare-footed at his entrance in, or at his going out of the palace, I having my head shaved every eighth day for that purpose; and not only his guards treat him with this submissive respect, but his whole court, consisting of his great officers and alcaydes, assemble every morning about eight or nine o'clock, all barefooted, to know if the Emperor has been abroad (for if he keeps within doors, there's no seeing him, unless sent for), or if he's returned in a good humour, which is well known by his very looks and motions, and sometimes by the colour of the habit he wears, yellow being observed to be his killing colour; from all which they calculate whether they may hope to live twenty-four hours longer.

If the Emperor comes out, their necks are all held out, their eyes fixed on the ground; and after this manner the crouching creatures pay their homage, and when they approach him, fall down and kiss the ground at his horse's feet. If he speaks, some swear by their god what he says is true; others, at every pause he makes, cry out, "God lengthen thy days, my lord; God bless thy life;" which once occasioned an accidental jest, for he was saying, "May I be called the greatest of liars, if I have not always conceived a great esteem for the English;" and making a little stop at the word "liars," his officious court cried out, "Yes, by G—d it's true, my lord!"

If he comes not out, he sometimes sends for some of them; at other times he has the door opened, and orders them all to pass muster, and they go one by one cringing by the door. If he only goes a little way out of the gate of his palace, they follow him on foot through the dirt; and he is a great man, and esteemed a great favourite,

who advances as far as his stirrup; and if he has occasion
to send a message, though never so trivial, the best of
them are ready to run, without respect to age, rank, or
favour (even his favourite Hameda used to make his
court this way), and return bespattered up to their eyes, at
least all over their white drawers, and other garments
which are white; nay, I have heard that Hamet Ben
Haddu Attar (who was ambassador in England in King
Charles the Second's time) was once surprised without his
shoes, walking barefoot in a great deal of dirt by his
horse; and without regard to his age, or the pretence he
had to his favour, was sent to the furthest part of the
town in that condition.

During all intervals from such my attendance, I was,
together with the rest of the guards, generally exercised
in shooting with a single ball at a mark, which was
generally a red cap set on the top of a high piece of
ground, distant about two hundred paces; at which we all,
to the number of nine hundred, and something more, fired
together at the word of command, the Emperor so ordering
it, thereby to make us the more expert, ready and dexterous, in case of any warlike action, whereto we might
happen to be suddenly called; though for my part, I
could never see who that person was that hit the mark,
if hit at all. It was, I think, impossible for any to
determine, though I must acknowledge it to be a very
good way in training up soldiers to their making of close
vollies; yet, indeed, I saw at other places these firings
single, and where the party was so lucky to hit it, he did
not fail of a suitable reward.

You may now perhaps imagine, that as I was altogether
at the Emperor's command, I was quite excluded the
sight and favour of the Queen; which I was not, often
receiving very valuable acknowledgments thereof, even

from her own hands, and certainly through her means I hitherto fared the better with the Emperor. For, in short, she thought she could not oblige me enough, and therefore was over solicitous in an affair which I had much rather should have been let alone, and such as I thought she would never have urged or consented with herself to have put upon me, it being quite the reverse of my inclinations ; yet did she urge it, and obtain it, and was, no doubt, some time in bringing it about with the Emperor.

One day, the Emperor being on the merry pin, ordered to be brought before him eight hundred young men, and soon after as many young women, who also instantly appearing (as being, no doubt, before ordered to be ready at hand), he told the men, that as he had on several occasions observed their readiness and dexterity in obeying him, he would therefore, as in some part of recompense, give every one of them a wife ; and which, indeed, he soon did, by giving some by his own hand (a very great condescension), and to others by the beckoning of his head, and the cast of his eye, where they should fix. After they were all coupled and departed, I was also called forth, and bid to look at eight black women standing there, and to take one of them for a wife. At which sudden command, I (being not a little confounded, as not at all liking their colour) immediately bowing twice, falling to the ground and kissing it, and after that the Emperor's foot (which is the custom of those who desire to be heard, as well as a very great favour and condescension to be permitted to do), humbly intreated him, if, in case I must have a wife, that he would be graciously pleased to give me one of my own colour. Then, forthwith sending them off, he ordered to be brought forth seven others, who all proved to be Mulattoes ; at which I again bowed to the ground, still entreating him to give me one of my own colour ; and then he ordered them also to depart, and sent for a single woman, full dressed, and who in a very little time appeared, with two young blacks attending her, she being, no doubt, the same he and the Queen had before particularly designed for me. I being forthwith ordered to take her by the hand and lead her off, which she holding out to me, I perceived it to be black also, as soon after I did her feet; at which I started back, like one in a very great surprise, and being asked what was the matter, I answered him as before; when he smiling, ordered me to lift up her veil (it being the custom of the country for women to go veiled) and look at her face; which I readily obeying, found her to be of a very agreeable complexion, the old rascal crying out, in a very pleasing way, in the Spanish language, " Bono ! Bono ! " which signifies, " Good ! Good ! " ordering me a second time to take her by the hand, lead her off, and keep her safe.

This artificial blackness of her hands and feet was laid on by a certain grass, first made into powder and mixed with water, alum, and the juice of lemons, and is called el bhenna, being brought from the river Draugh, about ten days' journey from Mequinez, and still further from Taffilet, and several other places.*

At our coming out of the palace, we found her father, mother, sister, and sister's husband, ready to receive us (the latter being a man of very considerable authority, as having under his command one thousand five hundred young men, who go under the name of " Kiadrossams," being all the Emperor's brothers-in-law, and are generally at his call in the palace), and received us very courteously indeed, desiring me, as it was the Emperor's pleasure to give me his sister, that I would always behave to her as a loving husband, so far as she

* *Note* 7.

deserved, and at the same time exhorting her no less in her duty to me. This we both readily promised to each other, and which was indeed by both of us as faithfully performed. Their next request being our acceptance of an apartment (as having none of our own) in this our brother-in-law's house, till such time as we were provided with one of our own which we as readily came into, and together with the old gentry went with them, though we were for the first night lodged in separate lodgings, as I suppose were the rest, being all first obliged to appear again the next day at the palace, there to receive a certificate from the secretary as a ratification or finishing stroke, and each couple fifteen ducats, each ducat 6s. 8d., making in all just £5 in English money, two thirds for the man and one for the woman, as the Emperor's bounty on such-like occasions, before our marriage could be completed. Which being paid, and our certificates delivered, each man paying for them (as the secretary's fee) sixteen blankeels (pieces of money of about twopence in value each), we were all dismissed to make merry with our friends, and celebrate our nuptials. As I and my spouse were well accounted of amongst the better sort, we did not want for plenty of wedding guests, nor they for plenty of good eatables, I having provided, at my own charge (over and above that of my brother-in-law's) a fat bullock, four sheep, two dozen of large fowls, twelve dozen of young pigeons, 150lb. weight of fine flour, and 50lb. of butter, with a sufficient store of honey, spices, &c. All which, our wedding holding three days, was clearly despatched with a great deal of mirth, and friendly satisfaction. Yet was it the soberest wedding you ever saw, for we had not, among all this great company, one intoxicated person, though they had all as much liquor as they would drink; but such, indeed, as might sooner break their bellies than operate in their noddles, being only water; wine being by their grand impostor, and great prophet, Mahomet, altogether forbidden. And though it is death by his law for any person discovered in drinking it, yet it is by some privately drunk, even to excess, there being great store, and very good in Barbary, besides what they catch from other countries.

This short way of marrying his guards the Emperor frequently put in practice, by often ordering great numbers of people before him, whom he marries without any more ceremony than pointing to the man and woman and saying, " Hadi yi houd Hadi," that is to say, " That take That;" upon which the loving pair join together, and march off as firmly noosed as if they had been married by a Pope. He always yokes his best complexioned subjects to a black helpmate, and the fair lady must take up with a negro. But the Moors in general, who are not married by the Emperor's command, use a great deal of ceremony about it.

When a man wants a wife, either his mother or some of his female relations must go a-courting for him (custom not permitting the man to visit the woman beforehand), and when the bargain is made, which is done before the Cady, or justice, the bride is to keep within for eight days, her friends coming to rejoice with her every day, and a Talb, or priest, also visiting her, and discoursing on that holy state; they pin the basket with a religious hymn appointed for that purpose. The husband, with his friends, repeats the same ceremonies for five days before the consummation in a house which he has, or must take to bring his wife to. The last day the bride is put into a cage, covered with a fine linen cloth, and carried on men's shoulders to the house of her intended husband; her friends, relations, and music going before. Her brother (if she has one) leads her into the house, where a room is

appointed for her and the women; the man remains also
in his room with his friends. When the evening ap-
proaches they are let loose by the company, and the
bridegroom goes to his wife's apartment, where he finds
her alone, sitting on a cushion of silk, velvet, or such fine
things as they can borrow (if they have them not of their
own) : underneath there's a silk quilt; before her stands a
little table, about a foot high, with two wax candles upon
it. Upon her head she has a black silk scarf, tied in a
knot, the ends hanging on the ground behind her; her
shift is made with large sleeves like the men's, and long
enough to hang behind her like a train. Her vest is of silk,
or velvet, buttoned close to her hands, and reaches to the
middle of her leg, adorned with lace at the hands, and all
over the breast. She has the same linen drawers described
in the women's dress, and collars of pearl or fine stones,
and (if she can get them) of lions' or eagles' claws tipt with
silver; in her ears she has great rings of gold or silver,
and the same about her wrists and ankles, sometimes set
with stones. Her slippers have thick soles made of cork,
covered with gilt leather, and edged with the same, which
is a mark of greatness among them, the Emperor and some
few more wearing them. Her cheeks are painted with
cochineal, which colours yellow at first, but being rubbed
presently turns red; with this they make one great round
spot on each cheek. Their eyebrows are painted black,
and continued quite round their temples, like a pair of
whiskers. They also make some small black spots, in
imitation of patches, near their nose and lips, a black snip
on the end of their nose, and a black stroke, the breadth of
a straw from their chin, reaching down below the pit of
their stomach, and how much lower I can't tell, for there
they begin to be covered; they paint their eyelids and the
sides of them with a black powder called Alchol [or anti-

mony], putting some of the same into their eyes with a little
stick; the palms of their hands are all blacked, and from
the top of their thumbs round the fleshy part is a black
stroke, and one from the end of each finger to the palm;
their nails are dyed yellow; they also have many fine
scrawls of black on the top of their feet, and their toe-nails
are likewise dyed yellow.

Thus beautified, the bride sits behind the table mentioned
before, with two wax candles upon it, holding her hands up
the height of her face, with the palms turned towards her,
about a foot distance from each other, and as much from
her face, upon which she is to look, and not on her husband. After this follows some other customs such as are
still practised to a certain extent in Spain, though they
do not call for minute description here. It need only be
remarked that the bridegroom is obliged to stay at home
for seven days, and the bride a whole year, who is kept ever
after so close from the rest of mankind, that not even her
father or brother can have the privilege of a visit unless
her husband is present.

All the women paint after the manner before mentioned
at their public meetings; they are extremely handsome,
and bred up with the greatest care imaginable in relation to
their modesty; the fattest and biggest are most admired,
for which reason they cram themselves against marriage
with a food called Zummith; it is a compound of flour,
honey, and spices, made into little loaves for that purpose.

And now I am soon about to enter from the sports of
Venus into the field of Mars, though indeed I had the company of my wife by intervals for some years after; for our
wedding being ended, I was on the fourth day, or day
after, ordered to prepare myself for my departure to a
garrison in the province of Tamnsnah,* about six days'

* Temsna.

journey from Mequinez, whence (after taking leave of our friends) I and my wife set out the same day, accompanied by six hundred of those who were so lately married with us, three hundred of them being put under my command, and the other three hundred under the command of Musa, or Moses Belearge, a Spaniard, they likewise taking with them their wives. These six hundred men were of different nations, French, Spaniards, Portuguese, and Italians, but not an Englishman amongst them, except myself. Bashaw Hammo Triffoe (half Spaniard and half Moor), Commander in Chief of that province, with two thousand men, went also with us, and being obliged to take with us a priest, the Emperor commanded me to find one, if possible, who was both blind and deaf, that if in case any of us should happen to take a cup of wine (as being used thereto in our own respective countries, and therefore might the sooner do so in his) he might not be capable of taking notice of it; for, added he, "though I will by no means encourage it, yet should I much rather be excused from receiving any complaints of that nature, whereby to give them any uneasiness." Though I made the best inquiry I could, yet I could by no means meet with such a one; therefore I recommended to him my wife's uncle, a seeming honest man, and one who was approved of by the Emperor, and by us as joyfully received. Then after being strictly charged to reside the first month at the castle of Tamnsnoe,* and the next at Stant, so as each garrison might have him by turns every other month, he cheerfully travelled on with us; and though he could both see and hear very well, yet was I under no apprehension of his giving the Emperor any uneasiness on our account, I having before seen him to drink wine in a plentiful manner.

We are now (women included) 3,206 on the road, all

* Tanisna.

well mounted, the men on fine horses, which, as they are
so famous for goodness, it will not be improper to say
something of the Moors' method of managing them. The
Moors take a great deal of pride in their horses, and order
them after a very different manner from us ; they back
them generally at two years old, and shear their manes
and tails till they come to six, thinking that makes them
strong. At grass they tie sometimes the two fore feet
together, at other times a fore foot and a hinder one. In
their stables they have two iron pins drove into the ground,
one before, and the other behind them, at the distance
of about three feet from their legs, which are fastened
together with ropes, like our traves, with which we teach
horses to pace, but being short, they draw their legs
together under their bellies, and two ropes come from their
hind and fore feet, which are so tied to these pins that they
cannot stir above one foot backwards or forwards. Their
collar is also made fast to the pin before them, which has
a ring for that purpose ; under them is a hole covered with
pieces of timber to receive their water, and a little on one
side a bed of sand, or sawdust, for them to lie upon. They
have no mangers, but eat their straw or grass off the ground.

All their horses eat grass in April and May, and, if it be
a good year, great part of March ; at other times they eat
straw instead of hay; their barley is given them in a
woollen bag, put over their heads. They are never dressed,
nor their manes or tails combed, but when dirty are
carried to the next running water and washed, and if they
design to have them look fine, they use a little soap. Some
will take it amiss that you touch a horse with the palm of
your hand to stroke him, and say there is venom in that
part which is hurtful to horses. They never crop their
tails or ears, nor geld them, for they like no maimed
creatures but eunuchs for other reasons.

They have one sort which they call " Noble Horses,"
who bow their heads about at the approach of a man.
Their love is so great for horses, that not only they are one
of the three things for which the Moors have a proverb, as
most esteemed, viz., " A horse, a woman, and a book," but
they keep even the genealogies of them for two or three
hundred years, and are nice in distinguishing the true from
the mixed generations. They have a base way of shoeing
them, cutting off the fore part of the hoof, and forming the
shoe into a triangular shape, with the two points almost
meeting at the heel, which points are made very thin, and
after the shoe is fastened with three nails on each side are
beaten as flat to the hoof as possible; but some time ago
the Emperor issued out an order that upon pain of death
all horses should be shoed with round shoes, a certain Turk
having persuaded him that was the best way.

They are not subject to distempers, and the Moors (as
Windus puts it) know not what you mean by a farsey
or glander, nor have I ever seen a spavin or mullender.
As for the Berebbers in the mountains, they never shoe
their horses; and their feet are certainly firmer than ours,
for a horse went to Tetuan from the camp, and came back
the next day, without a shoe, which is fifty miles, and notwithstanding he was forced to cross a mountain full of
rocks going and coming, not being able to pass the low way
for a river, it was not perceived he had the least crack in
his hoof, or made any complaint of his feet. Their horses
live to a great age, and are very fresh at fourteen or fifteen,
the reason of which seems to be their going so gently on
the road, where they seldom are put out of a foot-pace, but
when they exercise the lance they make them bestir them-
selve to some purpose. *

Our women rode on mules, and we got that day to the

* *Note* 8.

river Bate,* about five leagues, the second day to the castle Cassabjibbad,† the third to an old ruined castle called Phinseera,‡ and the fourth to the walls of Sallee, Hammo Triffe and his people encamping and remaining without three days, during which us new-married people had the liberty to go into the town, were lodged there, and most sumptuously feasted by the Emperor's order, as indeed were the Bashaw's men in their tents, there being great quantities of provision of all sorts carried out for that purpose.

The next day we again set forward, and got to Sharrot, all the way being very woody, and plentifully stored with wild hogs, and of them we killed some hundreds, which, perhaps (as their flesh is by the Mahometan law forbidden), may be imagined was either for pastime or antipathy, yet had we another reason, viz., by way of revenge on a very large boar assaulting the Bashaw, and killing his horse under him, though the beast instantly lost his own life by it. These boars, and especially those of a middle age, are very dangerous creatures, having very long tusks as keen as knives, and which, with the very great force and fury they execute their intention with, will rip up anything as soon. The tusks of the old ones generally turn up like a ram's horn, so that they cannot so well bring them to do mischief suitable to their rage. Here are also great plenty of lions, tigers, wolves, &c. However, we saw none of them that day.§

Sharrot is a river discharging itself into the sea about seven leagues to the southward of Sallee, and plentifully stored with many sorts of very excellent fish; and fording it the next morning we got that day to Gaebedad,‖ where are laid up for that part of the country the Emperor's

* Beth.   † Kasbah Jbad.   ‡ Fnsira.
§ *Note* 9.   ‖ Gabdad.

stores of corn, which the Moors have a way of preserving
without damage for a hundred years together by putting it
into pits, plastered within and over the mouth when they
are full.   The next day, at ten in the forenoon, we got to
the castle of Tamnsnah, where I, by the Bashaw's order,
immediately entered with two hundred of my men and our
wives, the old garrison marching out to make room for us;
and my other hundred men were sent with their wives to
Bevash,* another castle about three days' march from
thence, to be commanded by a deputy of my own appointment.

At my entrance into the castle, I found all things pretty
much in disorder, there being almost a general want of
everything, for what the old people had they carried (or
at least most of it) with them.   However, these wants
were, by the Bashaw's diligence (he remaining encamped
without sixteen days), very plentifully supplied by sending
us in provisions and stores enough for our subsistence for
six months.   This being done, he rose with his small
army and departed, as I was informed, for Stant, a garrison distant from thence about twelve leagues; where after
staying also about sixteen days, and settling Belearge
and his men therein for the better security of the
Emperor's stores of grain laid up there, he departed for
the City of Morocco, of which he was the governor.

Now have I and my comrades for some time nothing to
do but to contrive ways and means how to divert ourselves,
which we did after the best manner we could devise, living
in an amicable manner and passing our time very
pleasantly, here being to be our station for about six
years, though I was several times, with some part of my
men, ordered thence for the space of six or seven months,
and thither again, and once of almost two years at a time.

* Babash.

My first absence was about three months after my first
arrival, when I received a peremptory command from the
Bashaw to attend him with two hundred of my men as
soon as possible I could, and to leave my other hundred to
secure my several garrisons; in pursuance of which order
I drew out one hundred and fifty of my men, leaving the
other fifty to take care of the garrison and the women,
and immediately departed, and got that day to the castle
of Stant, where I found my old friend Belearge was with
a like number gone before me.   The second day I marched
to Geefaar, an old ruined castle, though well stored with
water and many other necessary refreshments, both for
man and horse; and the third day, about noon, to my
other castle of Broash, where I directly entered, and
found my other hundred men and their wives very well,
who received us very courteously; and I forthwith drawing
out fifty of them, which made my number complete,
proceeded, and got that evening to Cedeboazzo, in the
province of Talgror,* and the next to the river Tensift,
whence very early the next morning, the Bashaw meeting
us with good store of provision on the road, we were by
him conducted, with fine music playing before us, in great
pomp to the walls of Morocco, where I found my old
friend Belearge with the rest of the Bashaw's army,
encamped without the walls of the city, though as we
had before, by the Emperor's orders, liberty to go into
the town of Sallee, so were we now ordered to march
together into Morocco, and there treated after like manner,
with this difference only, the former being at the charge of
the Emperor and this at that of the inhabitants, as indeed
was also that of the whole camp.

The city of Morocco is very well situated, and reckoned
to be twelve miles in compass.   It is said to have had

* *Note* 10.

formerly a hundred thousand houses in it, but since the
kings of Morocco have removed their court from thence
to Mequinez, it is greatly decreased, but its palace or
castle is the stateliest of any in Africa, it being of a
prodigious extent, some of the rooms of which have large
fish-ponds in them, and the fishes may be seen swimming
in the looking-glasses, with which the ceilings are covered.
There are likewise in this city very fine gardens, and many
ancient and well-built mosques. The famous aqueducts,
which bring water to it from above forty miles, are a
stupendous work.

We rested seven days at Morocco, being ordered on the
eighth early to march out and join the army; when we all
rose, and marched that day to the river of Wadden
Enfeech, distance seven leagues, where we rested that
night, and the next day to Mesmeath,* at the foot of a
very high mountain, and where (on account of the inhabitants there and thereabout not having for some time back
performed the payments of their wonted tribute) we
settled our camp and rested fifteen days, during which,
notwithstanding they had before our coming refused to
pay it, yet did many of them at our approach, and
especially Tolbtrammet Mesmeasoy,† the head and chief
of that province, come to meet us; and declaring to the
Bashaw, after the most solemn manner, that he had no
hand in the rebellion, as he understood had been basely
and maliciously rumoured of him, the rebels having made
use of his name for the better carrying on their wicked
designs, he entreated that he would believe him innocent,
as in reality he said he was, having never made the least
advance that way, but, on the contrary, had done all in
his power to prevent it, even to the extreme hazard of his
life; therefore desired he would not look upon him as an

---

* Amezmiz.   † Taleb Hamed Amezmizi.

enemy to his country, but accept of the few presents he had brought him with as good a grace as they were offered by him with good will, and in all due obedience, being in truth those of one of the most loyal, most dutiful and obedient of his Majesty's subjects. These presents being somewhat considerable, as four very fine horses and furnitures, several Zurbees,* or Turbants, with a handsome purse of gold to usher them in, the Bashaw had not the heart to refuse. He likewise entreated the Bashaw to suffer him to send in provision for the army, which was also complied with, and plentifully performed during our stay there, with everything else in conformity to our demands. After a few days we rose and marched thence seven leagues further, along the foot of the mountain, and pitched our tents in the evening at Emsoeda,† keeping ourselves under arms for the first part of the night in great silence, and about midnight (drawing out six thousand men, our whole number being eight thousand, leaving the other two thousand to feed and keep safe our horses) we marched on foot up the mountain, where we had an account many of the malcontents had sheltered themselves; which being very woody, steep, and craggy, our horses could have been of no service to us, but rather a hinderance, and would have been a means of exposing us to be taken off separate from each other by the enemy in their lurking places before we could discover them.

* Mr. Meakin suggests " Erzez " (?).   † 'Msida.

CHAPTER III.

The Emperor's troops surprise the castle of Ehiah Embelide, and take vengeance upon the rebels—The march is continued and the revolted towns reduced to submission—Touching divers little places—A new mode of defence—A city is taken by storm—Fire and sword—The return to Morocco with hostages and booty—The Fast of Ramadan—The punishment of a Queen who failed to "nick the time"—Her expiation in the way of bridges and golden balls—Mr. Pellow attempts the madcap freak of trying to steal the latter—The palace gardens and the death of Muley Ar'scid (Reschid)—The march to Mequinez, and a description of the intervening country—The amount of plunder brought back from the Expedition—Treatment of prisoners—An English executioner—The soldiers meet with their wives—Shooting and fishing—Feasts regardless of the law—Wild beasts and their ways.

THIS being the month of February, wet, very cold, and the nights pretty long, the Bashaw marching at our head, we got under the walls of a castle called the castle of Ehiah Embelide, where we lay close, with strict silence and undiscovered, till sunrising. Then we saw several herdsmen and shepherds coming forth with their cattle, they being always at night secured within from the frequent incursions of the mountaineer Moors, and for fear of lions, tigers, wolves, and jackals, the sheep standing in as much danger from the latter as they do from the wolves, who are, in their voracious nature, sufficiently imitated by the jackals, of which there are vast numbers in Barbary. I had heard by several people in England that they were innocent though

subtle creatures, and served only for procuring prey for
the lion, by hunting before him, thereby to keep themselves in his favour and from his paws, yet have I often
seen them lay hold of an innocent sheep, and in a moment
tear him in pieces, and have very often shot them for their
pains and eat of them into the bargain.

On these herdsmen's discovering us they instantly
alarmed the castle, and no doubt to the great surprise of
those within, more especially when they saw us so near
their walls, surrounding them so as they might not in any
probability hope for escape; yet did they prepare for
defence, and fired upon us with small arms very briskly,
but cannon they had none, no more than ourselves, killing
in all but three of our men, we having got ourselves so
close under their walls that they could not bring their shot
to bear on us, we calling to them, "That in case they any
longer resisted, and did not directly deliver up the garrison
into our hands, we would put every one of them to the
sword."   To which we not receiving such satisfactory
answer as we had expected, and having by that time
almost finished three several mines at the foot of the
castle wall, and of which those within were not the least
apprised, we fired them all about one and the same time,
making such breaches as were wide enough for twenty
men to enter in a breast at each, and immediately began
to pour them in.   Upon which the rebels, being in a terrible
fright, submitted to mercy, crying out for quarter, and
humbly on their knees imploring pardon for themselves
and families, assuring us that, on receiving clemency, they
would make their future behaviour appear to be no less
deserving of the Emperor's favour than those of the most
observant of his subjects, alleging that they had been led
astray by those higher up in the mountain, and whom,
had they not come into seeming measures with, would

then have destroyed them to a man; therefore, said they,
" revenge yourselves on them, and you shall soon see that
we will not be backward with our assistance to subdue
them." Notwithstanding this submission we killed eighteen
of them, and amongst them the governor's brother and
his brother's son, whose heads were cut off by the
Bashaw's own hand, the latter being first obliged to
drag that of his father's round the army by a rope fixed
about his neck and to suffer a most cruel scourging from
most of them, and then both their heads, with the edge
of the Bashaw's sword, were set upon the castle gate;
at which the governor, as having five sons of his own,
was no doubt in a most grievous agony, and kept still
on his knees, desiring the Bashaw to believe him innocent,
and by horrid and repeated imprecations of it declaring
that he had no hand in that rebellion, and that his being
there was more by compulsion than inclination, and that
he hoped that he could not be accounted so stupid as not
to suppose the Emperor would soon make reprisals on
them, and that notwithstanding he had been so unhappy
to father the fictitious name of governor, &c. Yet he most
humbly hoped that the Bashaw would believe him and
permit him to use his utmost efforts by way of reducing
the remainder of the rebels who had compelled him to so
undutiful a behaviour, and whereby he might not only in
some measure make his royal master compensation, but
our future proceedings by far less hazardous, for that he
would directly send his messengers to acquaint them with
his own present condition; and in case they any longer
persisted in their rebellion and did not directly come in,
and with them bring in to him their respective tributes, he
was ready to spend the last drop of his blood in subduing
them. Then the Bashaw ordered him off his knees, and
after some short private conference their countenances

seemed to be on both sides more calm and serene ; and a
general pardon was, to the general joy, proclaimed. On
which many came in soon after with their presents and
arrears, as indeed did all in those parts, saving only four
little towns, which might contain in them about four
thousand men that bore arms, lying on or very nigh the
top of the mountain, then covered with snow and very
difficult to get up, which retarded our march sixteen days ;
when there falling a very great flood of rain, which
washing the snow down the mountain, so that there
appeared some likelihood of our being able to get up it,
though with great difficulty, we departed from the castle
of Ehiah Embelide, taking with us the governor, and
marched (or rather indeed climbed) up as fast as we could,
and got to the first of the towns that evening, very
sufficiently tired.   However, we soon entered, but found it
quite desolate, the inhabitants having all retired into the
next town, at about half a mile's distance ; which, as
their neighbours were joined with them, was no doubt of
more strength and security ; but the darkness of the
night coming on apace, the Bashaw was determined not
to attack them till the next morning.   However, we
carried off all we could find here, set the village on fire,
and retired to some distance, where we settled for the
night in an open camp.   About sunrising we took one of
their spies, who had that night been out upon the scout,
and brought him before the Bashaw, who, after threatening to cut off his head, told him that in case he would go
directly into the town, and on his honour immediately
return to him with their answer if they intended to deliver
up the town without resistance or not, he would give him
his life.   On which, and the late governor of Ehiah
Embelide's also vouching for the Bashaw's performance
of his promise, he went in and soon returned with an

answer to his message, and to challenge his pardon,
telling them that the inhabitants would not on any terms
surrender, but were resolved to fight it out, even to the
last man. Which (said he) they told me they had before
signified to the governor of Ehiah Embelide, by way of
answer to his message relating to their coming in with
their arrears; that he was a dastardly fellow, and if he
should happen to fall into their hands he should be the
first sacrifice to their rage. The Bashaw finding what he
had to trust to, ordered us directly to cut down and bind
up a great quantity of large faggots or bavins, which, as
I was then altogether a novice in affairs of that nature,
I really thought were for no other use than burning.
However, I soon saw my ignorance therein, and thought
them to be a tolerable safeguard from the shot of the
enemy, every other man taking one of them, and carrying
it lengthways before him and his comrade, who was close
at his back. Advancing after this manner till we got
within half musket shot of their walls, and notwithstanding they kept a continual firing from the walls of the
town upon us, yet did we not receive any damage thereby,
but intrenched ourselves breast high in a very little time.
About a dozen of our best miners and an engineer
advanced with their pick-axes and other necessary implements even close under their walls, and immediately
fell to work to undermine them. When they were to be
relieved they retired going backward, carrying their bavins
next their faces; and a fresh set, on the contrary, advancing, took their post. In the meantime the rest of us kept
a continual fire, so that the enemy did not so much as
dare to peep at those places of the walls where our people
were carrying on their mines at the bottom. And though
we were three days before we had finished them to our
engineers' minds (there being in all three), yet did they

through like means, brought under the Emperor's subjection; which was the last and finishing stroke of this our so long and dangerous expedition, in which we lost at the least fifteen hundred of our men, and amongst them sixty of my small number; myself, I thank God (though I had my clothes shot through in several places), escaping unwounded.

We now began our march for Morocco, where we safely arrived at the end of four days, having with us all our baggage, the greatest part of our booty, and three of the chief men out of every province to be carried with us to Mequinez, to give an account to the Emperor of their behaviour in the late rebellion, the Bashaw and the remains of his people encamping again without the walls of the city, Belearge and myself, with the remains of ours, being again ordered to march in; and we were by the citizens most courteously entertained, selling our shares of the booty, viz. bullocks and sheep in vast numbers, for what any would give us; I having myself, with several others in partnership, sold there and at several other places before on the road, four hundred sheep for so small a price as a blankeel each (which is twopence), and thought ourselves well off; for what could we have done with them, being obliged to take that or nothing; besides, we were glad at any rate to get rid of the very great trouble of driving them.

Now am I again in the city of Morocco, of which I do not doubt but it may be expected that I should give a particular description and an account of all its curiosities; which I could readily, and would as willingly do, did I not think it altogether inconsistent with my main point, and would enlarge my history to very little purpose, by only repeating what has been, without doubt, before made public. Therefore I shall, by way of digression, mention only two of the most agreeable curiosities which my own

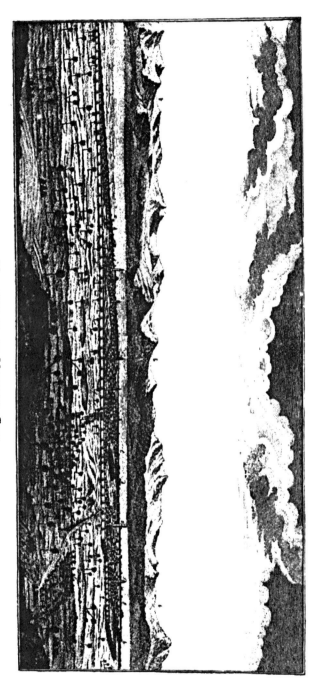

MARAKESCH, OR MOROCCO CITY.

fancy was struck with, the one within and the other without the walls, and refer my readers for the rest to the several books already printed ; and first of that within the walls, which was four golden globes of a large size and value, fixed on the top of the tower of the Emperor's palace, and which, according to common fame, were set up many hundred years ago on the following occasion.

Lulla Oudah,* daughter and widow to two of their ancient Emperors, happened one day to see in a woman's basket some very tempting peaches, and being at the same time with child, she took one of them, and after biting off a small part of it, and putting the remainder into the basket again, she went away, saying, "She had but just nicked the time ; " of which some of the bystanders taking notice and pondering thereon, it soon came into their minds that it must be very near the time of the commencement of their Ramadam, which is a very strict fast they observe every twelfth moon ; and during which, if any are known to eat or drink from an hour before the breaking of the day till the appearance of the stars, it is death by their law ; and they are not only obliged to abstain from all manner of food, but likewise from smoking, washing their mouths, taking snuff, smelling perfumes, or conversing with women.

Those who are obliged to travel may drink a little water ; and such as are sick may borrow a few days of their prophet ; but they must and do repay punctually, when they recover strength. In the towns they run about the streets and wake all those people they think are asleep, that they may eat and so be the better able to support themselves in the day ; they rise three or four times in the night, and sleep again. Such as are libertine, and used to drink wine, abstain from it at this time.

* 'Aoodya.

7

It is usual in the towns every evening, when the fast of that day is ended, for a trumpet to be sounded from the castle, to give notice of it; before which time it is pleasant to see the posture of the Moors, one holding a pipe ready filled, while he impatiently expects the sound of the trumpet; another with a dish of Cuscassoo before him, ready to run his hand in; some got close to the fountains, to be the first that shall drink. On the eve of their Lent they make great rejoicing, shouting and repeating the name of God, and watch for the appearance of the moon, at which they fire their muskets, then fall to saying their prayers, the Emperor himself sometimes at their head; who, to persuade the people of his great regard for religion, keeps this fast four months every year; but they are obliged to observe it only during that one moon.

The poor longing queen was, by a due inquiry into the moon's age, found to have transgressed in it by three hours, and immediate sentence was passed upon her, which put her under a grievous agony, as not knowing (though she was exceeding rich) how to get off; though at the last (on her promising to set up those balls, and to build four several bridges over two very rapid rivers, viz., three on Murbia,* and one on Wadlabbid,† wherein abundance of people had been before drowned, in their attempting to cross over) she obtained a pardon; and these promises were in her lifetime accordingly performed, together with several large buildings, and donations for schools, alms-houses, &c., over and above her very extraordinary and chargeable obligation.

These four globes are, by computation, seven hundred pounds, Barbary weight, each pound consisting of twenty-four ounces, which make in all 1,050 pounds English; and frequent attempts had been made to take them away, but

---

* Om-er-Rbia.   † Wad-el-'Abid.

without success ; for, as the notion ran, any attempting it were soon glad to desist from it, they being affrightened, and especially at their near approach to them, in a very strange and surprising manner, and seized with an extraordinary faintness and trembling, hearing at the same time a great rumbling noise, like as if the whole fabric was tumbling down about their ears, so that, in great confusion, they all returned faster than they advanced.

This did I often hear, yet had I a very strong itching to try the truth of it ; and to gratify my curiosity, I one night (having before communicated my intentions to two of my men, and persuaded them to go with me, and provided myself with candles, flint, steel, and tinder) entered the foot of the tower, lighted my candles, and advanced with my comrades close at my heels till I had gained at least two-thirds of the height, I still going on. Then really, to my seeming, I both felt and heard such a dismal rumbling noise and shaking of the tower (my lights at that very instant quite going out), as I thought far surpassed that of common fame. Yet was I resolved to proceed, and called to my comrades to be of good courage, but having no answer from them, I soon found they had left me in the lurch ; upon which, falling into a very great sweat, I went back also, and found them at the bottom in a terrible condition. And so ended my mad project, and which was, I think, a very mad one indeed, for had I obtained the globes, in what could it have bettered my deplorable condition, being always obliged to follow the Emperor's pleasure, and with whom it was a most sufficient crime to be rich. And so much for my foolish attempt on the golden globes.*

What I was most delighted with, without the walls of Morocco, was a most curious and spacious garden for the

* *Note* 11.

king's pleasure, when he came to that city, it being by far
the finest of all I had ever seen before, being kept in the
most exquisite manner, as to its curious and regular walks
and arbours, and laid out with large collections of most
kinds of fruits and flowers, the fruit trees being very large,
and dressed and pruned in a very elegant manner; so
that their wood, and especially that of the orange trees,
was always in a prosperous condition, almost ever green,
blooming and bearing fruit. In this garden I saw the
trunk of an old tree (which I was told was that of a very
large orange tree), with great spreading branches, which,
when in its prosperity, was the death of Muley Archid,
the Emperor's brother (who, about seven years before,
killed Muley Em Hamet, his elder brother, with his own
hand, to make way for himself to the Empire). He being
one day in his garden on horseback, and his horse running
suddenly out with him, so that he could by no means stop
him, carried him under this tree, in a moment appearing
on the other side without his rider; and notwithstanding
the quick approach of his attendants, they found him
quite dead, hanging by his head in a forked limb. On
which account there was, no doubt, no little hurry all over
the empire, he being reckoned one of the most famous
conquerors in those parts, having made himself master, by
the sword, of the kingdoms of Tafilet, Fez, Morocco, and
Sus, and by this means the old tyrant (whom I was
obliged to serve) came to the throne. However, this
accident was by all reckoned a just judgment.

And now being obliged to proceed immediately for
Mequinez, I shall, after so long a digression, which is
chiefly indeed from hearsay, return to my own story, and
be upon the spur with the tribute taken upon our late
expedition, together with that for one year, for the city of
Morocco; and which being somewhat extraordinary, I

think it may not be amiss to mention the particulars of it,
whereby the reader may in some measure guess at the
richness of the inhabitants.

It consisted first of 140 quintals, or Barbary hundreds
of silver coin; secondly, 204 fine horses, the latter four
being (over and above their wonted and required number)
a voluntary present to the Emperor, were the finest that
could be got, with saddles, bridles, &c., altogether as finely
set off, and especially that for his own riding, the saddle
being behind and before well strengthened with plates of
gold, and curiously inlaid with many very valuable jewels,
the stirrips of beaten gold, and the bridle and other
accoutrements in every point suitable, with a fine scimitar
and crooked knife, the hilts, scabbard, and sheath also very
rich, hanged to the saddle by gold chains; thirdly, 200
mules with pads on their backs, completely fitted with
stirrups, and their bodies covered all over with scarlet
cloth; fourthly, 200 blacks, males and females, a like
number; fifthly, 800 quintals of gunpowder; sixthly, 4,000
gun stocks; seventhly, 800 turrahs of fine dressed goat
skins, each turrah consisting of six skins; eighthly, 400
quintals of butter; ninthly, 400 ditto of honey; tenth,
400 ditto of oil; eleventh, 2,000 gun locks; twelfth,
2,000 sword blades; thirteenth, 2,000 powder horns;
fourteenth, 60 quintals of elhennah or black grass, the
same sort of that my duchess's hands and feet were dis-
coloured with at the time of our precipitate marriage; and
fifteenth, 400 quintals of dates. All which being packed
up, the muleteers proceeded with the caravan, and we
with the army as a convoy, and got the first day to the
river Tensift, about five leagues; the second day to
Ceedearhal,* seven leagues; the third to the river Tessent,
fourth to Boahgobah, fifth to the river Dernoe, sixth to

* Sidi Rahal.

Tedlah, seventh to Ceedelle Feellelle,* eighth to Tendrah, a very fertile and large plain, surrounded by vast mountainous woods,—and here many of the Emperor's cows (though no doubt it is a very dangerous place for cattle, on account of the very great number of savage beasts lurking hereabouts) are generally kept; the ninth to the river Gregrah, the country also very woody, and plentifully stored with lions, and I think the boldest I ever saw, coming that night even into our camp, making a hideous and terrible noise, killing two of our horses and eating them all up before daybreak; the tenth to the castle of Agoory † short of Mequinez about six leagues, travelling at the rate of about seven leagues a day; and the eleventh we came into Mequinez in good season, and secured all the effects of the caravan within the walls of the Emperor's palace; and after the Bashaw had acquainted the Emperor with our proceedings, and given him a particular account of the behaviour of the several prisoners, we were all (after making a plentiful supper) ordered for that night to rest.

The next morning, about eight o'clock, the Emperor ordered the Bashaw to bring the several prisoners into the yard before him, when myself and Belearge, by command of the Bashaw, immediately guarded them in. The old tyrant looking at them very furiously (after asking them a few questions), told them in an angry tone " that they were insolent traitors, and they should soon reap the fruits of their late rebellion." Then he ordered three of the most notorious of them to stand with their backs pretty nigh the wall. The victims obeying, the executioner was ordered, on the Emperor's signal, to cut off their heads, which (the signal being given) he instantly did at two strokes, two of them being cleanly severed at one.

* Sidi el Fileli.   † *Note* 14.

Then the Emperor ordered the rest of them to be removed
to some further distance; and though, no doubt, they were
every moment expecting to share in the same fate with
their neighbours, yet did the Emperor, on their promising
him to behave better for the future (contrary to their own
and every other body's expectation then present), pardon
them, though with this restriction, " Never more to return
to their old respective places of abode, but to reside at
those which should be by him allotted for them." Then
Belearge and myself receiving twenty-five ducats each,
and our men six, were ordered to depart and carry off
with us the prisoners; who after being stigmatized or
branded with a hot iron in their foreheads, were like
vagrants put the next day out of the city, every one to
inquire after the place of his allotment. What became
of them after I never heard.

The execution of these three captives was performed by
the hands of an Exeter man, whose surname I have forgot,
though I very well remember his Christian one was
Absalom,* and that he often told me he was by trade a
butcher; and he was, no doubt, a very bold man, for
before the execution the Bashaw offering him his sword,
he smiling told him, that he thought his own to be altogether as good, which he should soon see; and which,
indeed, was as soon made appear; he further adding,
that had it not been of very excellent temper it could not
have performed what he had hitherto done with it.

Now are Belearge and myself again ordered into the
palace, and by the Emperor commanded to lay open several
of the presents to his view. After taking particular
notice of them, and ordering also for the fine horses, &c.,
to be brought forward, he said, " These dogs are certainly
very rich; but what was this in comparison of what they

* Abd-es-Selam.

had yet behind, and that this was no more than their giving him a small part of what was before his own ; therefore, if they did not mend their manners by sending him more for the future, he would send his messengers to fetch it, with their heads into the bargain." Here we may see the dangerous consequence of arbitrary power, and thank God that we are governed by such wholesome laws as are those of this happy nation. Here every one is allowed fair trial in matters of life and death, as well as like equity in the recovery and keeping their own ; whereas, those unhappy people who are subject to arbitrary tyrants, are to-day rich and great, to-morrow beggars, often losing their lives with their estates, all without being heard, or any daring to inquire for why or wherefore.

If a poor man in Barbary gets but a pair of oxen to plough, he would not only be liable to be robbed of them by the next little mercenary governor, but forced to sell his corn to pay an arbitrary tribute. For which reason the land has no proprietor above two or three leagues round a town; and if you chance to spy two or three small cottages, you may be sure they belong to some Alcayde, and the poor people that live in them to till the ground are his servants, and, like the cattle, receive no other recompense for their labour but the wretched provender they eat.

The Emperor and his Alcaydes confound all trade in the country, by robbing such as have any reputation for riches. For which reason the Moors take it for a token that you design them harm if you say they are rich; and it is believed that there are abundance of Arabians who have concealed estates (for this country, fifty or sixty years ago, was extraordinary rich), and yet appear so miserable, that they have nothing but an Alhague* to cover them,

* Haik.

which serves for shirt, drawers, coat, cloak, bed, and everything. But those who lived in towns were presently ruined. I have heard that the people of Tetuan were very considerable traders, and some of them left off business when the Emperor came to the throne, thinking by that means to go off with what they had got and be quiet. But on the contrary, being once taxed for people of substance, the same continued till the fortunes they had got were exhausted, and nothing coming in, they are at present reduced to extreme want, and several of them have been shown without a bit of bread; for all those who are in any condition are such as continued to trade, because they had at that time no other means of subsistence.

In 1699, the Governor of Fez sent to a merchant to give him a hundred ducats for the tribute. He having before got off for a great deal less went to excuse himself; upon which he sent for four or five negroes, and ordered them to torment that man till he gave them a thousand. This he paid, after being stripped and left all day in the sun, hung up by the thumbs, and some other artful cruelties; and the condition of all the country is such, that any pretence whatsoever will serve the Alcaydes to rob and plunder their people.*—Thrice and four times happy the inhabitants of the British Isles. Here every man enjoys what is his own with the most undisturbed security, and without any fear of having it ravished from him by the hand of power. Here no haughty king dares to lay his hand, without the leave of the laws, on the meanest of his subjects; much less doom them to unjust and cruel deaths. Thankful, daily thankful ought we to be to Heaven for placing us where the inestimable blessing of liberty still exists; and how jealous ought we to be of it, and how careful that we never in the least contribute

* *Note* 12.

to overthrow the noble fabric of British liberty, by any imprudent or mercenary actions of our own.

And now for our departure for our respective garrisons again ; for which, after refreshing ourselves and recruiting our men, Belearge and myself departed, leaving Mequinez with our full numbers, and arrived at Tamnsnah—by the same road, and halting at the same places as we did at our first going thither—after the absence of seven months, without anything particular happening on the road worthy my notice. On our approach to the walls of the castle, all the women, and several of the men, came forth to meet us, which you may imagine to be a meeting both of a great deal of joy and lamentation amongst the fair sex—those who met their husbands rejoicing, and those who did not behaving like other widows on suchlike occasions. However, I remember that I entered very merrily with my girl, insomuch that I had forgot, as knowing her to be with child before our departure, to ask her if it was a boy or a girl, though, indeed, being settled within, this was my first question; to which she, smiling, answered me that she had had, about six weeks before, a daughter, but that a certain woman had taken it from her. At which—as not so soon seeing through the cunning of the wench—I was very much enraged, when the cunning gipsy ordered the child to be brought forth, declaring the thief to be the midwife; at which I was again pacified, and not a little pleased with the joke, laughing and embracing the child very heartily.

Now are some merry, and some seemingly sad, for a day or two; after which we lived again very comfortably together, Belearge and his people, with sixty of mine, being departed for their respective garrisons, where, no doubt, they were received with the like joy, mixed with lamentations.

Now are we again at liberty to divert ourselves, spending the best part of our time in shooting and hunting in the woods, as indeed we spent a great deal of it that way before our setting forth on our late expedition, but I being in such a hurry to join the Bashaw at Morocco, I did not then stay to mention anything of it; though here I shall not forget to tell you that we used to spend then, as well as now, usually four days in the week at that employment, here being vast plenty of game, as partridges, hares, and jackals. And though our sport was attended with great danger on account of the vast numbers of wild beasts, even to the extreme hazard of our lives. On which account some may think the game we got too dearly bought. Yet did not we so, as still thinking the profit to sufficiently compensate the danger, generally, I say, passing therein four days in every week, and with very good success, killing vast numbers of all kinds, coming home at nights laden, and seldom or never failing to refresh ourselves by a good supper of such as we liked best, and to wash them down with a cup of good wine, for which we never wanted, the inhabitants of the country round bringing us in several skins a week, together with many other presents, on account of our destroying the wild beasts, for which purpose we set every Saturday apart, the inhabitants joining us with their dogs, arms, &c., and amongst us all we made a notable slaughter. At our return home at night we never failed of three or four wild porkers roasted whole, nor of a fresh supply of wine, which, though two very presumptuous breaches of their law at Mequinez, yet did we—as being of other nations, and the Emperor winking at it—continue in it, stopping the mouth of the priest with a flowing bowl, though I could never bring him to eat pork.

Being now surrounded, as it were, with wild beasts, and

time upon my hands, I shall, by a short digression, acquaint you by what means any going the road about their lawful occasions may best escape them. And first for the tiger, which I take to be by far the most dangerous creature, though not so terrible as the lion, he generally lying near the roadside on his belly, with his legs under him in a proper posture for leaping, so that he is on his prey before it can well avoid him, and which cannot be done at all, but by a due observance of what I am about to tell you; and, in the first place, I hope you will allow it highly necessary for travellers in such countries to carry their eyes before their feet, whereby they may, before too nigh approach, the better discover the enemy, and which, if they do not, they may repent it when too late; and having so discovered him, to take their eyes instantly off him and continue to walk on their road, and if he is not hungry they are quite safe. Whereas, on the contrary, should they happen to make the least stand, and stare him in the face, he leaps directly at them, and it is a hundred to one if they escape with life. The lion, on the other hand, shows himself boldly sitting on his breech with a very sour look in the road, about twenty or thirty paces before travellers. In this case, instead of walking on and keeping their eyes off him, they must stand still and stare him full in the face, hollowing at him and abusing him all they can; and for fear he may not understand English, in the language—if they can—of the country. Upon this hollowing and staring at him, he gets him on his legs, and, severely lashing his loins with his tail, walks from them, roaring after a terrible manner, and sits himself down again in the road, about the distance of a mile or two, when both traveller and lion behave again in the same manner; and after proving them thus a third time, the lion generally leaves them without interruption. This I know to be true, having been obliged several times in my travels through the country to make the experiment, and which I shall hereafter have occasion more particularly to mention.* But to return to my history.

* *Note* 18.

CHAPTER IV.

Mr. Pellow goes with the troops to Guzlan, and shares in the siege of that town—He is wounded—The place surrenders and a number of the inhabitants are beheaded—Our author is advanced in the Moorish service and returns to Tamnsnah—He is now inured to the cruel wars of the Emperor, and takes part in most of his attacks on rebellious tribes and towns—He goes across the Atlas to Tafilet, and enters the desert—How the Royal children are disposed of—The wild Arabs or Bedouins and their ways of life—Bashmagh the negro and his extraordinary adventures—He is sold and sold again by his own request, and always returns with a good horse and weapons—The return to Tafilet—The march to the borders of Algeria—The author often visits his countrymen at Sallee, and begins to meditate his escape—The death of Muley Ismail.

ABOUT this time, that is to say, after about four months enjoying ourselves at Tamnsnah, there came repeated accounts to the Emperor of the revolt of a considerable number of his subjects in and about Guzlan, a strong town near the deserts, distant from Mequinez about twenty-three days' march, after the rate of twelve leagues a day, they having made very bold incursions into several parts of that neighbourhood, plundering all who refused to come into like measures with them, destroying the caravan of the Laurbs,* a wild sort of people, coming thither from the coast of the deserts for dates, killing sixteen of the Emperor's blacks sent there with his credentials to receive

* Arabs.

and bring to Mequinez their accustomed tribute; and, in short, having thrown off all obedience, stood upon their guard, fortifying the town with strong walls, and putting into it great quantities of warlike stores and provisions. On which so frequent alarms, the Emperor, being not a little enraged, immediately ordered an army to be in readiness to march against them, and myself and Belearge, with four hundred of our men, to hasten directly to Mequinez to join them. There we found the rest of the army, making with us eighteen thousand horse and eight thousand foot ready to march, sending before us four pieces of heavy cannon and two mortars, to be forwarded over the mountains at the expense of the several inhabitants, and guarded with all the foot. Early on the fifth day after we followed them with all the horse, lodging the first night at Agoory, the castle at the foot of the mountain, where we before finished our rout at in our march from Morocco; the second at the River Gregrah * ; the third at Tendrah; the fourth at Ceedeellee Feelellee; the fifth to Tedlah, where we rested two days; the sixth at the River Dernor ; † seventh at Inesergoe; eighth at Goahgobah; ninth at Ceedeaummorroh ; ‡ tenth to Ceedearhall; eleventh to Soakdegirgah,§ on a mountain about six leagues over; twelfth at Tinneough Gollowey, the foot of that mountain on the other side, and where we were most courteously entertained by Alcayde Abdestadick Elgolowey,‖ a very good man of the sort, and then Governor of that part of the country, he being in very high esteem with the Emperor, on account of his keeping his people under very strict order and good decorum ; thirteenth at Wadd el Mella, a very noted river, on account of its winding itself in a very intricate manner between the mountains, we being

---

* Gerygra. † Denooa. ‡ Sidi 'Amara.
§ Sók el Gergah. ‖ Al Kaïd Abd-es-Sadok-el-Gallowey.

obliged to cross it in one hundred and one several places, all in one and the same day; the fourteenth at Wourszessez, two or three small villages also between the mountains, commanded by Alcayde Bauhessey Elverzessey, who also behaved very friendly to us; fifteenth at a small river called Zouyet et Handore; sixteenth at Agadis, which is the head of the River Draugh, and where we found prodigious quantities of palm trees, with dates in perfection; seventeenth at Zooyet Burnoose; * eighteenth at the castle of Tanzulin; nineteenth at the castle of Tarhatter, commanded by Muley es Sherriff, one of the Emperor's sons, who was there waiting for our coming, he being ordered by his father to join us with sixteen thousand foot; and after refreshing ourselves there two days, he accordingly marched with them at our head, our whole army being now forty-two thousand; the twentieth we lodged at Taugahmadurt, in the province of Swagtah; the twenty-first at Fumulbungh; † the twenty-second at Binney Zibbah; ‡ and the twenty-third, about two of the clock in the afternoon, we got to Guzlan.§   Here the malcontents bidding us welcome twice that night, we soon found we had work enough to do.   For we had but just time to view the situation of their garrison, and by our engineers' orders began to work on our trenches, before the rebels sallied forth in number about twelve thousand, and began directly to fire upon us with small arms very briskly; which we as briskly answering, drove them back, and fell to work upon our trenches again.   Then, about ten at night, they having trenches without very near ours which we were ignorant of, they gave us on a sudden such a smart volley as in a very little time killed six hundred of our men, and amongst them were eighty-seven of mine

* Bénûs.   † Fûm-el-buągh.
‡ Beni Zibbah.   § *Note* 14.

and Belearge's. However, we gave them as smart a reception, killing many of them, and driving the rest quite
home in at their gates, and Belearge and myself, with the
remains of our people, followed them as far as we could,
sheltering ourselves as close as possible at the foot of their
outer wall, and keeping ourselves there in great silence till
daybreak ; when our General, seeing us there, and that
none of the rest of the troops had followed us, he seemed
to be highly enraged with them, calling them cowards, and
earnestly entreated our engineers to think of some safe
and speedy way for our retreat, for that, should we attempt
an open one, we must in all likelihood be taken off all to a
man by the shot of the rebels from their walls. Therefore
they, for the better and safer facilitating our retreat,
ordered to be directly cut down a great number of palm
and date trees, with which was thrown up a barricade
before a body of men, who carried on a trench of about
six feet deep towards us, through the sand, still covering
behind them with trees, and sand on the top ; so that they
got close to us, and we all safely retired through this
trench by eleven o'clock that forenoon.

This town of Guzlan lay in a flat and sandy country,
environed with three several walls and two ditches, one
within another, and without by millions of date trees,
spreading many leagues ; so that we are now obliged to
cut down many thousand of them with the fruit thereon,
and to carry matters on more discreetly and with less risk,
we having an undoubted account by several prisoners of
the enemy's strength and resolute defence, being at the
least eighteen thousand strong, and well provided with
provision, small arms, and ammunition. Therefore the
engineers said it was in vain for our men to expose themselves to the shot of the rebels, which they could fire upon
us all at once from their three several walls, and therefore

8

it would be mere madness in us to act any otherwise than upon the defensive, till we had raised a battery, in order for the better bringing our cannon to play upon them. But the sand sliding so fast from underneath us, it was a good while before it could be perfected to their minds, we being first obliged, to prevent the sand from running, to secure it by driving strong piles, and close buttresses thrown between the piles and it. By this means it was completed, our cannon mounted, and all that night we kept a continual firing from them, throwing many balls on their walls, though all without making the least breach, they being built of sand, strengthened with great limbs of trees in such a manner that we had only our labour for our pains; and the rebels, who knew they could not receive any damage from our firing, flouted at us after a very joking manner. Our engineers, perceiving their mirth and jokes, told the General that they would, in case his Excellency was so pleased, make them laugh the wrong side of their mouths; which he consenting to, they threw in a couple of bombs, which we soon found to take off the edge of their laughter, and to terrify them very much, they being followed by a great many more. And which, no doubt, did them a great deal of damage, they being thereat so highly provoked, that they made several sallies, though still driven back again with great loss of men on both sides; and though I was generally in the thickest of them, yet I escaped, thank God, hitherto unwounded, though indeed I could not, by the next day at noon, say I was invulnerable; at which time a Moor being brought by some of our men, who had been out a-foraging, in our camp with a mule laden with bread. The rebels seeing this from their walls, and knowing him to be one of their party, were so highly exasperated at, that they made a sudden sally; and notwithstanding they were as warmly received by us, yet did they kill of us fifteen hundred men, and wounded me by a musket shot lodging in my right thigh ; and which, though it was soon taken out by a German surgeon,* a man of great skill and diligence, and I was most carefully attended by him. Yet was it full forty days before I was again fit for action, and then I was again exposed to those hasty messengers, scarce a day passing without some of them coming even so near me as my skin, and carrying my clothes off in many places, and still the danger increasing, as was every day sufficiently manifest, and still the far more bloody part to come.

And now our General, on his seeing the malcontents so resolute, ordered our engineers to consider on ways and means for carrying on a mine under their several walls and ditches, which they instantly undertook to do from the trench already brought home for our deliverance, and as quickly set about it. However, it was a long time before it could be performed, the country being so very loose, that we were obliged to bind it every inch as we went on by firm timber and planks on the top, to support it, by which means it was at last perfected, and carried successfully on under their several walls and ditches, and at last blown up with that success as to make so wide a breach as we all, in a very little time, entered sword in hand. And now there was, between us and the rebels, for the space of two hours, bloody work, when the remnant of them retired to one end of the town, which they had so well fortified against our fury, that we were in a manner glad to give out for eight days, though during this time we often saluted them with our cannon and bombs, and they us by frequent sallies ; and which, I think, was by far more bold and noble. But they being reduced to a very great degree, and seeing their longer resistance would be in vain, their provisions being

* *Note 15.*

quite spent, and ammunition very short, they having un-
advisedly left the greatest part of it without, and which was
now in our hands : so that they began, for want of it, to
grow very faint, and many of them dying of hunger, the
remnant beat a parley, humbly imploring the General that
they might be spared with their lives, and promising, on
such terms, to surrender and behave to the Emperor for
the future with the most dutiful obedience.   To which they
were very reasonably answered, that rebels reduced to such
a condition, after so long and bloody a resistance against an
army of their sovereign prince, and from whom they had
thrown off all allegiance, and in a most insolent and con-
temptuous manner bidden him defiance, were not in any
wise to be allowed to become their own choosers.   Therefore
they should submit to the will of the General, who would,
no doubt, soon order such punishments to be inflicted upon
them as he was before ordered by his father to do, according to the merits of the case.

And which, poor wretches, they, being almost all starved
and miserably wounded, were obliged to submit to, and had
all their heads instantly cut off on the spot ; by which, I
think, rather than to continue longer in such misery (as
being thereby at once freed from all their calamity), they
were by far the better off.   Thus ended this long and
bloody rebellion, which took us up about seventeen months,
and with the loss, on our side, of fifteen thousand of our
men.

And now our General, as not having thought, in the heat
of blood, to preserve some few of them alive for triumph,
orders vast numbers of heads, already cut off, to be carried
in lieu thereof to his father, as a present ; though at last
they became stinking to that degree that he was obliged to
be contented with their ears, which were all cut off from
their heads, and put up with salt into barrels.   For we had

carried so many stinking heads so long a way, it must
certainly have very much annoyed the whole army, and
probably have bred an infection in it.

Now are we obliged, on account of our wounded men, to
remain here six weeks longer; when we struck our tents,
and, after burning the town and demolishing the walls,
departed with some of them on handbarrows for Mequinez,
resting at Tarnatter six days. After which we proceeded,
leaving Muley Sherriff there with his people, marching back
so fast as we could, all the way diverting ourselves by shooting and killing many lions, tigers, and other very dangerous
wild beasts, the inhabitants all the way striving to outdo
one another in all good offices, bringing us in every day
sufficient of all kinds of provisions, both for ourselves and
horses. So that we fared very well, enjoying ourselves
with the produce of this plentiful country, having every
day fresh supplies of bread, butter, and honey, with abundance of very good beef and mutton, corn, &c., and all
without plunder or rapine.

The Emperor received us, at our arrival, very courteously,
and gave every soldier twenty ducats, he being highly
pleased with the conduct of Muley Sherriff, who he said
had sent him his reasons in writing, for not sending him
so many heads so long a way, and therefore he was highly
contented with the ears; though not, as he said, but that
the sight of the heads would have given him a great deal
of pleasure; yet, as they were stinking, and might possibly
prove of ill consequence to the army, he thought them to
be by far better left behind. He then ordered the barrels
to be opened, and the ears to be turned out before him;
and after looking at them for some time, he with a pleased
though stern aspect ordered them to be again put up and
laid by till another rebellion, when he would, he said, send
them to the rebels as a present. However, they were all

at last strung on cords, and hanged along the walls of the city.

Now are Belearge and myself ordered, after recruiting our men (as having in this so long and dangerous expedition lost at least one half), to be again in readiness, as the next day, to depart for our respective garrisons, though this my old and very good friend was not destined to do, he being, poor man, that night poisoned by a woman, as was generally supposed, in order to her getting his post for her husband. But in this she was very much mistaken, all his men being put under my command, and all of them the next day marched with me, getting safe to my castle of Tamnsnah, after the absence of twenty-one months.

Now, after visiting and settling my new men in Belearge's old garrison of Stant, I again returned to my wife, and stayed with her and her daughter in peace for four months. For as I was now so far inured in their bloody civil wars, I was seldom exempted from making one, and receiving many wounds therein. Nor had I (during the remainder of the reign of old Muley Ishmael, and the short reigns of Muley Hammet Deby, and Muley Abdemeleck, two of their succeeding emperors, and until Muley Abdallah, who succeeded the last of them, was a second time by the Black Army driven out) any rest therefrom, unless by these little intervals at Tamnsnah, and some few others at our garrisons, which I shall take notice of in their proper place. But being, as I said, now again with my wife at Tamnsnah, I endeavoured to make the time as agreeable to my inclinations as I could possibly, never failing to employ myself, according to our usual days, in our old sport of shooting and hunting, and still bringing in plenty of game, and many skins of good wine ; though this, indeed, as I had now many new people to deal with, was under closer cover. Not but they might have been all soon brought to drink

wine, but being seldom or never faithful to their promise,
I was thoroughly resolved not to trust any of them in that
way; and indeed I thought wine too good for the best of
them, and therefore I was fully determined not to run any
hazard on that account.*

Now are my four months expired, and I am again ordered
directly, with two hundred of my men, to Mequinez, where
we were soon joined with two hundred more, we being all
light horse; and we were immediately ordered by the
Emperor to proceed for Taffilet, and thence, as a convoy to
the caravan, to the castle of Toal, seventy days' journey
in the deserts, to convoy and bring safe to Mequinez his
wonted tribute from those parts. We proceeded according
to the following route :—The first day to Bittitt; second to
Suffrooe: third to the river Gregoe; fourth to the mountain Ceedehamsou † ; fifth to the river Melwea; sixth to
Cassavey, a castle commanded by Muley Hasham, a near
kinsman to the Emperor; seventh to Embetsgurvan;
eighth to Buiny Menteer; ‡ ninth to Cassersook, in the
Province of Endoughrah; tenth to Fumulhungue, and the
eleventh to the city of Taffilet, where we rested four days;
here being the beginning of the deserts this way.

The kingdom of Taffilet is famous for dromedaries, which
will travel as much in twenty-four hours as ordinary horses
do in eight days. It is much more barren than any other
part of Barbary, and has only this one city in it, in which
reside many of the Emperor's sons; for when they are of
such an age that he is apprehensive they may be a cause
of trouble at home, he no longer lets them live in the
palace. But they are disposed of as the interest of their
mothers prevail, either in some post about the Court, or
sent to Taffilet, where the Emperor gives them a plantation
of dates, on which they live. But those who have the mis-

* *Note* 16.   † Sidi el Bamsoo.   ‡ Beni M'tir.

fortune to lose their mothers, or are out of favour, come to want, and are as much neglected as if they had not been born, never returning to Court again.*

In Taffilet vast quantities of most sorts of commodities, coming out of the deserts and country round, are laid up in storehouses, till they are by the Emperor's orders otherways disposed of.

We now entered with our pilot and the caravan into the deserts ; who, after seventy days' travel over this sandy ocean, he still directing us by the compass, brought us in safety to the castle of Toal, a garrison kept by Moors, always residing there, and where the Laurbs or Arabs, people inhabiting those parts of the deserts, bring in once a year their wonted tributes, as gold, ivory, indigo, &c., which they traffick for on the coast of Guinea.†

These Laurbs are an awkward sort of people of an olive colour, and wearing the hair of their heads and beards without ever cutting or topping, it runs naturally up into rings or curls, so that their heads look all one at a distance as if they had growing on them large bushes of furze. Their only clothing, is a blue linen shirt, and a pair of drawers reaching a little below their knees, with which they are furnished by the Moors. Their habitations, or tents, are made of the skins of tame and wild beasts. Their food chiefly the flesh and milk of camels, as being of all others most in esteem with them, though sometimes they eat mutton, having many sheep of a large size, bearing a long spiry hair instead of wool ; antelopes, and, in short, any other sort of flesh they can catch, as lions, tigers, ostriches, &c., and dates instead of bread. Their language, called Laurbea,‡ is much the same with that of the Moors, as only differing some small matter in the pro-

* *Note* 17.   † *Note* 18.
‡ El Arbya or Arabic.

nunciation, so that they understand each other perfectly
well.

The cattle here (that is to say, camels and sheep) are
tolerably well fleshed ; which I think to be pretty strange,
there being but here and there scarce anything of pasture
to be seen, and that chiefly in and about those places where
the springs of water rise, and where you may see vast
herds of those creatures almost continually browzing on a
long spiry weed, bearing a seed much in colour and taste
like that we call worm-feed.

When the natives kill a camel, they make him first kneel
down on his knees with his nose close to the sand, and then
they cut his throat in that posture, always beginning to
take off his skin from the bunch on his back (which is all
fat) and so downwards. Then they cut him into small long
pieces, drying all but what they reserve for present use by
the wind and sun, and then it is hung up in their tents ;
and though it is not at all salted, yet will it, if kept dry,
remain good for a long time. In short, their stomachs
being pretty much upon the cannibal, they are not very
squeamish, generally (to save themselves the trouble of
dressing) eating it raw.

We had with us in this expedition several blacks, and
amongst them one (a very stout, active, cunning fellow)
named Bushmough, a native of the Brazils, to whom one
of the chief men amongst those Laurbs had a very great
fancy, and was several times very desirous of buying him ;
and which the negro perceiving, and seeing the Laurb one
day coming again with some of his people to our castle, he
asked me why I did not sell him. "Sell you," replied I,
"why so ? No, no, Bushmough, by no means." "Foh,"
said he, "sell me for good gold and mutton, and you shall
see I will be soon with you again." "Oh but," said I,
"when once they have got you into their clutches, they will

not again so soon let you go as you may perhaps imagine;
therefore, good Bushmough, be content to remain as you
are rather than to run any such hazard." "Oh no, no,"
said he, "you need not, as to that, be under the least
concern; for you may depend on Bushmough's soon finding his way back again." Upon which, and on my seeing
that I could not be at quiet from the Laurb's so pressing
and frequent importunities, and I having before received
orders from the Emperor to sell any of the blacks, by way
of furnishing the army with provisions, I sold him for
twenty gold ducats (which is just nine pounds English)
and sixty sheep; and after I had taken the Emperor's
clothes off him, and had in lieu thereof given him an old
blanket, and the money and sheep were delivered to me,
he was, by his new master, mounted on one of his own
horses, which I had the day before (by the Emperor's permission also) sold him, together with several others past
our service.

And now is honest Bushmough about to depart with his
new master, calling to me in Portuguese that I should not
be under any the least doubt of his honour. For that if he
could not, according to his inclinations, get off so soon as
he intended, and I might expect, yet I might depend on his
coming back so soon as he possibly could. And then the
Laurb turned about his own horse to be going, looking
very chary at Bushmough, ordering him to ride on before
him, and was, no doubt, not a little pleased with his
bargain, bidding us all farewell; and Bushmough played
a thousand antic tricks, as long as he thought himself in
our sight.

And now is honest Bushmough gone with his new master,
with whom we must leave him seven days on hard drudgery,
he coming back to us again on the eighth, about day-break,
mounted on one of his master's best horses, and a long lance

on his shoulder, dressed only in a blue shirt and drawers, according to the Laurbish mode, calling to me to be let in; of which I being acquainted, hasted as quick as I could to receive him, accosting one another very friendly, and laughing very heartily; and after we had laughed our fill, I asked him what he thought of the gold ducats, and if he was not afraid I would keep them for myself. "No, no," said he, "that is the least of my fear, I being, if you please, determined with myself, that they shall be laid out for the good of so many of us as you shall think fit;" adding that unless it was my own fault, I should sell him again and again. In which, indeed, he was soon after as good as his word, for I sold him again to two other several masters, as will be related presently. I inquired of him the particulars of this comical adventure; first asking him what reception he had met with there. "What reception?" said he, "oh, very good, very good; I was used very courteously indeed, and wanted for nothing they had." After he had related to me some of his pretty pranks among his late owner's household, "Very well," said I, "but are you not afraid your old master will be soon here again to inquire after you, as you may depend he will? And how will you manage then?" To which he (walking on tip-toes laughing) told me "that he would leave that to me, and that if I should let him go, it might not be in his power to get his friends any more gold ducats or mutton." Then in an angry tone I told him that he was a very pretty fellow, in intending to carry on the droll further; but I could not forbear laughing, no more than himself, I being really surprised to see the subtlety of the creature.

However, I told him in good earnest that he should take especial care not to let any of them see his face, for that I was very certain that his late master would be again with us very soon; as indeed he was the next morning very early at our gates, inquiring if his fugitive was come back: of which Bushmough himself brought me the news, running hastily, and saying to me in a soft, though pleasant manner, "My old master Laurb is come! my old master Laurb is come!" "Your old master come," said I; "pray what old master?" "Why," said he, "I tell you my old master Laurb." "No!" said L "Yes, indeed," said he, "he is, for I saw him myself with the great bush upon his horns." "Very well," said I, "and don't you intend to go with him?" "Oh no, no," said he; "but you shall see (if you will suffer me to put on a rich dress and to mount a good horse) that I will ride out, and soon make him glad to depart again without me; but you must be sure to tell him that I am a very near relation to the Emperor; which," said he, "will be very pretty, and then I will ride out and make some very good pastime." Therefore, to try his dexterity, he was soon rigged in a very rich dress, a turban on his head, a scimitar by his side, a lance in his right hand, and mounted on an exceeding fine horse richly accoutered; and then I, with some others of our people, rode out, and Bushmough in the midst of us, appearing very grand, bold, and as unconcerned as you please; and after my asking the Laurb what he would have, he told me that he was come to inquire after the black that we had sold him about eight days ago; who was, he said, gone off in a base manner with his best horse and lance, and that he was seen riding that way. "Indeed!" said I, in a seeming surprise; "but how came you to let him go? Certainly you must have used him very ill." "No," said he, "he had all the encouragement imaginable." "Oh, the rogue," said I; "a most ungrateful base rogue! he knew better than to come here. I wish I could light on him, that I might make an example

of the base villain, to the terror of all his countrymen."
Bushmough was all this while close by the Laurb, whistling
and behaving after the most unconcerned manner, though
hearing and understanding our discourse on both sides
perfectly well; when casting my eyes round, I soon found
the Laurb had fixed his on Bushmough, muttering to himself that he thought him extremely like him.

At which I asked him what was the matter; when he said
aloud that the black riding the fine horse was very much
like his, and that had it not been for his rich apparel, and
grandeur of his fine horse and furniture (by which he
appeared to be a man of much higher rank), he should
actually have concluded him to be the same. When I
telling him in Portuguese what the Laurb said, he
answered me, "I know it already," still keeping his
countenance, without the least alteration of temper or
behaviour, and riding up and down by the Laurb as close
as he could, till he seemingly agreed that it was not the
same black, asking if he was to be sold. "Sold!" said
I. "Oh fie, what are you talking of?" "Why," said he,
"what harm is in that?" "Indeed," said I, "the harm is
not much between us; yet, as he is a very near relation to
one of the Emperor's wives, should he know what you said
of him, he would no doubt be very angry with you; and,
as he is a man extremely passionate in his nature, making
no more of killing a man than looking him in the face, it
might not only prove of very ill consequence to you, but it
is even a hundred to one if he did not cut off your head."
At which he seemed, and was, no doubt, in a very great
hurry to be gone, and glad if he might depart in a whole
skin, desiring me not to tell the Emperor's cousin of his so
scandalous opinion of him, bowing to him with the most
profound reverence, and Bushmough behaving like the
Emperor's cousin indeed, not so much as giving him one

nod in return, but in a scornful manner turned upon him his back, soon after laughing very heartily to see, as he said, how disconsolate he went off, and how much like a fool he departed, throwing himself even in an ecstacy on the ground, and crying out, so well as his excessive laughter would permit him utterance, "Laurbs! Laurbs, Laurbs! Oh, poor silly Laurbs!"

Bushmough's first adventure proving so lucky and diverting, and being finished so well, he had now in a manner nothing else to do than to look out sharp for another chap, and which indeed he on the second day after had the luck to meet with. He running hastily in and telling me that he had just then spoke with some gentlemen Laurbs without, who had a very great mind to buy him, and that they lived in a quite different part of the desert from that of his old master, I went out immediately to them and asked what they wanted. They told me, to buy the black by my side; and finding them to be very eager for a purchase, I seemed altogether as indifferent and unwilling about it, by which I screwed them at last to forty gold ducats. There was now a dispute between the Laurbs, for some time, which of them should have him. However, it was at last agreed by them, that as they lived all, as it were, together, they would buy him in partnership; which indeed they did, and honestly paid me down the forty ducats for him.

After he had given me sufficient satisfaction as to his intentions of coming back (which he hoped would be in three or four days at the furthest), he merrily departed with his new masters, and was indeed better than his word, he coming to us again the next day in good season, and when I again asked him concerning his reception with them, he said it was not in anywise so agreeable with his inclinations as was that of his former masters, there not being, he said, so proper objects of his observance; therefore he was obliged to remain their debtor, till they were otherwise provided better to his mind. "Well, but," said I, "you don't, I hope, intend to go back to them, nor again to braze it out with these as you did with the former. If you do, I think it is high time for you to be dressing, for if I am not very much mistaken, I see them coming," pointing with my finger at some people I had discovered at a distance; whom Bushmough also discovering, he seemed to be highly delighted at it, and turned himself about to be going off; and then I asked him where he was going to. "Going to?" said he; "why, going to dress, for they will be soon here," intending to play again his old gambol. I told him, "No; for that I thought he had on that subject carried on the droll far enough before; therefore he should, at his peril, keep himself close within till they had an answer to their errand and were again departed."

However, I kept him in discourse, till the Laurbs came so near us that we plainly made them out to be the same; and then Bushmough cried out, "Oh yes, yes, they be my second masters indeed," humbly desiring me to give him leave to make them some pastime, "for that," he said, "was all they were like to have for their money, therefore it would be very unconscionable in me to deny it them. However, I still persisted in my former resolution, and told him, with seeming warmth, that in case he should offer to play any further pranks of that nature, I was thoroughly resolved to deliver him up to them; for that I was very certain all his art would not be sufficient to conceal from them the knowledge of his noble phiz, nor had these masters horns (so far as he could tell of) to stand in their light, as the former master's stood in his. So he was at last constrained to submit and tarry within, till I had heard the result of their message, and given them an answer; though this,

I am sure, was very much against his inclination, and he would, no doubt, have attempted some prank, had not I, by several repeated commands, ordered him to the contrary; and then I rode out with a few of our people, and asked them what they wanted. To which they answered me, that they wanted the black whom I had sold them the day before, and who, they said, ran away from them in a short time after they had him at home. "Run away!" said I, in a seeming surprise; "I can scarce believe you. Pray which way did he run?" "Nay, that," said they, "we cannot tell; however, we thought he might have been come hither." "Hither!" said I; "that you know he dared not, therefore you only jest with me."

, On which they confirmed it in the most solemn manner, assuring me that he was actually run away, wringing their hands, and lifting up their eyes together, as though they had at once lost all they had. And thus they continued to do for two days, still expecting his return; when I telling them what countryman he was, and that probably he was beating his way home, and their provision quite spent, and having no encouragement of getting any more from us, they returned in a very heavy and discontented mood without him; which Bushmough perceiving, he called after them from the castle wall, in Portuguese, "Here he is, here he is!" though this indeed he knew they did not understand.

And so an end was put to his second adventure, they giving him quite over; and he was now at liberty again to look out for a third, in which he managed so well, that on the sixth day following he got a new chap to purchase him, and I sold him for the like sum, viz., forty gold ducats, but again charged him on his life to make haste back again; which, if he did not (as we should be soon moving with the caravan), we should be obliged to leave him behind us.

"No, no," said he, "never fear that. Do you but take care
to set up at night a lighted torch on the top of the castle
wall, and never fear of my being back again before the
next daylight." And which, indeed, he was, coming to us
soon after midnight with two of the Laurbs' muskets, and
all their ammunition in two leather pouches, stealing with
them, he said, out of their tent whilst they were sleeping.
However, they were soon after daybreak back again to our
castle to inquire after him, sadly lamenting their loss, and
especially that of their ammunition and arms; to all which
we only gave them the hearing, they being at last no
better off than the others of their brethren had been
before them.

And now, after having had sufficient profit and pastime,
through means of honest Bushmough (though having a
very great mind to sell himself once more, he did not think
so), and all other matters finished to our satisfaction, we
packed up our treasure, and in seventy days got safe back
to Taffilet, making of it a very pleasant journey; which
I must in a very great measure attribute to the jocular
behaviour of honest Bushmough, seldom a day passing
without our meeting some of his old friends, and his suddenly crying out thereon, "The Laurbs! the Laurbs!"
running and skipping in the most comical manner, though
he had not the pleasure of meeting with any of his old
masters, which I dare say he of all things desired. Here
we rested seven days to refresh ourselves and cattle, and
then we proceeded, and got safe in eleven days more to
Mequinez, where we were well received by the Emperor,
sumptuously feasted by his order, and had every man
twenty ducats; and then he directly ordered us for our old
garrisons, with his service to our wives, where we safely
arrived, after the absence of six months.

Now am I again at my old sport, and busy killing plenty

9

of game, which was but for a very short duration, I being
all on the sudden soon after hurried away to try my fortune
in another part of the country, after a more hostile manner;
for at the end of the sixth week I was expressly ordered by
the Emperor again to hasten to Mequinez with two hundred of my men, where I found ready to march, on some
secret expedition, an army consisting of sixty thousand
men, horse and foot, commanded by Bashaw Gossoy, with
whom we were joined, and the next day marched with
them, our route being, as I then understood, for Binnisness,*
on the River Wadzeetoon † or River of Olives, near the
borders of the Morocco dominions, and the country of the
Argireens, on account of their denial of paying the Emperor's agents their respective tributes, which they had
refused to do for a long time back, after a most insolent
manner.

The first day we marched to Fez, the second to Keessan,
third to Tessan,‡ fourth to a skirt of the deserts, and after
three other days march thereon to Wishaddah,§ a strong
garrison, to keep the Argireens in awe, and wherein the
malcontents had as strongly fortified themselves. We
lying at a convenient distance for the night, our Bashaw
sent in a messenger the next morning, requiring them to
surrender the fort to the Emperor's pleasure, and to send
him out immediately sufficient pledges of their performance.
To which he was answered, "That they were thoroughly
resolved to the contrary, and that he should find he had
not children to deal with." With which answer the messenger in a very short time returned, and then we were all
ordered to entrench ourselves. But before we could finish

* Beni-Snous.

† Wad-el-Zeitoun, a branch of the Isser, so called from the great
quantity of olives gathered in its vicinity.

‡ Tsara, Tezza, or Tazza, still a considerable town and fortress.

§ Apparently the Hadaha of the old geographers.

our work, the malcontents sallied forth, in number about
ten thousand, who discharged their muskets on us, and
were returning again towards the castle, when six thousand
more of them within also sallying forth, and joining them,
they all of them turned upon us again, and there ensued
between us a cruel slaughter for the space of three hours,
thousands falling on both sides; and thus they continued
by frequent reliefs from the castle, to skirmish with us in
and out for three days. At they end of which, they (the
greatest part of them being already, by the force of our
superior numbers, cut off) surrendered to the discretion of
the Bashaw, Torogolgh their chief, with many others of
their principals, coming out to him with their excuses,
presents, and arrears, and amongst the former several very
fine horses, and a large sum of money for the Bashaw's
own particular use, and which, no doubt, was sufficiently
made good to them, by saving some of their lives, though
some indeed only to live a little longer.

And now am I again at leisure to look about me, as
indeed it was high time, being grievously wounded in our
last bloody skirmish by a musket shot lodging in my left
thigh, the Bashaw receiving another in his arm, much
about the same time. Mine proved extremely painful to
me, it being even to the end of the third day before my
surgeon could conveniently take it out, notwithstanding he
was a very ingenious man; and though the remains of our
army rested there two months, yet could I not ride till just
before our departure. However, I thought myself to be far
better off than a great many of our army, we having lost
therein full fourteen thousand men.

And now am I travelling back, in a great deal of pain,
with the remainder of our army for Mequinez, and with
us forty of the principal rebels in this rebellion, to give
an account of their behaviour to the Emperor. Being

brought before him, he forthwith ordered them for execution, the victims standing all in a row, and the headsman ready with his sword drawn in his hand, only waiting the word of command, or signal, which being given, he struck off seventeen heads at so many strokes, when he was ordered to stay his hand, and the other twenty-three were pardoned, and sent back to behave with more prudence for the future; and I, after I had recruited the men I had lost (in all twenty-six), so fast as I could ride for Tamnsnah, and my other three garrisons, getting thither again after about three months' absence, finding my family in good health, and increased by a brave boy.

Now am I, after my late skirmishes and sad wound, again with my wife and family at Tamnsnah. There I happened to remain with them for some considerable time in peace and plenty, spending most of my time in my old sport in the woods, though I went pretty often to Sallee, and where I met with several of my countrymen, with whom I soon got well acquainted, yet could not I (although I very heartily endeavoured it) meet with any opportunity to my mind, wherein I might in any probability make my escape; and for me to make any foolish attempts that way, I thought was by far better to let alone. Therefore, after making merry with my countrymen sometimes for three, four, or five days, I returned to my family and my old sport. But as pleasure never comes sincere, a dash of water is now thrown into our wine, our son, at the age of ten months, dying; though after this we lived without any uneasiness almost to the end of two years, when a sudden rumour ran, that the old Emperor was dead, as indeed he had been at least two months before, though kept private for certain reasons of state, no doubt to strengthen the interest of some of the competitors for the empire.

And here, before we go on to relate what happened on the death of the old tyrant, Muley Ishmael, it will not be amiss to add some further particulars of his character and method of governing.

CHAPTER V.

The rise of Muley Ismaïl—His character a mixture of vice and virtue
and piety and cruelty—How he made himself master of the kingdom—He clears the country of robbers—His empire—His mode
of government—How the governors of provinces are called to
account—Degrading ceremonies incumbent on officials before they
enter the Imperial presence—His supposed sanctity—His severity
against law-breakers—His disturbed sleep—The terror his attendants had for telling him whom he had killed—His duel with a
woman—His Bokhari, or Black Guards—His esteem for them—
His fickleness—The story of an attempted assassination of him—
The influence of Maestro Juan over him—His mania for building
in an economical fashion—His attention to the affairs of State—
Civil war on his death—The contrast between Muley Hamet Deby
and his brothers—Character of Muley Hamet—How Mr. Pellow's
career was influenced by these turmoils.

THE Emperor came to the throne in the year 1672,
upon the death of his brother, Muley Archid,* by
opposing his nephews, the sons of Muley Archid, being
then only Alcayde of Mequinez; but aspiring to the crown,
he raised what forces he could, and by his courage and
vivacity, with the help he met with from the Jews, particularly Memarran, their governor, who supplied him with
money to carry on the war, he overcame both his nephews,
one of whom, Muley Hamet,† being Bashaw of Morocco, at
his father's death, had caused himself to be proclaimed
king there, and the other, Muley Aran,‡ set up in the
kingdom of Taffilet.

* Ar'scid or Er-Reschid.   † Ahmed.
‡ Hharùn, sometimes " Hispanised " into Arrani.

An Audience of Sidi Mohammed, Emperor of Morocco (1760).

An excessive cruelty, a great capacity, and a perfect knowledge of the genius and temper of his people, preserved to this Emperor the throne for so long a space of time as fifty-five years, and death alone took it from him. By strictly observing, even to the nicest particulars, all the ceremonies of the Mahometan religion, he made himself respected by his subjects for his virtues, at the same time he was feared for his cruelty and vices. He always brought his projects to bear, and if he saw there was danger in using violence, he knew how to employ cunning. Voluptuous, covetous, passionate, treacherous, more than a tyrant, he tamed the natural savageness of his subjects, by showing himself still more savage than they.

After the death of his nephew, Muley Hamet, his cruelty began to appear. The first scene of which was acted by the side of a river, to which he came with his army, but could not pass, where he ordered all the prisoners to be killed, and woven into a bridge with rushes, for his army to pass over upon.

In 1678, he made himself master of Taffilet, and three years after that took Mamora from the Spaniards, where he found eighty-eight pieces of brass cannon, fifteen of iron, ammunition of all sorts, more than he had in his whole dominions before, and a great prize of pearls and jewels (belonging to merchants who then were in the town) fell into his hands. He also took Larach from the Spaniards in 1689, clearing all the sea-coast of his territory, but Massagan,* Pennon de Velez, and Ceuta, the latter of which (though always blockaded with ten thousand men, and so strictly pressed that the Bashaw cannot stir from before it without leave from the Emperor) has defied all attempts for thirty-four years together. In 1701, he

* Mazagan, spelt in another page as Marcegongue.

fought a battle with the Dey of Algiers,* but coming off with the worst, a peace was concluded, which has continued ever since.

At the beginning of his reign the roads were so infested with robbers that it was dangerous to stir out of the towns without being well guarded, but he so well cleared them that now it is nowhere safer travelling.

He maintains his large empire (which consists of several kingdoms joined together) in peace and quietness, although of so late an acquisition to the family. In his empire is contained all that country called by the Romans Mauritania Tingitana, with other provinces to the southward, as far as Cape Blanco, where it is bounded by the Negro country, as it is northerly by the Mediterranean Sea. It has on the east the kingdom of Algiers, and part of the country of Bildulgerid, and on the west the main ocean, including the kingdoms of Fez, Morocco, Taffilet, Segelmess, Darha, Suz, and Tremezen, over which he rules with so severe a hand, and has struck such a dread into all men by his terrible executions, that none of the remnants of the royal blood of the before-mentioned kingdoms or any of his bashaws have dared to take up arms against him. All the disturbance he ever met with at home (since his establishment after the conquest of his nephew) was the rebellion of his son Muley Mahomet, who causing himself to be proclaimed King of Morocco, plagued him for some time, but sending his son Muley Zidan against him, Muley Mahomet was overthrown; and the Emperor having got him into his clutches ordered his right hand and left foot to be cut off, after which the prince soon died, not suffering the blood to be stopped, but tearing off the plasters.

His manner of governing is by alcaydes, who have no

---

* At Zenboudj-el-Aousat, in the Beni-Amer country, near Tlemcen (Tremezen), an arrondissement of the province of Oran.

commission, but receive their authority only by his saying, " Go govern such a country; be my general or admiral." At Court he has five standing officers. They are the Grand Mufti, for affairs of religion ; the chief eunuch, to take care of the Seraglio ; a treasurer for his revenue ; the superin- tendent of his buildings, and the Bashaw of Mequinez, who is the first minister, or supreme alcayde, of which there are three sorts. The first and chief are those who, in the nature of viceroys, are sent to govern the provinces, to whom, for their greater honour, is sometimes given the title of Bashaws. They have an unlimited power, and it matters not how much they tyrannize, if, upon their return to Court, they bring riches enough to satisfy the Emperor. Another sort are the generals of his armies, and com- manders over small parties of horse or foot. The third sort are governors of cities or towns, and are either made by the Emperor himself, as are the Alcaydes of Morocco, Fez, Sallee, and other cities, or by the governors of the provinces over small towns and cities. A fourth sort may be added, which are titular only, and therefore called Alcaydes of their Heads.

The governors of the provinces are ordered to Court every two or three years to render an account of their government; that is, to bring the Emperor all that they have by an arbitrary and tyrannical power plundered the people of ; by which means he gets little less than their whole wealth, which never circulates more, but is thrown into his treasury, and remains there an unprofitable and useless hoard, he never parting with it again upon any account whatsoever—for neither his armies, fleet, or build- ings cost him anything. When he has occasion to raise forces, the alcaydes of the provinces are obliged to find and maintain them, each providing for a number in proportion to the extent of his government. The ships also that are in his service are fitted out and maintained by the alcayde of the port to which they belong. Nevertheless he has half the prizes, and takes all the slaves, remitting part of his moiety of the prize goods in consideration for the slaves, who did not belong to his share.

When the alcaydes return from their governments it is with the greatest fear imaginable, as I have before hinted, for if the Emperor thinks they do not bring him the whole profits thereof, but keep something for themselves, they are in danger of being put to some cruel death. Before they go into his presence they pull off their shoes, put on a particular habit they have to denote a slave, and when they approach him fall down and kiss the ground at his horse's feet. If he speaks to them, they bend forward and hold their heads a little on one side in token of offering their life, which great degree of subjection proceeds partly from fear and partly from superstition, for they believe him to be the true branch of the Xeriphian * family, who draw their descent from the prophet Mahomet, and there-fore think he was particularly favoured by Heaven, and could do nothing amiss, but imagined all who died by his hand went to Paradise ; in which opinions he confirmed them by a long continuance of tyrannical power, by artifice and by hypocrisy, never doing anything of consequence without first falling down upon the ground with his face close to the earth for a considerable time, making believe that he then received inspiration and directions from God, or Mahomet (for which purpose he had a great number of praying places contrived in different parts, not unlike niches laid horizontally in the ground), and that he performed the will of God in everything he did.

The Emperor certainly punished all breakers of their law with great severity, and carried his hypocrisy so far that it

* Shereefian is the more general spelling.

was the most religious age that ever was in Barbary by the King's example, whose commands were esteemed sacred, for the least breach of which he had often inflicted the severest death; so that what from the dread of punishment and the opinion the people are brought up in, no prince was better obeyed.

He was an early riser, whether from his natural disposition, or the horror of the many murders, exactions, and cruelties he had committed on his poor subjects and slaves, I cannot determine; but those who have been near him when abroad in camps (for in his palace he was waited on by women, young wenches, and eunuchs, who dare not tell tales), report that his sleep was very much disturbed and full of horror, when, starting on a sudden, he has been heard to call upon those he had murdered, and sometimes awake he used to ask for them whom he had killed but the day before; and if any of the standers-by answered, "He is dead," he presently replied, "Who killed him?" To which they answered, "They did not know, but supposed God killed him," unless they had a mind to follow.

I have heard he used once to call often on Hameda, a great favourite of his, when he was walking alone, and nobody could be supposed to hear him. This Hameda was the greatest favourite he ever had; he was the son of the guardian of the slaves, and came a boy into the Emperor's army, when he was besieging his cousin Muley Hamet in Terudant, and doing some action before him he took notice of him and gave him a horse. The man still continued to do good things, and being a merry buffoon fellow the Emperor grew into great familiarity with him, insomuch that he could take the liberty to go into his gardens when he was with his women, which no man ever did before or since. He had the title of Bashaw by way of pre-eminence above all other bashaws. The Emperor used passionately to tell him that he could never be heartily angry with him, and that it was impossible he should be provoked to kill him. And it was thought he did not design to do it when he gave him so many blows with the butt-end of his lance, that he died of them the next day. The Emperor afterwards showed a great deal of sorrow at it, confessed he repented of what he had done, sent him and his physicians a bag of money, and desired him to live.

As soon as his first prayer was over, which was before the morning star disappeared, he used to go to his works, which were of a vast extent within the walls of his palace. There the poor people (whether Christians, negro slaves, boys who attended him, alcaydes, or overseers of the works), all tasted of his anger in their turns, beating, killing, or giving good words, according to the humour he was in. This was one of his top pleasures; in some of these places and never within his palace he gave audience to ambassadors, conversed sometimes sitting on the corner of a wall, walked often, and sometimes worked.

In the year 1690, before he was master of Sahra,* there came a woman from that people to him, who, hearing of her coming, went to meet her on horseback, at the head of twenty thousand men. She told him the people of Sahra were desirous to put themselves under his protection, but that he must fight her at lance-play, if he had a mind to have her, at once the pledge of their fidelity and the prize of his victory. She set him hard at first, but afterwards suffered herself to be overpowered, was put among the rest of his women, and troops were sent to protect the frontiers of Sahra.

When he was abroad, there used to be carried after him a stool, a kettle of water, and a skin, which was his table-cloth. This belonged to his eating. And if he was out at

* The Sahara, or desert country to the south.

dinner time, his dinner was carried after him upon the head of a negro, in a great wooden or copper vessel, which he did not take from his head till the Emperor asked for it. The manner of his eating did not differ from the ordinary Moors. His other travelling utensils were two or three guns, a sword or two, and two lances, because one broke once as he was murdering. Both the swords and lances were carried with their points upwards. These were all carried by lusty fellows; his boys carried short Brazil sticks, knotted cords for whipping, a change of clothes to shift when bloody, and a hatchet, two of which he took in a Portuguese ship, and the first time they were brought to him, killed a negro without any provocation, to try if they were good.

Although the natives of his dominions are whites, yet they are not so much esteemed by him as the blacks and the copper-coloured, to whom he commits the guard of his person, and was so fond of their breed, that he took care to mix them himself, by matching them to the best-complexioned of his female subjects.*

Thus he took care to lay the foundation of his tawny nurseries, to supply his palace as he wanted, into which they were admitted very young, are taught to worship and obey that successor of their Prophet, and being nursed in blood from their infancy, become the executioners and ministers of their wrath, whose terrible commands they put in execution with as much zeal and fury as if they had received them immediately from Heaven. Their manner was—as soon as the word came out of his mouth—to seize on the wretch ordered for execution like so many lions, whom, if he was not to be executed on the spot, they almost tore to pieces before he got to the place of execution; and by the fury of their looks, and their violent and savage

* *Note* 20.

manner of using him, made a scene very much resembling
the picture of so many devils tormenting the damned.
They were so ready to murder and destroy—even while
young—that the Alcaydes trembled at the very sight of
them, and the Emperor seemed to take a great deal of
pleasure, and placed much of his safety in them, for they
surrounded him almost wherever he was.   They are of all
ranks and degrees; some were the sons of his chief Alcaydes, others picked up by chance, or taken from a large
negro town joining to Mequinez,* which the Emperor had
filled with families of blacks and tawnies for his use.   If
they were well looked and strong, they needed no other
quality; some who had relations that were able were fed,
clothed, and lodged by them; others who had not were
lodged in the outskirts of the palace, in great rooms,
where they pigged an hundred or two together.   They
wore only a short and small coat without sleeves, which
did not reach to their knees; their heads were shaved and
always exposed to the sun, for he affected to breed them
hard.   Most, and sometimes all of them, were employed
in his buildings, where they took off their clothes, and
laying them all in a heap, every one took a basket and
removed earth, stones, or wood; when they had done, he
ordered them to go to his Jew and receive so much soup;
the next day they appeared gay and under arms.

He beat them in the cruelest manner imaginable, to try
if they were hard; sometimes you should see forty or fifty
of them all sprawling in their blood, none of them daring
to rise till he left the place where they were lying, and if
they were discountenanced and out of heart at this usage,
they were of a bastard breed, and must turn out of his service.   I never heard that he killed but three of them, one for
a heinous crime, and two for hiding a piece of bread in the

* Close to the Jews' quarter, but now dismantled.

hole of a wall, which it was supposed they could not eat, for they are great reverencers of bread, and take up (as all Mahometans do) the least crumb, wherever they find it, and kiss it. When they wanted clothes, the Emperor thought of somebody that had too much money, either Moor or Jew, and bade them go to him, and receive each a coat or shirt.

They were generally about eight hundred in all, who lived with him in a sort of subordination to one another; several had the names of Alcaydes, as the chief of them who waited on the Emperor's person; others were made overseers of some task or work the Emperor had ordered them to finish; some he made perpetual Alcaydes over a certain number of his companions, and such a one was to answer for the rest, as to their diligence, cleanly and good deportment in all particulars; and it was wonderful to see the indolence, state, and gravity of these young rogues, and how they aped the old Emperor in their way of government; for though they could only inflict blows, yet they used the haughty phrases of command, and talked of cutting throats, strangling, dragging, and so forth.

The first mark of their preferment, after they were grown too big to serve the Emperor in this nature, was giving them a horse—a horseman being in the highest esteem imaginable among them, and the foot the contrary, insomuch that those who commanded thousands of them were not esteemed equal to the commanders of fifty horse. Then the Emperor either recommended them to some of his Bashaws or great Alcaydes employed against the Christians, or the Berebbers that inhabit the mountains, or kept them near him, and then they were ready to be entrusted with all important messages, as to carry the Emperor's letter of thanks to any officer who served him

well, or to call him cuckold, spit in his face, give him a
box on the ear, strangle, or cut off his head.

When they had waited a considerable time, if no commands or government became vacant, he sent them to
gather the tribute of some country, with the title of an
Alcayde; and if any remained by him without any employment after performing this service, he was called
Alcayde of his head, which was a sort of an Alcayde titular
or Reforme, as I have noted above. But perhaps the
Emperor suspected that he had put something more in his
pocket than ordinary, then he bid him build houses of such
or such dimensions, and that he might seem something
more reasonable than the Egyptian taskmasters, used to bid
him take his lime and stone. The poor man begins with
a good heart, and when he has spent all, despair forces
him to go to the Emperor, and tell him he is not worth
one farthing more, lest he should find his work standing
still, and bury him alive in one of the walls. The Emperor
then used to pick a quarrel with him, cut him with his
sword, wound him with his lance, or take off his clothes,
all but his drawers, give him five hundred blows on the
buttocks, put him in prison, or load him with two great
chains, and send him to labour at the house he was
building, and ordered somebody else to finish it. Now you
must know the Emperor never beat a man soundly, but
the man was in the high way of preferment, and it was ten
to one but His Majesty passing by him in chains a few
days after, and finding him in a sad pickle, he called him
his dear friend, uncle, or brother, and inquired how he
came into that condition, as if he knew nothing of the
matter, sent for a suit of his own clothes (which was a
great compliment), made him as fine as a prince, and sent
him to govern some of his great towns; for by this means
he was sure he had not left him worth a groat, and made

a careful computation of what he might get in his government, till it was his turn to be squeezed again.

They tell a story of a Spaniard who was esteemed a
good marksman, and bribed to shoot the Emperor: he so
missed his aim, that the two balls he had charged his gun
with, flew into the pommel of the Emperor's saddle. The
man was immediately seized, and when it was expected he
would be put to a cruel death, the Emperor first reproached
him with his base design, asking him what he had done to
deserve being used so, whether he was no more beloved,
and people were tired with him; then calmly sent him
to the works among the rest of the Christians. The
Spaniard, fearing he should not come off so, and thinking
it a means (if there was any) to get his liberty again,
turned Moor, but continued in his Christian habit. Some
years after, the Emperor, going among the workmen
where he was, asked him why he did not pull off his hat.
He answered, he was a Moor; and the Emperor, being
informed who he was, ordered him to be freed immediately,
asked him a thousand pardons for keeping him at work so
long, dressed him from head to foot, and made him a
governor of some country.

A little more or less this was the treatment of his
grandees: to-day hugged, kissed, and preferred; to-morrow
stripped, robbed, and beaten. Many of the people about
him bore the marks of his sword, lance, or short sticks:
and the face and arms of the negro who carried his
umbrella when Captain Norbury was there, was scarred all
over with cuts that the Emperor had given him, it was
supposed, for letting the sun come upon him; for he was
exceeding nice in his tyranny, and when he had done with
his lance, he darted it suddenly into the air, and it must
be caught before it comes to the ground, or he would kill
the man appointed for that purpose.

If he chanced to kill anybody when he had not determined their death—as it frequently happened—he civilly begged their pardon, and said he did not design to kill that poor man, and laid the fault on God, saying his time was come, the powers above would have it so.

If he designed the death of a Christian whom he cared not to pardon, he shut the gates of his palace, that Maestro Juan should not come; for it was very singular that this Maestro Juan, a Christian slave of Catalonia, by his good works, temper, and sincerity wrought so much upon the Emperor, that he once swore he would never see him but he would give him something, and that he should never ask him anything but he would grant it; and that, being desirous to keep his word, made him fear that Juan should come to beg such a man's life; nay, sometimes having seen him first, he cried out he must give him something, for he had seen him.

The Emperor was wonderfully addicted to building; yet it is a question whether he was more addicted to that, or pulling down; for they said if all his buildings were now standing, by a moderate computation they would reach to Fez, twelve leagues off. And those who had been near him since the beginning of his reign, have observed him eternally building and pulling down, shutting up doors and breaking out new ones in the walls. But he told them this was done to occupy his people. "For," said he, "if I have a bag full of rats, unless I keep that bag stirring they would eat their way through." He also dug many strange caverns in the earth of all sizes, some for corn, others for powder, arms, brimstone, and money, of which latter it is suspected he left no witnesses, when finished.

The Emperor never parted with any money, to defray the expenses of war or building, and caused his large and magnificent palace to be erected, without expending a

blankill towards it. But instead of money he gave the
Alcayde of his buildings a government; which then was
all that country lying between Mequinez and Tremezen, a
large tract of ground, and a very fruitful soil; but considering the continual employment and unlimited expenses
which his office obliged him to, it was thought he could
not get anything for himself, more than what sufficed for
his maintenance.

Although this Emperor had eight thousand wives, nine
hundred sons, and about three hundred daughters, yet he
was always attentive to the affairs of the State, and never
committed the care of it out of his own hands.

Muley Hamet Deby,* one of his sons, whom he had
designed for his successor, hearing of his father's illness,
came with all despatch from Tedla (where he resided) to
Mequinez, to see him. It was not but with much difficulty
that he got the liberty of speaking to him, and he was at
last but badly received. The father, persuaded that interest
rather than affection was the motive of this visit of his
son's, told him to moderate his eagerness for the crown;
but the son protested to his father, that the pleasure of
seeing him was the only motive of his coming.

Hamet Deby found, by the condition in which he saw
his father, and from the opinions of the physicians, that
he could not live long, he therefore took all possible
methods to prevent disturbances, and to assure himself of
the crown; for he had many rivals for it, and amongst
others two of his brothers, Muley Abdallah, and Muley
Abdemelick,† who was accounted one of the most able
generals in the kingdom. These had all been secretly
making great preparations; but Deby had, by his prudence
and vigilance, disconcerted all their measures. He had
brought with him only a thousand men, but as soon as he

* Afterwards Ahmid (Hamid) IV. Ed-dehèbi.   † Abd-el-Malek.

knew of the different parties which were forming in the
kingdom, he drew from the provinces of his jurisdiction
five hundred foot more, and six hundred horse, whom
causing to enter privately in the night into Mequinez, he
seized upon all the advantageous posts therein, and obliged
the governor to render to him an oath of fidelity. During
this, the disorder of the Emperor Muley Ishmael, together
with his great age, put an end to his life the 22nd of March,
1727, in the 81st year of his age.*

The moment his death was known, all the inhabitants of
Mequinez retired every one to their houses, abandoning all
the public works on which Muley Ishmael had unprofit-
ably kept them incessantly employed. The same day the
Bashaw Mesael presented the keys of the city to Muley
Hamet Deby, who, without losing any time, went to take
possession of the palace, and the apartment of his deceased
father. He ordered him to be buried in the night, in a
place he himself had fixed on, and gave orders for erecting
a monument over him, according to the fashion of that
country, viz., a large tower, on the summit of which were
placed five balls of gilt copper.

The measures which Deby had taken were not useless.
The very day that the death of his father was made public,
he was acknowledged by the inhabitants of Mequinez as
King of Morocco, notwithstanding the attempts made to
defeat it by his brother Muley Abdallah; who being informed of all that passed by his mother, waited in vain for
a favourable opportunity of having himself proclaimed
King; and with this design he drew together some troops
in the neighbourhood of Mequinez, expecting that seven
thousand men in the city, who had promised to espouse his
part, would come and join him. But the vigilance of Deby,
and the zeal of the Bashaw Mesael, hindered these from

* *Note* 22.

putting their design into execution; so that the troops which were with Abdallah seeing this reinforcement did not join them, abandoned that prince, leaving only sixteen horse with him. This desertion entirely ruined his affairs; so that to save his life he fled to a sanctuary. Deby caused him to be sought for, and learning that he had taken refuge at Fez, in the Mosque of Muley Idris, which is held in great veneration by all the Mahometans, he caused it to be told that prince, that he might with all safety repair to Court, giving him his solemn oath that he would neither hurt him, nor any that should accompany him. Abdallah trusting to the King's promise, went to pay his respects to him. Hamet received him with kindness, and having pardoned him and embraced him, gave him, as a token of his friendship, a very fine horse, most richly caparisoned. It was by this act of generosity that Deby signalized the day of his coronation, the ceremony of which was performed in the Mosque of the great Seraglio.

The principal officers of the Army of the Blacks assembled together, crying out, "Long live the King!" and threatening death and destruction to every one who would not acknowledge him. Hamet Deby went out from the palace, to hear what they had to say. They told him they were deputed by the Army of the Blacks to assure him they were ready to execute his orders, and if necessary to shed their blood in his service. The King was so pleased with this deputation, that he gave these officers two hundred and twenty thousand ducats to distribute among the Black Army, and ordered that they should march immediately against the Alarbes of the province of Duquela, who had not acknowledged him.

The deputies immediately returned to their camp, pitched about six leagues from Mahmora, and distributed among the soldiers their shares in the King's liberality; so that

the whole army were eager to march on the expedition they
were ordered upon.

The Alarbes * did not let themselves be surprised.
Hearing of the march of the Blacks, they prepared themselves for an engagement. The two armies soon came
within sight of each other. The Blacks resolved to attack
the Alarbes in their camp, which was entrenched by camels
and other animals, lying down. However odd such a
fortification might appear, it was not without a great deal
of trouble that the Blacks could force it. Both sides fought
with great fury; at length the Blacks, equal in courage to
the Alarbes, and superior in numbers and discipline, gained
a signal victory. Sixteen thousand of the Alarbes were
cut in pieces, with the loss only to the victors of fourteen
hundred men killed, and sixteen hundred wounded. The
loss of this battle prevented the provinces, who had taken
part with the Alarbes, from continuing in their revolt. The
Black Army overran them in fifteen days, without meeting
with any considerable resistance. At length the Alarbes,
having desired a suspension of arms, submitted to the
clemency of the King; who, though he gave them a pardon,
did, notwithstanding, give secret orders to his generals to
drain the riches of these rebellious provinces, without,
however, depopulating them. And these orders were indeed
punctually executed, being highly agreeable to their natural
avidity.

The first certain intelligence I had of the advancement
of Muley Hamet Deby to the throne, was by Alcayde
Larbeet Benabbo Woldernjottlee,† then head governor of
that province; who, with 1800 horse, came one morning
within musket-shot of my castle; to whom I sent one of
my people, to know his pleasure, and to tell him, that in
case he had anything to say to me he should advance with

* Arabs.   † El' Arby Ben Abou Oold Enjiotlee.

a few only to the foot of the wall, and let me know it ; but if he, on the contrary, persumed to draw his main body on any farther, I should be obliged to fire upon them. And which he well knowing to be my positive orders, and that I would actually have performed it, he came with a very few, and told me, that the old Emperor was actually dead, and that Muley Hamet Deby was, by the general consent of the Black Army, proclaimed at Mequinez in his room.

This Muley Hamet was a man of a most generous, though very sottish nature, being almost ever drunk, giving the Blacks a great deal of gold, and many other valuable presents, insomuch that their hearts were for the present entirely his. The governor advising me to go directly to him, and submit myself to his will, telling me that he thought it in all likelihood to be by far the better and safer course ; and which I also thinging to be so, I (after giving my people very strict charge concerning the garrison) accordingly did, the governor going also with me ; and we were both of us very kindly received by him, and I directly ordered back, and again to return with all my men.

And now am I soon about to leave my old, so much beloved habitation, for such as my future chance might happen to allot for me ; and after bidding adieu to all my rural diversions, and merry-makings thereabout, and settling my garrisons under the care of the country people, who had been trained up to arms, much in like nature of our trained-bands, we departed together after a very disconsolate manner, though we got all well to Mequinez, and were by the new Emperor all most kindly received, and each man immediately presented with new clothes, fire arms and swords.

Here we stayed about four days ; then we were sent to Hartan, a castle about six miles out of the city, where the ambassadors of foreign princes generally lodge at night, before they make their public entrance into Mequinez; where we stayed six days, and then were sent to the castle of Agoory, and from thence, after having been there two months, to the siege of old Fez, the inhabitants there and thereabout, on the death of the old Emperor, throwing off all future allegiance to any of his successors, as thinking themselves thereby entirely delivered from their so long grevious bondage, now acknowledging no lawful king, killing Alcayde Boel le Rosea,* their old Governor, boiling his flesh, and many, through spite, eating thereof, and throwing what they would not eat of it to the dogs, killing also thirty-six of his head servants, whom they said had also committed many insolencies against them. All which coming to the Emperor's ears, he forthwith ordered an army, consisting of one hundred and twenty thousand men, horse and foot, to be in readiness to march from Mequinez against them, myself and all my men being of the number; and it being but twelve leagues, we marched the first day to Emhaddumah, and the next, in good season, to the walls of the city, where we entrenched ourselves. Here we had shrewd skirmishing with the malecontents in and out for forty-eight days, and during which were slain on both sides many thousand men; when Muley Mustada, one of the Emperor's brothers, arrived at our camp with a commission from him to offer the malecontents quarter on the following easy conditions, viz., that they should immediately surrender, and promise to him future obedience; on which he was ready to pardon them for all that was past. These terms, indeed, they accepted of, though I think I never saw anything of that nature accepted with so much seeming indifference, they bringing him out only such presents to be carried back to his brother as they pleased.

* Al Kaid Bou el Roseo.

And now we were all ordered to march back again to
Mequinez; and though I lost in this expedition several of
my men, yet did I, as to my own part, escape for this bout
unwounded, as indeed I did soon after in an affair of a far
more dangerous though quite different nature; and which,
I hope, will be by all allowed to be a very extraordinary
providence, and which I shall, after I have finished the
small remainder of my present expedition, give you a
particular account of. During our stay at Old Fez, came
Captain Russel to New Fez, who lodged there a night or
two, visited our army, then went to Mequinez, and in a
little time redeemed the few English captives then there.*

* *Note* 21.

CHAPTER VI.

Mr. Pellow makes a determined attempt to escape from Morocco—He
succeeds in reaching Mazagan, then in the possession of the
Portuguese—He unfortunately, however, mistakes the Moorish
outposts for the Christian, and is seized and sent to Azamoor—
He is thrown into a dungeon and is threatened with execution—
A friend saves him, and he is able to reach his family in Agoory—
The revolt of the Black Army—The author takes part in the
Siege of Fez—He is sent to Sallee to bring new carriages for the
field-guns—Arrived there, he plots another attempt at freedom—Is
betrayed by another Christian renegado—He saves himself with
difficulty, and abandoning the plan returns to Fez with the gun
carriages—Is well received by Muley Hamet—The author is
wounded, and while thinking of returning to his wife and
daughter hears of the death of both.

AND now I am soon about to give a relation of my so
wonderful preservation; for I had just returned with
the remains of our army to Mequinez, received of the
Emperor twelve ducats, and ordered back to my wife at
Agoory (where I found I was very likely to be exempted
from any of their bloody actions for some time), before
my mind ran altogether upon escape; and after I had
with myself agreed on the means, which was to go first
for Sallee, and if I could not to my mind speed there, to
travel on to Marcegongue* to the Portuguese garrison there,
if I could bring it to pass, several to my knowledge having
before made their escapes that way—as indeed so should I

* Mazagan.

now, had I not most unhappily precipitated myself into the enemies' hands.

For as I could find no ship at Sallee, I travelled on to Marcegongue, which is about three days and a half's journey further to the southward, and where the fourth following night I got without any accident, and, to my most unspeakable joy, even close home, or within a hundred yards at the utmost, of the castle walls. And here we may soon see the lubricity of mundane affairs; for I was, even in the height of this my excessive joy, laid hold on by four Moors, who had that night been upon the plunder in the gardens, but had been disturbed therein by the Portuguese sentinels. But the night being excessive dark and windy, they in a narrow passage between two garden walls ran right against me; and laid fast hold of me. When I telling them I was a Christian (as supposing them to be some of the Portuguese, a very unhappy mistake) I was carried by them in a little time back to their main guard, and confined in irons, and early the next morning conducted by a strong party of them to Assamoore, a town to the northward of Marcegongue about five leagues; and where, after being severely handled by them, I was carried before Simmough Hammet Beorsmine,* their then commanding officer, (Ellemensore,† their Governor, being, on account of the people's rising against him, fled to the Emperor for assistance), who ordered the Moors to put me in prison till his return, when he told them I should be very severely punished. "When he returns," said they, "who can tell how long that may be, or if it may be ever; for if he meets with his reward, the Emperor will there cut off his head, and therefore this fellow shall be put to death directly." "No," said Beorsmine, "I tell you he shall not now, neither

---

* Si Mohammed Smâbyn ?   † El Mansoor.

shall he be at all till the Governor's return, and which may
be sooner than now you imagine." Upon which they cried
out I was a Christian, and about to make my escape to
Christian-land. To which the Governor made them no
answer, neither had they the power to tell him that they
had it from my own mouth, at their first surprising me.
However, it was at last agreed between the Governor and
them, that I should be kept till their next market-day, when
I should be put to death in the market-place; and as that
would be on the next Thursday, and it being then Sunday,
it could not make any difference, and during that time the
neighbourhood might be acquainted with it, and come in
and see the execution.

And now am I, as any may suppose, under a most
grievous agony, the next Thursday being the peremptory
day fixed for my execution; and for their better securing
me, I was directly guarded away by a multitude of those
bloodthirsty villains, and put into a very deep and dark
dungeon, there to be kept without any allowance from them
besides bread and water, though the Governor sent me in
the evening a servant (in whom he could confide) with some
meat, and to tell me that I should not be under any apprehension of danger from the mob, for that he had truly
considered my case, and that he would deliver me from
their rage, even to the hazard of his own life. And this
he, by his servant, repeated twice every day, till the appointed day for my execution came. And when he early
brought me my breakfast that same morning (to which I
then had but little stomach) he told me that I should not
despair, for that his master still continued his friendly
resolutions towards me, and that he was very well assured
he would deliver me out of their hands, for that he had
often told him so in the most positive manner.

This, I must own, moderated my fear in some measure;

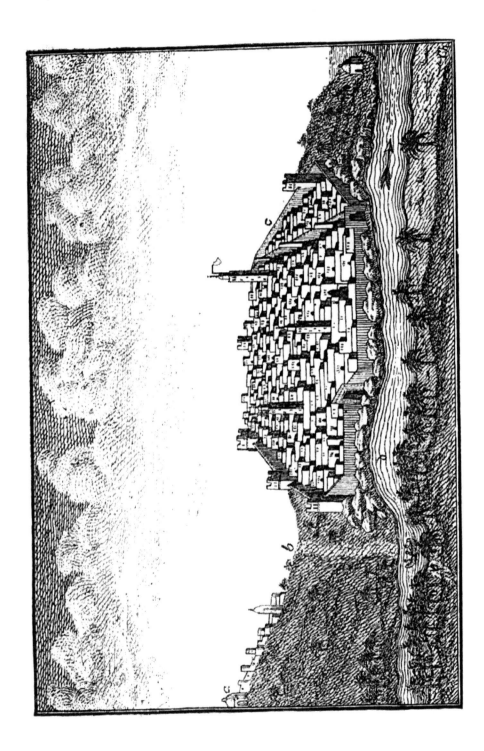

but as it was but the promise of an infidel, and at second hand, which made it the more uncertain, how could I otherwise choose but be still under a very great agony, as indeed I really was, and more so, when about ten o'clock these bloodthirsty villains came, hauled me out of my dungeon, and led me through the street to the market-place, being attended by an insolent mob, still increasing as we went, so that by the time we got to the market-place, which was sufficiently crowded by the barbarians, to feast their eyes with the blood of an innocent Christian, I was almost ready to expire. And now, notwithstanding I saw Simmo Hammet * amongst them as indeed, I did from the moment of my being first hauled out of my prison, yet could not I help, at sight of a long murdering knife in the hand of the executioner, being stricken with a very great terror. Nay, so great indeed, as is scarce possible to be here expressed. For though Simmo Hammet had faithfully promised me all the assistance in his power, yet was it at such a time very much to be doubted if that power would be sufficient to save my life, and especially as I was exposed to the rage of an insolent mob; who, though they be in some cases accounted good servants, yet are they, I think, on the other hand (like wind, fire, and water), bad masters; therefore I expected nothing less than death. The executioner had now his knife ready in his right hand, and with his left hand had taken fast hold of my beard, the better to hold back my head to cut my throat, when my guardian angel stepped forth, and took the knife out of his hand; and which, had not he done that very instant, he would, no doubt, therewith have soon taken from me the small remainder of life that was left in me, without any addition to my pain. For, in short, had he then cut my throat, I was

* "Si" Mohammed,—the namesons of the Prophet having always this honorary prefix.

before so much stricken with the thoughts of immediate death, that I should not have felt it; and though I had seen death before in so many various shapes, yet could not I then for my life behave with better courage.

And now is there a very hot dispute between the mob, whether I should die or not being the question; insomuch, that had not Simmo Hammet procured a good party from the neighbouring parishes, it would in all likelihood (notwithstanding his office) have gone very hard with me. However, it was at last agreed by all of them that I should be again sent back to my dungeon, and there to remain till the next market day, and which they plainly told the Governor should actually be my last. Therefore I should not feed myself with vain hopes and fancies, for that it should not then be in the power of him or anybody else to prevent it.

But, on the other hand, I was by the Governor altogether as much encouraged, and plainly told not to despair, for that he would deliver me out of their hands, even to the hazard of his own life; and lest they might offer me any foul play in my prison, he solemnly promised me that he would order a good lookout about it. Which you may imagine, as I had hitherto found him so punctual to his honour, made my imprisonment much more supportable, though I was again the next market day hauled by the mob to the market-place, and by my guardian angel again brought back, as indeed I was a third time. After which he came that night to my dungeon, desiring me to be of good courage, for that I should no more be hurried by the mob to the market-place; that he expected Elemensore's return in a very little time, which he said (as he understood he had been very favourably received by Muley Hammet Deby) he hoped it would be to his satisfaction, as well as that of

all his friends. However, it was to the full expiration
of two months before he came, and then he came with
sufficient strength indeed, and in open daylight delivered
me from my nasty prison, and set me again at liberty to
depart where I would, out of the reach of my cruel
persecutors. And as I had promised them, upon my
honour, to return again to Agoory, so I did, and got
thither again (even beyond my own expectation) after
the absence of about four months. And, what I·was
much surprised at, I never once heard the least syllable
from the Emperor concerning this my attempt to escape.

Now am I, instead of entering the walls of Marcegongue,
returned safe to my family at Agoory : and which, though
quite the reverse of my intentions, yet must I ever
acknowledge it to be, even in the highest degree, very
extraordinarily providential, and what I could never have
expected. But I never told my wife the least word of this
affair. Whilst I was in the middle of these reflections,
I received an account from Mequinez, that the Black
Army had all of them revolted from Muley Hammet Deby,
in favour of Muley Abdemelick, and that they had surprised Muley Hammet in his own house, keeping him
there, under a very strict guard, close prisoner, and, as
most thought, very sufficiently guarded, though he found
means to escape. And Abdemelick, though he was then
at Terridget,* and it was six weeks before he came, yet
he was immediately proclaimed Emperor of Mequinez,
with the general approbation ; and after, at his coming,
no less received. The first thing he did was a bloody,
and I think most unaccountable, revenge on Muley
Hammet's servants, putting so many of them as he
could light on instantly to death, sending me with four
hundred light horse to the castle of Tessout, about two

* Terrijet.

days' journey short of Morocco, there to join some other troops, to cover and demand the Emperor's dues. And this, though my heart was with Muley Hammet, I was directly obliged to do. On our first coming thither we were received by the inhabitants in seeming friendship, but soon finding them beginning to play tricks with us, as allowing us no more than half a pint of flour a day for two men, and using us thus for seven days, and stripping our people going out singly to fish in their rivers. This not in the least pleasing us, and knowing it in our own power to redress our own grievances, we soon made such reprisals as our necessities required, and they deserved, killing about eighteen of them, and they seven or eight of us; and had not Bashaw Belide Shawey suddenly alarmed us that Muley Hammet Deby was within a day or two's journey of us with thirty horse only, again going back to try his fortune at Mequinez, we should soon have taught them better manners. On which we left them and went directly to him, and marched with him to Mequinez, where he expected sufficient forces ready to receive him, and where, indeed, the Black Army, who were all again revolted from Muley Abdemelick to him, and all encamped without the walls of the city, waited his coming, Muley Abdemelick being within with most of the citizens, making what defence they could to keep him out. But at the end of forty-eight hours, or thereabout, Muley Hammet's forces, still increasing, got in, and, after a faint resistance, put vast numbers of them to the sword, and him again in possession of the city. But as to Muley Abdemelick, he was obliged to seek further after before he could find him, he being with a few fled thence through a by-gate in the night-time, as was rumoured, to Old Fez. And which, indeed, proved to be true, though on confirmation of this report, and of

his being there well received, he was, by a body of Muley
Hammet's army, consisting of sixty thousand men, soon
followed, costing much blood, time, and expense before
we could get him thence.

Now am I one in the above number before Old Fez,
Abdemeleck being within strongly fortified, resolutely
resolved and well provided, bravely defending himself
six months and fourteen days, and during which scarce
a day passed without skirmishing and much slaughter on
both sides. But I am, to my very great satisfaction,
even to the middle of the siege, unwounded, and sent
very unexpectedly (though to my great content) to Sallee
with a few of my men, there to forward, with all possible
expedition, the making new carriages for our field pieces,
the old ones being, through the so frequent shocks of such
weighty and high-metalled cannon (thirty-six pounders of
brass), to that degree shaken, as they were become in a
manner unserviceable. So, after taking the dimensions,
I was hurried away with a strict charge therewith to
return as soon as possible. The second day I got thither,
and delivered my charge to Amberk Foolan,* a black, the
then Governor ; and by him the shipwrights were directly
ordered to work, and to be as expeditious as possible. Yet,
supposing all hands at work, the carriages being in all
thirty-six, they could not finish so soon, but what I might
again have time sufficient to gratify my curiosity in the
old affair, and from which I was thoroughly resolved never
to desist so long as I could see any possibility remaining.
For, notwithstanding my so late miraculous escape from
the bloody knife at Assamoore, I say I was then thoroughly
resolved to pursue it, and on my road thither from Fez
had so confirmed my resolutions, that rather than go
back again to the army I was fully determined to make

* 'Abd er Foolan.

11

all imaginary efforts that way, be the consequence what it would. For as the country was then in very great confusion, and the place I was then in very likely for my purpose, I thought I could not desire a more favourable opportunity.

And now are mine eyes busily employed in looking sharp out after the ships then in the harbour, and my thoughts (in case I could not in any probability perform my design by myself) on what other help I might with safety procure me; and which, indeed, I soon found to be the most difficult and dangerous point; though to do it alone, if I could, I was thoroughly resolved upon. Notwithstanding I made all the inquiry I could, yet could not I to my mind find any proper assistance, though on the other hand such a glorious opportunity offered as could not but be accounted, with the assistance of one or two more, a very plausible and easy undertaking, and which was as follows :—Early the next morning, after my arrival at Sallee, I took a walk to the seaside where ships' boats generally put in at, and where I met two Moorish sailors just landed with a few empty barrels to fill with water ; and, after a very courteous salute, I asked them what vessel they belonged to, their lading, and whither bound. To which they answered, To such a sloop (pointing at her), bound to Santa Cruz, and laden with gums, beeswax, and copper. "Very well," said I, "but have you on board no good wine or brandy?" "No, indeed," said they with a sigh, "so far as we can tell of, and in short if there was, very little of it would fall to their shares." "Alas !" said I, "poor hearts, I thought that sailors could not live without it." When they, shrinking up their shoulders, telling me, "There was no help for it," I left them, seeming for the present to take no further notice of them, till they had filled the water and got the

casks again into the boat, and then I came to them again,
telling them "that I thought the few casks they had
with them held but a small matter of water for their
ship's company, as being, no doubt (as the sloop was
upwards of fifty tons), five or six." "Oh," said they,
"we are in all eight, though no more kept on the vessel
than us two, the other six being constantly on shore
waiting a fair wind. Our main sea store of water is
already laid in, and this (without our using of that) only
for us two for present spending; and if it is not enough,
you know it is not very far to fetch more." "Really," said
I, "that (as none can tell how long your voyage may be)
is very well considered, and, as all must agree, to leave
than lack is by far the better policy," turning from them
in a seeming manner to be going off; but I turned me
quick round again, and told them, "If the wind stood
out of the way till the next day, it should go very hard
if I did not find for them a dram or a glass of wine,"
seeming again to be going off; when they, to my very
great satisfaction, and as, indeed, I really expected, asked
me if I would go off with them and see their vessel.
"Why, really," said I, "that is what I would do with all
my heart, but that then I could but badly spare so much
time. However, as I had not been on board any vessel
for a long time, and in case I was certain of my being
again in a little time brought back, I could even find in
my heart to go with them." "Well," said they, "as to
that it shall be even as you please." So I stepped into the
boat, went with them, was kindly received, and treated
with such as they had. And after I had employed my
tongue so far as I thought fit in telling them my present
state, as how I was one of the Emperor's soldiers, that
under him I bore an office of some distinction, and
mine eyes in viewing the dimensions of the sloop, sails,

&c., so nigh as I could guess, and given them my hearty thanks for my so kind welcome, I humbly entreated them to put me again on shore; and which they, after telling me they should be very glad to see me there again, instantly did, kindly for that time bidding one another farewell.

Now is my heart to that degree inflamed, that every drop of the blood in my veins is upon the ferment how I should manage in this affair. To do it alone I found was impossible, and to communicate it to others exceeding dangerous; though which I must be obliged to do, or let all drop; not but I could of myself easily manage and overcome the two Moors, but to sail and navigate the vessel was the main point. And now am I at a greater debate with myself than ever who those associates should be, though I very luckily thought on one in a very little time, named William Hussey, a Devonshire man, and whom I soon determined in myself to be a very trusty and honest man. And as he was then one of my soldiers, and in Sallee with me, I could let him gradually into the secret when I pleased; and which, indeed, you may suppose I did the first opportunity, for in less than an hour after I singled him out, and began to discourse him after the following manner :—" Now, Will," said I, "I desire you will answer me sincerely to a question I am about to ask you." " That," said he, " you may depend I will, be it what it will." " Then," said I, " do not you think yourself to be better off here than to be in the camp before Fez, where are, no doubt, some even this moment expiring of their wounds, others receiving fresh ones? Would you not still think it safer and better to be in your own country? And would you not rather run some small hazard to make your escape, than to go back again to such bloody dogs to run a greater?" "Yes," said he, " to be sure; and could I find any probable means for it, they should never see my face in their country more; that it was what his soul had for a long time longed after; and he was ready, even at the expense of the last drop of his blood, to make the experiment."

" Then, honest Will," said I, " if I am not very much mistaken, I have at last found one, and which I do not in the least doubt, by our prudent management, will answer both our expectations, even without our losing any blood about the matter; " telling him every particular wherein it consisted, and which he also approved of greatly, alleging the only difficulty to be our procuring of a third person that might be trusted, for that two were not sufficient to work the vessel and steer her well over to the Spanish shore, or to any other coast, in case the winds would not permit us to go thither. " Well, Will," said I, " cannot you tell where to look out for such a one ? " " Yes," said he, " I could soon name one, but I cannot altogether answer for his fidelity, though I never heard anything to the contrary of his being an honest man." " Very well," said I, " name him, and then we will consult further whether he may be trusted; " and then he told me it was William Johnston, his comrade, a Kentish man. " Very well," said I, " then let us not trouble our heads about any other till we have at a distance proved him; " which we instantly went about, and on our finding him very desirous to make his escape, we (on his swearing secrecy) let him into it, and which he seemed very highly to approve of, and eagerly pressed the execution.

So having consulted and agreed on the means, we were the next night fully determined to put it into execution, and which we ordered after the following manner: I, having, as aforesaid, very highly ingratiated myself with the two Moors,

and taking with me a bottle of brandy, went down to the
landing-place; and where I had not been but a very little
time before they had from the vessel (which was not more
than a hundred yards off the shore) discovered me, and
came with their boat directly to me, thinking (as they
said) I had a mind to go again on board. I told them,
" No, for that I had then only borrowed so much time as
to be as good as my word with them," seeming to be in
an extreme hurry; then privately conveying them the
bottle, I turned me about to be again going off, as if I
had for that time nothing further to say to them; when
they, calling to me and expressing their gratitude in
hearty thanks, I turned me round again, and said, " Poor
hearts, I wish with all my heart it had been a greater
quantity; but that you know would at this time of day
have been very dangerous to bring; therefore, if you will
come to-morrow night by ten of the clock, I will meet you
here, and bring with me some more brandy, sugar, and
lemons, and (if you please) two of my comrades, as
honest cocks as any in Barbary, and we will go on board
together and heartily enjoy ourselves." Which they
seemed very highly to approve of, and earnestly desired
that I would not fail in it.

Now is my heart by far more light, seeing myself, as it
were, already safely landed on some Christian shore, flying
to my comrades with the news, who seemed therewith (and
especially Johnston) no less pleased than myself; and that
night and the next day we got all our little matters in
readiness, as two pair of pistols, the brandy, &c., and the
time appointed for the boat's coming just at hand; when
Johnston, to my very great surprise, told us he could not
by any means go that night. However, Hussey and I went,
and found the Moors just landed, telling them that as we
had good reason to believe there were then some people on

the watch, we had deferred our going on board till the next
night; however, in point of good manners, we had brought
them a couple of bottles of brandy, sugar and lemons,
which we thought ourselves obliged to, rather than to
suffer them to wait our coming in vain. And with which
they were, no doubt, highly delighted, telling us, after a
most pleasing manner, that they would go on board and
drink our healths, and that we might depend on their
coming again the next night; as indeed they did, but
Johnston again disappointing us, we could not then go with
them no more than the night before. Therefore, after
thanking them for their civility, desiring them to accept of
a couple of bottles more of brandy, &c., and telling them,
that when we saw the way clear we would give them notice,
we parted, they again on board to make merry, and we on
the contrary back to our loathed apartments, in a very dis-
satisfied mood, though resolving, before we let loose our
rage, to lay us down, if we could, to compose ourselves.
But alas! sleep fled us, rising again at daybreak as we lay
down, without so much as closing our eyes; when we went
directly to Johnston, taking him aside, and telling him,
that in an affair of that nature, to do as he had done, was
using both us and himself very ill; and which, had he
gone about as heartily as he promised, we should in all
likelihood have been then safely landed on some Christian
shore, quite out of the power of the Moors, and with a
rich prize, to the value at least of five or six thousand
pounds, in our possession. This might, in some measure,
make us a compensation for our so long and grievous captivity; and as the opportunity was still in our power, we
hoped he would mend all, by going heartily about it that
night. To which he, after a short pause, answered, " That
he had again considered maturely of the affair himself, and
that he found it to be quite different from what it had first

appeared to him ; therefore we should urge it to him no further, for that it was only a foolish whimsey come into our heads, impossible to be executed ; and for which, if we did not desist, he would inform the Governor. " Why, thou vile villain," said I, " thou can'st not surely be in good earnest." " No," said he, " but indeed I am," and confirmed it with many horrid oaths ; when I, being quite overcome with passion, could no longer forbear him, but directly drew my sword, and gave him a very deep cut across his face, which I verily thought, and really hoped, had done his business, at least so far as that it might not be in his power to tell any tales. However, the dog recovered ; but let him come home when he will, I warrant he will bring with him the mark, which I told his sister, who was with me in the river of London, inquiring if I had seen him in Barbary ; together with what it was that he complained of to the Governor about me ; how I got off, and him confined close prisoner ? For after my giving him this shrewd cut (which I must own to be intended in another manner), he went directly to the Governor, holding his wound so close together as he could (though bleeding prodigiously), complaining against me, and telling my reasons for serving him so. And then I was forthwith ordered before the Governor by a file of musketeers, who offering to lay hold on me, I put them by, telling them that they should not, at their peril, lead me like a dog, for that I had done nothing anywise deserving of such usage. However, if they would walk on before, I would follow them ; and which they consenting to, I was soon before the Governor, who looking at me very fiercely, and turning up the white of his eyes sullenly, told me that he never thought me to be so much a villain, always having had of me before a very high opinion ; that he thought I would be the last person guilty of such an action. "Pray, sir," said I, "of what action?" "Of what action?" said he. "Why you know already better than myself; and therefore I do not see what occasion there is of my repeating it. However, since you plead ignorance, I desire to know what could induce you to cut Johnston across the face." "As to my cutting him across the face," said I, "I cannot deny; and as to the induce- ment, I was only sorry that it had not ended his days." "A very pretty inducement indeed," said he, "to kill a man, for not joining with you in your wicked design in running away with the sloop and cargo." "I run away with the sloop and cargo," said I; "the villain could not have the impudence to say so!" "No," said he, "but he will say it to your face, and you shall be punished in a way deserving of so notorious a crime," ordering the guards to carry me directly off, and to put me into safe custody.

When I humbly entreating to be heard, and that before he let loose his rage he would be pleased to inquire into the truth of this second part of Johnston's story, it being quite reverse and notoriously false, he asked me what I could say to justify myself. I told him I could say enough to con- vince him, and all other impartial judges, of my innocence; and which, if I did not make very plainly to appear, by most undeniable evidence, he should proceed against me, and I was willing to undergo such punishment as the nature of the case deserved, and his Excellency should think fit to inflict; and that in order thereunto, he would be pleased to suffer Johnston to be confronted, and in both our presence to examine such evidence as should be by me produced.

On this Johnston was directly ordered forth, and soon appeared in a terrible condition; and being asked if I had not often prompted him to run away with the sloop and cargo, and if I had not, on his refusing to join

me in so foul an action, given him that cut, he as well as
he could answered in the affirmative. At which the Governor, looking again at me very fiercely, said, "Now are not
you a very pretty fellow?" I told him yes, and that when
he had heard my evidence, I did not doubt but what he
would think me so in good earnest; and for me to tell him
myself that he had the word only of a perjured villain,
who would not stick to say anything, even to the prejudice
of his own father, so he might thereby accomplish his
wicked designs, would signify nothing. Not but he had
most basely reversed the story, himself being the only
aggressor; for that he had of a long time back continually
teazed me to join with him in escape, and very particularly
during the last three days, concerning the sloop; and at
last, finding that notwithstanding my often denials and
representations I could not be at quiet for him, and his so
wicked importunities, I gave him the cut. And of all which,
if his Excellency doubted, I could make most undeniable
proof, by means of another person, whom he also prompted
to the same undertaking. "Indeed!" said the Governor.
"What may the person's name be?" I told him William
Hussey." "And can you produce him," said he. "Yes,
sir," said I, "I can, for he is one of the people who came
with me from Fez for the carriages, and cannot be far off,
but very likely in the yard with the carpenters, where my
men generally, by my orders, gave their attendance."

Then a messenger was sent for him, and soon returned,
and Hussey with them, Johnston being all this time, no
doubt, in a fearful condition, it being then too late for him
to bring in Hussey for a party; through which omission,
Hussey's evidence carried with it by far the greater weight,
and he had his lesson, as you may suppose, at his tongue's
end, though he said never a word till he was by the Governor asked if he knew anything concerning Johnston's

wound, and of the party giving it? When he answered
yes, it was Pellow, and that if I had not given it, he had
fully designed to have given it himself. "Pray," said the
Governor, "for what reason?" "For what reason, sir,"
said he, "for reason enough, I think; and no doubt, when
I have told you the truth of the story, you will also allow
it." "Very well," said he, "proceed, and let me know the
very truth of the matter. "Then the matter, sir, in short
is even this:—Johnston and myself are soldiers, you must
know, under Pellow's command, and therefore consequently
generally together; and for a long time back I have not
been at quiet, on Johnston's frequent importuning me to
join with him in escape, and very particularly since coming
to Sallee, in carrying off a certain sloop; alleging that
Pellow had already given his word, and that if I would
likewise consent to it, it would be strength sufficient. This,
sir, I must confess very much surprised me, I having
always found Pellow very easy under his present condition;
and as not knowing what such falsities might tend to, I
could not be quiet till I had it either confirmed or denied
from Pellow s own mouth, and for which I this morning
found an opportunity, and told Pellow in Johnston's hearing what he had said of him. Indeed (said Pellow, in a
very great surprise), Will, had not I a very good opinion of
you, I should have no small difficulty with myself to believe
it; and now I cannot very well tell what to make of it, it
being, I think, almost impossible for any one to invent
such an abominable falsity, looking sternly at Johnston,
and asking him if it was true; to which he making no
answer, Pellow asked him what he meant by it, thus (the
better to colour his so wicked designs) to make use of his
name; at which Johnston being so confounded that he
could make no answer, Pellow said, 'You dog, you are
going the right way to take away my life; tell me what

could induce you to it, or if ever I had any discourse with you tending to the affair. Speak, had I, or had I not?' And being still silent, Pellow drew his sword and gave him the cut; and this, sir, is the very truth of the matter." Here the Governor was silent for some time, looking very fiercely at Johnston, and at last telling him that he could not imagine how he could invent such a damnable lie! and which, had not Providence interposed, by Hussey's being let into the secret, must in all likelihood have taken away the life of an innocent person, ordering the guards to carry him off and put him in irons. As for me, their attendance on me was no longer necessary, for that I had sufficiently cleared myself, and that I was again at liberty to depart when and where I would.

Now having overreached Johnston, and for his villainy procured him a close prison, and of which I think he was in more respects than one highly deserving, and which (as proper for the keeping the knowledge of the affair from the public whereby it might probably spread and reach the Emperor's ears) was, I think, the fittest place for him. However, to prevent all this, I humbly desired the Governor to pardon him, and that he might in the prison be taken care of, and cured of his wound, and that the matter might be all hushed. For notwithstanding he had so dealt by me, yet would not I on any account, as I was then so far in the Emperor's good graces, that he should know it, thereby to give him any uneasiness, or the least doubt of my fidelity. "Therefore, pray, sir," said I, "forgive him, and be pleased to accept of the small matters in this purse, as an acknowledgment of so great a favour:" giving him forty gold ducats (which I had been a long time before scraping together), and which he very greedily accepted of, telling me, with a pleased countenance, to keep my own secrets, and all should be well.

And here, before I proceed any further, I shall, by way
of a short digression, ask my readers if they think we
used Johnston in anywise ill, or otherwise than they would
have done, had it been their own case, unless by my extraordinary care of him, after he was made a prisoner, which
I think to be no way suitable to his deserts, notwithstanding
our so wrongfully turning the tables upon him ; therefore,
I say, the nature of the case being duly considered, and
when I tell them that it prolonged my captivity eight
years, I hope my treatment of him will be rather approved
of than censured.   Though Hussey was so lucky to get off
in a short time after, and he has, I am sure, gratitude
enough to acknowledge that I was therein very instru-
mental, though it was not my fortune (I having yet a
much longer and very severe servitude to encounter with)
to go with him, he getting with success to Marcegongue,
and thence in a Portuguese ship to Lisbon.   But to
return.

The carriages being all now finished, and all of us
ordered to be at the next morning in readiness to depart,
I that night waited on the Governor, to thank him for all
his past favours, and to intreat his future remembrance of
my so late misfortunes, and as Johnston was not then able
to undergo the journey, he would order such care of him
as to send him after us, so soon as he was; not that I ever
desired to see him any more, but in case he might happen
to be required at our hands, we might know where to find
him ; though indeed he never after cared to come where I
was, neither did I see him but very seldom.

Now are we on the road with the carriages, having with
us a sufficient number of the inhabitants from Sallee, to
the next town, and so from town to town, relieving one
another till we got well to the camp, and where I was by
Muley Hamet most kindly received, and told by him that

he had an account from Bashaw Belide Showey, of my
readiness in following him from Tessent, in order to assist
him in his restoration at Mequinez, and that he would
always have a kind remembrance thereof. And now are
our cannon all mounted, and for a month's time we kept
almost a continual battery upon the town ; and though I
had the good fortune to escape hitherto unwounded, yet
was it my mishap soon after, the malcontents sallying, to
receive two musket shots within a minute's time of each
other, one passing through my right thigh, and the other
through my left shoulder, and at such a time as I had but
the moment before received a shrewd cut in my left hand,
and disengaged myself from a party fighting sword in hand.
And now am I in a bloody condition, I being tapped in
three several places, insomuch that from my excessive loss
of blood from them all, I really thought that I could not
have long survived it ; and thought the wound in my hand
might not be in anywise reckoned dangerous as the others,
yet could not the surgeons prevent its bleeding little or
more for three days, though they staunched the others in
a very little time.

Now am I laid on a bier, in order to be carried to an
hospital in New Fez, for the better conveniency of cure ; and
which Muley Hamet seeing, he rode forth, and asked who
I was, and after being told, he said he was very sorry for
me, and that it was his pleasure I should be particularly
taken care of, and ordered three surgeons to go along with
me, and to use the best of their skill for my recovery, and
a Genoese servitor to be always in my apartment with
me, giving me out of his jibbera,* or purse (which he had
generally hanging at his saddle before him), fifty gold
ducats, and strictly charging that I should have a quarter

* The "chkâra," or leather bag, slung over the shoulder, which
serves the purpose of a pocket, haversack, and purse.

of fresh mutton brought in every day, or anything else the
surgeons should approve of for my subsistence. Then,
after wishing me well, he turned from me, and my bearers
proceeded ; and they had not carried me far before a Moor
(just arrived in the camp from Agoory) stepped forth,
telling me that he was sorry to see me in that condition,
that he hoped my wounds were not mortal, and so forth ;
that though he never cared to be the bearer of ill news,
yet he could not forbear telling me that my wife and
daughter were both very lately dead, dying within three
days one of the other. One of Job's comforters indeed !
though I must own that it gave me very little uneasiness,
as I thought them to be by far better off than they could
have been in this troublesome world, especially this part of
it ; and I was really very glad that they were delivered out
of it, and therefore it gave me very little uneasiness.

CHAPTER VII.

More uses for wine than one—Mr. Pellow and his renegade attendant
find little difficulty in trying how far Malaga is potent to cure
wounds—He amazes his surgeon—Doctor and patient, their
adopted faith notwithstanding, have a merry evening over the forbidden cup—The surrender of Fez—The humiliation and murder
of Abdemeleck—A general beheading *more Mauritiano*—Muley
Hamid Ed-dehèbi is poisoned by Muley Abdallah's mother—This
prince seizes the throne—A new master but old habits—War again
—Fez once more in rebellion—A terrible siege of seven months—
Famine compels the Fasees to yield and meet their retribution—
Hopes of escape again disappointed by a fresh rebellion and a
long march—How malcontents are brought to book.

NOW am I brought to my apartment, and my wounds
in my thigh and shoulder were carefully searched
and dressed, and the blood staunched. Yet, I say, they
could not with all their skill (though they applied all the
medicines they could think of), prevent that of my hand
from bleeding for three days, and which was at last
staunched by applying (as I may say) some of the same
blood, it being first put into a receiver, and by a continual
stirring over a pan of fresh coals burnt into a powder, and
a small matter thereof laid on the wound put an end to the
bleeding, which I thought might not be unuseful to mention. Now am I in a very low, painful, and disconsolate
condition, and my spirits sunk to that degree that I really
expected every day to be my last; and, indeed, had I not

by way of my Genoese attendant borrowed a point of the law I must actually have been dead in a very little time; it being otherwise impossible for me to get over it. For not-withstanding I was so miserably low, and my so often telling my surgeons of it, yet would not they allow me to drink anything stronger than water.

Therefore I, considering my own case, told my keeper (whom I knew to be a trusty person) if he did not instantly look out for some comfortable wine for me, or something that was stronger by way of cordial, I could hold it but very little longer. Therefore, said I, pray hasten and see what you can do for me, giving him a gold ducat, with which he departed, and was in a very little time back again with two leather bottles concealed under his robe, the one full of brandy, and the other of excellent old Malaga wine, with which I that night made pretty free, drinking, I believe, of both sorts, as a be-ginning, about a pint, and slept after it a hearty nap, I not having shut my eyes before from the time I was wounded. At my awaking I found myself another man, my spirits being to that degree exhilarated that never was there a more sudden and surprising alteration; and then I took another moderate tiff, by which I was soon again composed, and slept till the next morning sunrising, when my German came to look at and dress my wounds, asking me how I felt myself, and if I had taken any rest. I told him, yes, I had slept many hours, and that I found myself very much revived. "Very well," said he, "I am glad of it with all my heart." "But sir," said I, "I hope you will be pleased to allow me something by way of cordial, to cheer my spirits, for you cannot but suppose them, after so great a loss of blood, to be very low." "Well," said he, "I will consider of it, but first let me feel your arm wrist," when he, starting back as one in a very great surprise,

12

" Something," says he, " to raise your spirits; why your
spirits are now ten times higher than they were yesterday,
therefore I hope there will be no occasion for any spirituous
liquors, and I very heartily wish there may not, it being
the most dangerous thing in the world; therefore," said
he, " I would by all means have you to content yourself
without it till to-morrow, and if I find any further occasion
for it then than I do at this time, I give you my honour to
procure some for you, and to trust to yours for the event."

I told him it was very well, and that I should be thereby
highly obliged to him, desiring him to look at my wounds.
To which he answered me that he would willingly first
stay a little longer, for that he every moment expected his
brethren—who indeed came in a very little time after, and
by consent fell to opening the bandage, and after a very
short time looking at that in my shoulder (which, as being
so near my heart, they thought to be by far the most
dangerous), they in a very pleasing manner told me that
they had never before seen, in so short a time, so great an
alteration for the better, for whereas it was the day before
inflamed to a very high degree, it was then wonderfully
altered, and the inflammation almost quite off; and then
they looked at the other two and found them the same, so
after dressing me they, having many other patients to go
to, departed together. But the German coming hastily back
again told me that he really thought my wounds to be in a
very promising way, and so it would be mere madness in
me to drink any spirituous liquors till the inflammation
was quite over, and they had brought them to a better
matter; and which, if I did, it would not only be the un-
doing of what they had hitherto done for me, but put it out
of the power of all the surgeons in Barbary to cure me.

" Well," said I, with a sigh, " I remember you told me so
before," and then he left me, but he was not gone out of

the room two minutes before I and my attendant drank
each of us a bumper to his good health, and between us,
before night, finished all the wine, burning most of it with
sugar and spices, which threw me into a gallant sweat and
sound sleep. In this I continued the best part of that
day, and at night had our wine bottle replenished again,
when I took another hearty tiff, and fell again into a sound
sleep, napping it in and out till six of the clock the next
morning, when my surgeons came in a full body to dress
my wounds, which they instantly went about, and still
found them growing better in a surprising manner, saying
that the inflammation was quite off, and there was a very
good digestion, asking me if I did not find my spirits to be
very much restored. I told them yes, to a very high
degree. "Well," said the German, "keep but a good
heart, and never fear of a cure in a little time," and after
telling me in a low voice he would bring me some wine the
next morning, he departed with his brethren.

Now is my stomach again craving after meat, and soon
began to relish it tolerably well, eating a good mess of
mutton broth two or three times a day, and which, with
the continuance of my wine, and a good bowl of cuscassoo
now and then, I found to bring me on apace. My German
coming again the next morning before any of the rest,
bringing with him a bottle of wine concealed under his
robe, after sending my attendant out of the room, he asked
me if I would venture to take a tiff. I told him yes, if he
pleased, with all my heart. "Then," said he, "here, take
the bottle and drink," giving it into my hand, though
after it had been but a very short time at my mouth he
cried out, "Hold! hold! you have drunk enough," when
I took it off, telling him that I thought it to be very
excellent wine, and that I found it very comfortable.
"Well," said he, "don't you by any means make too free

with it, but now and then take a little by way of cordial," to which I had but just time to tell him that it was very well, and hid the bottle in my bed-clothes, before my other surgeons came in, and fell to opening my wounds; still finding them for the better, and soon again left me, when I fell to work with the doctor's bottle, and which (as being but a quart) my attendant and I drank clear out that same day, designing no longer to impose upon my benefactor, but to bring him in the next morning, if I could, for a third man; and when he, coming again before any of the rest, very opportunely asked me how the wine had agreed with me, and if I thought it had done me no harm, "Harm!" said I, "no, no, but has, I think, on the contrary done me a great deal of good, and which, if I had more of it, you would as well as myself soon find to be true, and to work a perfect cure on me in a very little time." "Some more of it!" said he, in a seeming surprise, "why you have not, I hope, finished all I brought you yesterday." "Indeed, sir," said I, "I have, and, to be plain with you, a great deal more, or I should not be now here to tell you so." "Now here," said he, "to tell me so; in short, that you are is the greatest miracle." And when I told him the real truth, how much I had drank, the benefit I had received by it, and how I must have been inevitably dead without it, "Well," said he, "God is all sufficient, but of all the ways I ever saw or heard of curing wounds before, yours is the most uncommon one."

Then I called to my attendant to bring forth one of our own bottles, and drank a hearty tiff to my doctor's good health, delivering him the bottle, and he as heartily pledged me, telling me that he thought it to be very excellent wine, and that he was very glad it had so well agreed with me; however, he believed that nobody before had ever been that way cured. "Oh, doctor," said

I, " you are in that very much mistaken, I having many times before made the experiment on myself." " Very well," said he, " I hope all this is under the rose." " Yes, yes, doctor," said I, " that you need not fear, and if you will be pleased to come in with us for a third man we may innocently enjoy ourselves over a bottle, without doing any harm to anybody else." " Very well," said he, " I understand you, and as to my answer I will give it you in the evening." His comrades coming in at once upon us, we had not time then to talk any further about it, and after they had dressed me, and told me that my wounds were bettering apace, they again for that day left me.

And now is my German doctor soon about to come in for a snack. Coming at the beginning of the night, when all was pretty quiet, and bringing with him two bottles of excellent old Malaga wine, he sat down, took a cup out of his pocket, filled it to the top, and drank it off to the good health of our Christian friends, myself and my attendant following his example; and after we had drank a round or two more, he told me that he thought I might think myself very happy under my present circumstances, and to be much better off than a great number of my comrades, who, during my lying sick, had been exposed to many dangers and hardships, and a great many of them slain. Of which, indeed, I had before repeated advices, and therefore my life was in all likelihood entirely owing to my wounds, and which, indeed, was very likely to be true, for during my cure were many thousands on both sides slain, and amongst them of my small number at least one hundred and fifty.

Now are my wounds healing apace, being able again to sit up and walk a little, and my strength every day very apparently increasing, insomuch that my surgeons told me that they did not doubt but that I might in three weeks more be again in a capacity to return to my duty in the

army. Though indeed I thought myself fit at the fortnight's
end, and should certainly have made my appearance then
had not they prevented me, telling me that they thought
my wound to be still too green, and not sufficiently
hardened, and therefore I was obliged to remain there
another week ; at the end of which I waited with my surgeons on Muley Hamet, who seemed to be highly pleased
at my recovery, and thereof gave my surgeons very liberal
acknowledgments, ordering me immediately back again to
my old apartment.   For as the malcontents were then
reduced to the lowest ebb, he said he could not see what
service I could be of there, and after making most humble
acknowledgment for his so very great care of me, I obeyed
his orders, went back, and there continued six days longer,
at the end of which he sent me word by one of my own
people that the city had surrendered, and that it was his
pleasure I should come directly and see the rebels march
out ; which, so well as they were able, I soon did, being
really all of them reduced to a very miserable condition.
Yet, notwithstanding, many of them (especially their ring-
leaders) had their heads chopped off on the spot, and
Abdemeleck, with forty principal men, were put into safe
custody, in order to be safely conducted by the army to
Mequinez.

Before Abdemeleck was brought into Hamet Deby's presence he was searched by the captain of his guards and
some other officers, who found a poniard and a small pistol
concealed in his pockets, which they took away, and then
conducted him into Hamet Deby's tent, who, instead of
venting his wrath and vengeance upon him, contented
himself with making some reproaches, and those without
sharpness. " What," says he, " after having taken the
crown from me, are you now cruel enough to seek to take
away my life ? "

Now have we a general muster, by which we found we had
lost in all on our side in this siege thirty thousand men;
then we struck our tents, and with the remainder of our
army marched with our prisoners to Mequinez, where the
forty principal men were beheaded in the market-place,
which was a much milder fate than those met with who
were before taken in Mequinez, for there the governor of
the city and some of the principal men were nailed by
their hands and feet to one of the gates of the city, in which
miserable manner they lived three days, except the governor
of the city, whose hands and feet were so torn by the weight
of his body (being a lusty man) that he fell down from the
gate some time after he had been nailed thereto, upon
which they had the mercy to dispatch him with their
sabres. And at this time, indeed, the Emperor ordered the
Governor of Sallee to be served in the same or worse
manner, for he had first his skull cracked with the blows
of a pistol, and was then hung up by the feet at one of the
gates of the city, in which deplorable condition he remained
alive four days.

Abdemeleck was put under the custody of Emshael,* the
black Bashaw, who was strictly charged to keep him close
prisoner in his own house till further orders; and indeed
he never got free from thence, being at the end of six weeks
strangled by two of his own brothers; and lest he might
not be dead enough, they gave him each a stab with their
long murdering knives through his body, Muley Hamet Deby
dying about an hour before him. His death was occasioned
—as was by all supposed—by his drinking a small bowl of
milk at his entrance into Mequinez from Fez—according
to custom, after obtaining any signal victory—it being
poisoned by Muley Abdallah's mother, in order to clear
her son's way to the Empire, he languishing from the very

* 'Mshael.

moment of his taking it, even to his last hour. Muley Abdallah was accordingly proclaimed as soon as Hamet Deby was dead, his mother Lela Coneta, who had been one of the wives of Muley Swine, or Ishmael, having—by distributing three hundred thousand ducats amongst the Black Army, besides fifty thousand given by her own hands to their chief officers—engaged them in his interest, notwithstanding Hamet Deby left a son named Muley Bouser,* who was capable of reigning, whom Muley Abdallah kept in prison some time, but he at last found an opportunity to escape.

Now am I to prepare myself for swimming through a fresh sea of blood, the scene opening in new and deeper colours indeed, for though Muley Abdallah was in my time driven out twice, yet was there scarce a day passed without his murdering some of his subjects, more or less; he having, I believe, killed with his own hands, besides those most unmercifully butchered by the hands of his executioners, at least fifty thousand men, he having his old father the devil so riveted in his heart, as that it was impossible for anybody to tell when he was in jest or in earnest, being always bent on bloody enterprises, and unhappy I, seldom exempted from making one therein—I mean in his inhumane bloody wars. But I was for the present sent again to my old station at Agoory, and where I had a short interval of about six weeks, often reflecting on the loss of my wife and daughter; for though I said before their death gave me very little uneasiness, yet could not I help now being under concern for them, and especially the child, who always used, at my coming home wounded, to clasp her little arms about my neck, hugging and bemoaning her poor father, and telling me that I should no more go into the wars, for that she and her mother

* Bou Azza.

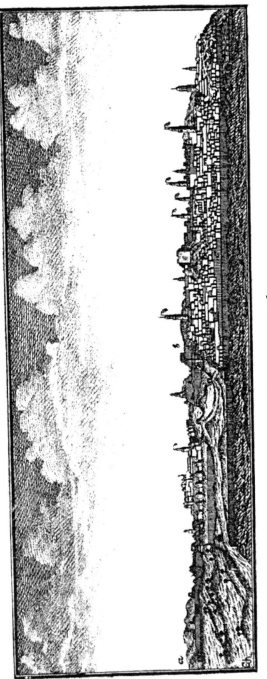

MÉQUINEZ IN 1760.

would go with me to England, and live with her grand-mother.

These reflections, I say, gave me some concern ; however, I soon endeavoured to forget them, for, in short, what could I do ? To bring them back again I knew was im-possible, and as they were—as far as lay in my power—instructed in the knowledge and, I hope, true belief in Christ, and my intentions were fully bent upon escape, I was really glad that they were dead; and I plainly told myself that as I could find in my heart in their lifetime to endeavour to leave the country, I had now no room left for excuse, but ought to pursue it ; and therefore I was thoroughly resolved to lay hold of all opportunities, and as soon as my strength was a little better restored again, to push all for all. My resolutions thus settled, I am again at peace with myself, diligently employing my time in bathing my wounds with such ointments as my doctors had directed me.

But I was again on a sudden ordered, with all my men, for Mequinez ; and though I was in a very indif-ferent condition, sore against my inclinations, and full two of the clock in the afternoon when my orders came, yet was I obliged to obey them, and to be there, if possibly I could, that same day ; and which, though very short notice, it being in the month of July, I punctually performed, we being all on horseback by four, and without any hurry got to Mequinez in good season, where I found Muley Abdallah at the head of an army consisting of 140,000 men, chiefly blacks, ready to march for Old Fez. With whom we were joined, and early the next morning marched with them, the malcontents having gathered together there, refusing to acknowledge him, and yet setting up no one else ; so that I verily believe it was merely for the sake of rebellion, and I easily foresaw that, if they

chose to be obstinate, their blood would be poured out like
water; and I must own I heartily wished—seeing they
were of so cruel a nature—that their insatiate eyes might
be never satisfied with blood, till the last of them had seen
the last drop of all the rest, himself expiring with the
utter extermination of that so barbarous and most un-
christian monarchy. And which is, indeed, now in a very
fair way of being accomplished, they having a most insatiate thirst after each other's destruction, attended with
sad devastation and famine, and the times still growing
worse and worse upon their hands; and which may God
continue, till they are either brought to a true sight of their
errors, or the utter extirpation of themselves and principles.

For as their country is so very rich, spacious, and popu-
lous, it is much to be regretted that it should go under any
other denomination than that of a part of a Christendom;
and whereto should all Christian princes but set their
helping hand, Christianity would not only flourish and
abound, but many poor ignorant souls who are now,
through means of their following false lights, in a most
dangerous and deplorable condition, be in a little time
brought by the light of the Gospel into a true knowledge
and belief in Christ, and to the utter abhorrence and
detestation of Mahometism; which, through the ambitious
artifices of cunning and designing men, hath for so many
ages been so grossly imposed upon them.—But whither
am I wandering? These digressions are quite out of my
way, as well as a subject far beyond my abilities, and
altogether out of my way to meddle with; therefore I
shall again return to my old road, travel gently on, and
leave the event of all these things to God; who, no
doubt, hath in a great measure ordained them for wise
purposes.

Now am I again one in this large army before Old Fez,

where Muley Abdallah offered the malcontents free pardon, in case they would surrender, and promise future obedience to him. To which they answered, being but too well acquainted with his deceitful nature, that, considering their resistance was for liberty and property, they thought it as good or much better for them to die then, than at another time; therefore they utterly despised his offer, which they directly confirmed from the mouths of their muskets. And now is the bloody scene opening apace, nothing but death and horror reigning here for the space of seven months, during which I was not backward in acting my part even in place of greatest danger, insomuch that I was very willing—in case I might escape with my life—to compound for a smart wound or two; and which, indeed, was both my bad and good hap, as you will by and by hear.

Now is there scarce a day without close skirmishing, and on both sides great slaughter; and notwithstanding our cruel treatment of those we took alive, as unmercifully cutting some to pieces, and hanging others up alive by the heels, till they were dead through anguish and hunger, and others by many other cruel inventions of tortures, and all within sight of the garrison, yet did they seem to make no manner account of it, unless growing thereat more desperate. And which, indeed, by their future behaviour and bold attempts of reprisals, they made soon to be very apparent, behaving to the last with an undaunted resolution, selling their blood with their lives, to the very great expense of that of our army. Had not their provisions and warlike stores failed them, they had certainly done us far greater mischief, we having from several prisoners repeated accounts that, as long as their stores lasted and people continued, they were thoroughly resolved to hold it out. But when their provision was exhausted, their horses had eaten up all their provender, and they at last eaten up their horses, the remnant were resolved to sally forth together, and sell their lives at the rate of those of the bravest soldiers, which they deemed much better, and by far more honourable, than to drag a miserable life, attended with grievous servitude, and continually exposed to the capricious humour of a bloody tyrant.

Therefore they were resolved to deliver their country from his tyranny, or perish with it. And in which, indeed, they were in a great measure as good as their words, for they fought us to the last with a noble resolution, and desperately sallied so long as they had anything remaining whereby to support their sinking spirits, their horses being at last all eaten up, and the remnant of themselves so miserably weak through famine, that their lives were scarce worth the taking, not having strength enough left them to make an honourable pile for burial, which was what they fully intended, and, like Samson, to have killed more at their deaths than they had before done during all the time of their lives.

But as their strength could do no more, they were at last obliged to submit to the mercy of a merciless tyrant, marching out, or rather, indeed, crawling out—as being scarce able to stand—in one body of six thousand and thirty-six. The 36 were instantly on the spot beheaded, and the remaining 6,000 led by the army in a miserable condition to Mequinez, and ever after exposed (so long as any of them remained) in the fronts of the tyrant's bloody battles, and most of them were killed in my sight. This was my third battle at Fez. We lost 40,000 men ; and of 1,500 Christians in this siege and the former, no more remained than 660, myself being likewise wounded by two musket shots in my left shoulder and fleshy part of my buttock, though these wounds did not keep me from my duty more than five weeks.

Now am I, after this my so very great fatigue and narrow escape of my life, sent again to Agoory, where I could not again help thinking on my late wife and little prattler, ruminating on the many hazards I had hitherto undergone, and the no less miraculous preservations I had met with, fully intending to pursue my intentions of escaping, and to put my trust in Providence for deliverance, as soon as my wounds were somewhat hardened, my strength restored, and a convenient opportunity should offer.

But alas! I may as to that set my heart at quiet for some very considerable time longer, I having first many more tedious and hazardous exploits to encounter with. And first I was by Muley Abdallah, even, as I may say, before I had time to look about me, very unexpectedly hurried away on the following expedition. He having repeated accounts of a great body of malcontents, consisting to the least of 100,000, gathered at Itehuzzan,* in the province of Itemoor,† and that they behaved after a most insolent manner, he therefore directly ordered 70,000 horse to be got ready to march with him thither to correct them, and of which number myself and men, as a part, were forthwith ordered to Mequinez, where we directly joined the rest of the army and marched towards the rebels; and the second day following we got to Itehuzzan.

Here we soon found the grand assembly had divided themselves into several parties, flying before us as fast as they could into the heights of the mountains, so as we were at least two months before we could light on them to any purpose, and then, being driven to many hardships, they sent to the Emperor twelve of their chiefs, and with

* Aït-Hassan?
† The district of the Aït-Zemour, a still rebellious tribe?

them sixteen fine horses as a present, with full power to tell him that if in case he would send a small party of his people back with them, they would so order matters, as that they should return again in little time with their respective dues. In order to which he sent with them the next morning six thousand men, who were treated by them for some time in a seeming friendly manner, and a great many of them, in conformity to this offer, accordingly brought in the tributes, though the greatest part of them, as not at all liking such heavy impositions, joining in grand consult, sent thirty-eight of their chiefs to the Emperor to tell him that they had not as then brought in their several payments, according to their promise by their former messengers; not but they fully intended to do it, and were then ready to do so, provided he would make an abatement. At this the tyrant was so enraged, that he answered them in a most furious manner, "An abatement, you dogs! I'll soon make an abatement of you," looking at them very fiercely, and beckoning to his own people to hem them in, and then, on giving a sign, they had all their heads in a moment cut off, saving one only, who through wonderful chance escaped to carry this so unexpected answer back to their message: and which, for some time, put the remainder of them into a most terrible consternation, as not thoroughly resolving for a day or two what course to take; though it was at last agreed by them to surprise and cut off the six thousand of our people, who lay encamped near them, and accordingly they fell directly on them, and notwithstanding they made a gallant resistance, yet did they kill of them four thousand on the spot, the other two thousand flying in great confusion back to our army, with this so unwelcome and unexpected news.

Now is the tyrant most highly enraged, insomuch that he directly ordered most of us up the mountains on foot,

and to give no quarter to all we could light on ; which was
punctually obeyed, though we found at first but very few
of them, as only here and there a small number tarrying
behind the rest of their brethren, under a pretence of being
shepherds or herdsmen to look after their cattle, the main
body (of about 30,000) flying from mountain to mountain
before us, and so continuing for seven days. On the eighth
day we got so near them, and to that degree so hemmed
them in, that we in a very little time destroyed them,
putting them all to the sword with very little loss on our
side ; and then, after breathing some short time, we
marched to the castle of Mint, in the province of
Itehacam,* lying at the foot of a very high mountain, and
wherein we had an account that 50,000 more of the rebels
were entrenched ; and very early the next morning we were
all ordered up on foot, to pay them a visit, and so surrounded
them that we attacked them in their trenches sword in
hand, and in a short time killed of them 30,000 more, the
remainder in great confusion flying before us to the mountain of Ceedeboazzo Multorria,† where they were in such a
manner sheltered from our fury, that it would have been
in us not only a mere madness to follow them, but also
very hazardous, as well as altogether in vain.

Therefore we marched to the river Cuscasoe,‡ about four
leagues farther on between the mountains, lying between
Ceedeboazzo § and Mint, there intending to settle our camp
for some time ; and which was indeed forthwith marked out,
and our tents pitched there ; but on the eighth day following our camp was very accidentally set on fire by a coal
of fire sticking at the bottom of a cake of bread, just taken
out of a hot oven, which falling amongst the fodder (of
which there was a prodigious quantity, very long and dry)

* This is probably another form of Beni Hassan.
† Sidi Bou Azzua Multorria.   ‡ K'sksoo ?   § Sidi Bou Azza.

the fire quickly spread itself to that degree, that notwithstanding all our haste in removing our tents, &c., yet were many of them, with several of our horses and all our stores, burnt, the fire still spreading towards the Emperor's pavilions, wherein were fifty of his concubines, who were with great difficulty carried off by the eunuchs, covered all over with cloaks, and shrieking after a dismal manner, before the fire reached them.

Now are we, on account of this sad accident, both as to our provision and ammunition, in a very great strait, and there was very little dependence of having a fresh supply from the country, any further than what we got by foraging. Therefore we were obliged to send expressly to Mequinez for such as we wanted, and which was full twenty days before it came to our hands ; though during this (after the fodder was all burnt up, the fire extinguished, and all the ashes cleared off, for fear of a second accident of like nature) we settled the remainder of our tents, which we had preserved from the flames, again in the same place.

Our stores, &c., being arrived, we rose with our army, and marched out in four days to the castle of Cassavah Amarisu,* in the parish of Juzob, in the province of Tamnsnah, after the following route : The first day to the other side of the river Melhah : the second to Mersaidore † ; the third to Zeebedah ; and the fourth, by three o'clock in the afternoon, within two leagues of the castle. Here we met with a great party of the malcontents ; and though they were double our number, we forthwith attacked them, and by ten of the clock that same night cut most of them off, when we marched on to the castle, and settled our camp without the walls, where we remained for the space of two months, ravaging and plundering the country all round us of their corn, fruit, cattle, &c., after a most

* Kasbah Amarisoo.   † Mers-el-Abiod ?

shocking manner, the inhabitants (all but those of the parish of Meduna) * flying from us into the heights of the mountains. Indeed it would have been much better for them had those of Meduna also done so, for notwithstanding their so ready compliance in sending in to the tyrant four hundred horse all gallantly mounted with the prime of their youth, and almost laden with vast sums of money for his service, yet did he instantly order them for execution, and had all their heads cut off on the spot. The rest of the inhabitants in those parts, on seeing this sad disaster of their neighbours, compounded for their own lives by bringing in vast sums of money. Then our army rose, and marched thence with much booty and several prisoners to Milce,† about six leagues, where we again pitched our tents, and settled four weeks, still making in the country grievous havoc. At length we rose and marched thence, after the following route for Mequinez: The first day to Invelghummeese; ‡ the second to Inemocoon; the third to the river Sharrot; the fourth to Wilgehiah Ben Hammo; the fifth to the river Bate; and the sixth, in good season, to Mequinez, the tyrant still (as we passed along) plundering the country and murdering his subjects.§

* District of Mediuna.   † Mils.
‡ Invelg-Khamiss.   § *Note* 22.

CHAPTER VIII.

War is exchanged for commerce—Pellow is sent with the trading
caravan to the coast of Guinea—The route taken by him—Privations from want of water—How to find it—Wonderful acuteness
of the senses displayed by a blind Arab—Lions and ostriches—
How the latter are killed in the desert—Business being finished
on the coast the caravan returns to Morocco—Displeasure of the
Emperor Muley Abdallah at the results of the journey—He, as
usual, slaughters a great many innocent men—He kills a plotting
Marabout or Saint—An expedition to the River Draa country—A
cruel sight—The deaths of Jerrory and Bendoobash—Treachery
of the Emperor—An easy life again—Hunting and fishing—To
Mequinez—War once more.

NOW am I again returned to Mequinez, where this
bloody villain is for the space of a month employed
in nothing but contriving ways and means how to put his
people to death, scarce a day passing without his exercising
his cruelty more or less. But I could not (very much to
my dissatisfaction) find any likely means to escape, and
therefore I found myself of necessity obliged to follow his
so evil genius till a more convenient season, and to content
myself under it so well as I could, I being at the end of
five weeks a second time ordered with a good number of
troops for Itemoor, and after following the malcontents
into the mountains for eight weeks, killing all we could
light on, and plundering their cattle, &c., we again returned therewith to Mequinez; and where I had not again

remained no more than three weeks, but I was ordered forthwith with the caravan to the coast of Guinea.

This really gave me some disquiet, as being (I was very certain) work cut out for me for at least two years. However, to show any dissatisfaction I knew would not be in the least availing, and therefore with seeming cheerfulness set out thence in company with 12,000 camels (our numbers still increasing on the road), and got the first night to the river Bate ; the second to Dyefroome ; * the third to Bolegrig and Grove, where two rivers meet ; the fourth to Amwoodermel ; the fifth to Waddon Enkeese ; † the sixth to Meetheor Obeor, ‡ the hundred and one wells ; the seventh to Broash ; the eighth to Emshrah Dellia ; § the ninth to Menzet ; and the tenth to Morocco, with our caravan very much increased. Here we rested ten days ; the eleventh we came to Wadden Enfeese ; the twelfth to Zouyet Belhoul ; the thirteenth to Kishour ; the fourteenth to Algorarsassa ; the fifteenth to Itewaddel ; the sixteenth to Sofeegofulee ; ‖ the seventeenth to Afford ; the eighteenth to Agroot, a small fishing cove ; the nineteenth to Tammanert ; the twentieth to the river Souze, three leagues to the southward of Santa Crux ; the twenty-first to Messah ; the twenty-second to Agolooe ; the twenty-third to Ceedehammet Benmoosa, ¶ where one of their famous conjurers, formerly called after that name, was buried ; the twenty-fourth to Ofran ; the twenty-fifth to Wadnoon, ** and which is the last that way, where the inhabitants live in houses ; the twenty-sixth to Shebeccah, and the twenty-seventh to Segeeahamrah. ††
Thence entering the deserts, our numbers now being 30,000 men, and 60,000 camels complete, each soldier having the charge over two ; and we were all of us (saving a few that

---

* Dayat-er Roumi. † Wad Enkees. ‡ Meat Bir oo Bir.
§ 'Mshrah Dallia. ‖ Safeegosoolz. ¶ Sidi Hamid ben Moosa.
** Wad Nûn. †† Sejea Hambra.

died on the passage) safely conducted by an old blind
Laurb in five months' time over this sandy ocean, to the
castle of Shinget. This castle of Shinget belongs to a
better sort of Laurbs, as they are generally termed;
though I think they are all of them a pack of thievish
bloodthirsty villains, insomuch that whether of them or the
Moors are the better I shall not take upon me to determine. Though indeed, in the original, I take them to be all
one and the same people, yet is there here a Moorish
governor always residing, and the plunder and tribute is
there brought in during the stay of one caravan on the
Guinea coast till another caravan arrives, and then the
old ones march off with their booty, and leave the new
comers the possession.

In and about this castle was our general rendezvous,
though we marched thrice to the Wadnil, or river Nile,
and all such as made any the least resistance we brought
under subjection with the sword, so that they were either
obliged to bring in the tyrant's exorbitant demands, or
to suffer the severe plundering of the army, stripping
the poor negroes of all they had, killing many of them,
and bringing off their children into the bargain. At
our first coming to the river, we found on it a French vessel
of about eighty tons, and manned by twelve sailors, which
the Moors swam off to, boarded, and hauled to the shore.*
But before I proceed any further, I shall first beg leave to
go back, and tell you of a most extraordinary thing trans-
acted by our old blind pilot, in our travel over the deserts,
into which we being entered about fifty days, during which
we never failed of meeting every day, or every other day
at the furthest, with some very refreshing springs of water,
whereby we and our cattle were very much cherished. At
one of those springs the old man told us that we should

* *Note* 28.

not fail there to fill so many of our skins as would hold
water sufficient for all of us for three days at the least, for
that we should not meet with any more of them during
that time; which we did accordingly, and at the third day's
end we got again to other springs where he told us that
we should not neglect doing the same, for that we should
not for a fortnight meet with water oftener than every third
day; and which, indeed, we did not.   However, we passed
over those stages without any great matter of murmuring,
and at the last of them he told us that we should there be
sure to fill all our skins, and let our cattle drink their fill,
for that we should not meet with any more water for some
considerable time, and therefore we should be on our march
as sparing as possible.   But the weather being according
to the season of the year (it being in the beginning of
Autumn) exceeding hot, about the sixth day following, we
being about to pour the water out of our skins, to our very
great astonishment found them (or at least the greatest
part of them) quite empty, the excessive heat of the sun
having exhaled the water through the pores of the leather,
insomuch that we to that degree suffered for four days,
that had not our old pilot cheered us in a wonderful manner,
it must certainly have been attended with very ill conse-
quences, it causing amongst us a general murmuring.
But he desired us to be as easy as we could under our sad
distress, for that he was well satisfied we should again in a
short time have water enough, desiring one of our people
to take him up a handful of sand and hold it to his nose;
and after he had snuffed upon it for some short time, he
pleasingly told we should before two days' end reach other
springs, and have water enough, travelling on, and encouraging us all in his power.

In the morning of the second day following he desired
that another handful of the sand of that place might

be taken up and held to his nose; on which the party
taking that which he had smelt of two days before (he
having still preserved it in a piece of old linen cloth)
stepped forth and held the same for him to smell to
again; and after he had snuffled on it for a much longer
time than at first, he told him that either the army was
again marching back, or that he had most grossly and
basely imposed on him, for that was actually the same or
some other of the sand of that place he had smelt of two
days before, and therefore he thought him highly to blame,
and that he did very ill thus to go about to deceive a dark
old man. However, it was not in his power, notwithstanding he had so much like a fool endeavoured it. "Therefore," said he, "throw it away, and on your honour take
me up a handful of the real sand of this place," which,
after just putting his nose to it, he said in a most pleasant
manner, "Now, sirs, this is something like," giving us all
to understand that we should, about four o'clock that afternoon, have water sufficient; which was, indeed, at this
time as comfortable news to me, as my trusty Genoese
servitor's assurance of procuring me some comfortable
cordials, when I was sick with my wounds at Fez.

About noon he desired a fresh handful of sand, which
putting his nose to, he said, "Ay, ay, this is as it should
be," ordering us to keep a good look out if we could see any
wild beasts, ostriches, eagles, &c., and in such case to tell
him of it; and before we had travelled half a league further
we saw several eagles in the air, and soon after many wild
beasts and ostriches, flocking together on the sand, and on
our telling him of it he told us to march directly thither,
and there we should find several shallow wells of excellent
water, covered over with the skins of wild beasts. "But,"
said he, "take care you don't disturb it, by pressing on too
eagerly, but go gradually on, and you will find sufficient

for you all ; and I further promise to bring you to-morrow
evening to a very large pond, where yourselves and cattle
may all drink at once, and where we may again fill our
skins, so as no more to want water during the remainder
of our journey, for we shall afterwards meet with little or
more every day." At last we got up to these so very much
longed after wells, which we found according to the old
man's assertion, close covered, but soon hauled off the
skins, and all of us, to our very great satisfaction, in course
drank our fill, and then we fell to settling our camp there
for the night, and there being for a good space round, store
of pasture, our cattle were as well off as ourselves.*

By the next morning we were gallantly refreshed ; when,
after covering the wells (having first filled our skins with
water, sufficient for that day), we with fresh courage travelled
on, and got that evening, according to promise, to the spacious
pond ; and here being also good store of provender, with
vast numbers of wild beasts, ostriches, &c., we rested two
days, and through means of our old pilot we killed a great
many of them after the following manner. On our seeing
those creatures hankering after the water, and telling our
pilot of it, he ordered us to dig holes in several places
round the pond, deep and large enough to hide two or three
musqueteers in each ; then to draw off the army, when he
said they would come to drink, so as we might shoot them
at our pleasure. After which method we in a little time
killed a great many of them, committing all to pot, as
lions, antelopes, and ostriches together ; though I think the
latter by far too good to be thus misused, as being alone
most excellent and delicious eating, and of all other birds
(if it may properly be so called), in the way of serving a
great many people, by far the most preferable, as weighing,
no doubt, at the least two hundred pounds weight, and in

* *Note* 24.

a manner all one lump of fat, so as one of them decently handled will no doubt suffice two hundred men.

When the native Laurbs are minded to kill an ostrich, they generally go out in a party, and at a distance surround him, drawing nearer by degrees, driving him from one to another till he is at last so tired as that he can seemingly do no more harm ; which, as he cannot fly, may seem to those who are therewith unacquainted to be a very easy matter, yet is it, I assure you, a very difficult point. For when he is pursued, he runs so swiftly as few horses in Barbary can keep up with him : and when he finds himself beginning to slacken his pace, and the enemy to gain ground upon him, he to that degree spurs himself with his spurs (which he hath growing under his wings, prodigious long and sharp) as that he soon again recovers his pace, his wings being always extended, and though of no benefit to him by way of flying off the ground, yet no doubt of a very great addition to his speed in running, he being at last run down much in like nature of a hare before a pack of hounds, with this difference only, that being generally close hunting, this altogether in open view.

And now to return to the French vessel ; which, after taking out some elephants' teeth and blacks (their gold being all thrown overboard), was directly burnt, carrying the prisoners with us to Shinget, four of them dying in the desert on our way homeward, and the other eight we carried with us to Mequinez. During our stay on the Guinea coast, which was in all about twelve months, we got together a very great booty, as gold, ivory, blacks, &c., though it did not satisfy our insatiate master, as you will by and by hear.

Our time being expired, and another caravan arrived, we packed up our treasure, and set out for Mequinez, getting well to our old pilot's pond without anything happening worth my noting, where we again gallantly refreshed ourselves during the space of two days, regaling on our wild dainties. And after filling all our skins, we set forward, and got that evening to our so late longed after wells, where we again took up our quarters, without impairing our main stock of provisions, we have several ostriches and antelopes, which we brought with us from the pond for our supper. The next morning at daybreak we were again on the march, myself and six more, in pursuit of some antelopes, staying about a mile behind the rest of the caravan; when all on a sudden we saw twenty of the wild Laurbs riding on camels towards us, they having during the caravan's passing by hid themselves behind some large sandy banks, of which were here and there several thrown up by the violent winds, and again the next storm very likely removed to other places. The Laurbs being between us and the army, thought no doubt to have made of us sure prize; six of them advanced within a hundred yards of us, and discharged their muskets on us, one of their shot grazing along the side of my head, and another wounding a Moor close by my side. On which we fired at once and killed two of them, when we directly rode off to charge, and fired at them again, killing the other four, when again riding off we saw several of our people coming back to our assistance.

However, before they came up with us, we had fired twice round on the other fourteen, and killed most of those, and then we saw many more of their party advancing; though on their seeing those of our people come back they turned from us and fled, and lest we might happen to lose sight of our army we pursued them no further, but hasted forward as fast as we could. After this skirmish we travelled on unmolested, taking most special care of our water, so as we might not be again reduced to so sad a calamity, I riding as often as I could alongside of the old Laurb, asking him a great many questions, and particularly concerning his so wonderful and surprising knowledge in smelling to the sand. To which he, after a most courteous manner, answered me that this was his thirtieth journey over this ocean, therefore in going and coming his sixtieth time; that in his last four journeys, finding his sight gradually declining, he had, by often making the experiment (as having a wonderful faculty in smelling), attained to this so wonderful knowledge, he being, he said, well satisfied that the loss of his sight was thereby in a very great measure compensated, insomuch that he would engage at any time to tell in what part of the desert he was. One day as I was riding pretty near him, my camel happened with one of his feet to hit against something which sounded very hollow, which I telling the old man of, as wondering what it should be, he told me it was a mummy. "A mummy," said I, "pray what is that?" "It is," said he, "a human corpse, which hath for some time lain buried in the sands, till through the excessive heat thereof it is dried to a kecks; and if our surgeons knew it, they would not suffer it (if they thought it fit for their purpose) to lie any longer there." "Fit for their purpose," said I. "What, is one of them better than another?" "That," said he, "is according to the time of their being buried, or of their being more or less dried." "Well, father," said I, "if I should be so lucky to light on another, I think I should have curiosity enough to take it up." And riding again the next day near the old man, he bade me to get off my camel, for that his camel had with one of his feet struck against a mummy; which, by his directions, I with the point of my sword soon found, and with a spade digged it up in a little time. It was as hard as a stock-fish, had all its limbs and flesh (though shrivelled) entire, all the teeth firm in the gums; and as to its being

any way nauseous, a man might without offence have even
carried it in his bosom.

After this, we travelled on without anything else happening particular, till we safely arrived at Tedlah, where we
found Muley Abdallah waiting our coming, diverting the
time in plundering the country, and murdering his subjects.
And after he had strictly examined into the value of our
treasure, he being not at all pleased with it (though no
doubt it was to the value of some millions of English
pounds sterling), killed Monsore, our Bashaw, and seventeen
more of our principals, with his own hand, and the next
day twenty-seven chiefs, who came thither to him in all
humility from several parts of the country with their
presents, and, to my most unspeakable grief, my deliverer
from the bloody knife at Assamoor.

When the tyrant was glutted with blood, we marched with
him at our head to Mequinez ; whence, after the caravan was
separated and sent home to their respective habitations, I
was again at the end of six weeks hurried away on the following expedition :—The tyrant having repeated advices of a
vast number of credulous poor souls being (through the
means of one Enseph * or Joseph Haunsell, a noted conjurer)
stirred up to rebellion in and about Tedlah, he having
before shown many of his magic pranks, and had then so
far insinuated into the giddy multitude as to make them
believe they should be invulnerable from Muley Abdallah's
shot, and suchlike stuff, and they pinning their faith so
far on his sleeve, that they were gathered in a little time
to a body of at least two hundred thousand men, doing
even as he commanded them, committing many insolencies,
and with a high hand (like a great torrent) bearing all
down before them. All which, I say, coming to the
Emperor's ears, I am, in company with eighty thousand

* Y(J)usuf.

regular troops, and Salem Ducullee * at our head, ordered
directly to march against them ; and notwithstanding the
vast number the conjurer had with him, and those spirited
up by his pretended conjurations, yet could he not hinder
them from flying into the heights of the mountains before
us. However, we followed them so close, that we by the
sword and musket killed vast numbers in a very little
time ; and after we had at last conjured the conjurer into
our custody, we marched with him to Tedlah, where the
Emperor then was, and gladly received him at our hands,
telling him that he was very glad to see him there, and
that as he had hitherto heard so very much of his famous
conjurations, if he could tell him what death he had within
himself determined for him, he would, notwithstanding all
his past villainies, pardon him. To which the conjurer
making no answer, he told him that he thought his con-
juration to be then at an end, and that himself was become
the better conjurer of the two, for that he was very sure
his hands and feet should be cut off to the arm-wrists and
ankles ; which was immediately done, and his body thrown
on a dunghill naked, guarded by fifty soldiers till dead, and
afterwards left till it was eaten up by the dogs.

This Enseph Haunsell was actually in his days not only
a noted magician, but had therein performed many strange
and very unaccountable things in favour of Muley Hamet
Deby, as raising to all human appearance vast numbers
of armed men, and in the Emperor's palace at Mequinez
making most surprising doings, the doors in and throughout it, when they were to all people's seeming close shut
and firmly bolted, flying open on a sudden of themselves,
and on the top of the palace walls many armed men
appearing on horseback, sometimes in grand order, riding
in ranks, and sometimes in great confusion, rallying and

* 'Abd es-slam—or Salêm—Eddoukkâli.

charging one another sword in hand. This did I myself
see, as well as many thousand others; though indeed I
could not at that time have any further opinion of it than
that it was a trick or delusion, yet I must confess that I
had afterwards (when I was about to make my escape for
good) some reason to believe there was somewhat more
than imaginary, as shall in its proper place be set forth.

This way of putting the conjurer to death was premeditated by the tyrant, though I had never before seen any
of his subjects despatched by his order that way; not but
it was (when they were up in arms one against another in
their civil wars) cruelly practised, and of which indeed I
had one night a very melancholy instance. I being out in
pursuit of some of those rebels, and straying a little from
my party, in passing by an old ruined house I heard a
most dismal groan, and which I very attentively listening
to, I soon heard to be repeated in different accents; when
stopping at the entrance, I was soon given to understand
that there were four brothers (stout young men) lying on
the floor, having all of them their hands and feet cut off,
through the cruelty of their enemies of a neighbouring
town, humbly imploring me to go to their father's house
and acquaint him with it.

And after they had given me directions, I went, found
the house, and was in a little time back again with their
father and mother, and with them sufficient help and
light; and at our entrance we found two of them dead, and
the other two almost ready to expire. However, they had
time enough to tell them by whom they were thus used;
so that I was, to my very great satisfaction, freed from all
suspicion of having any hand in it; of which, had they all
died in my absence, I might very reasonably have lain
under a very great one, and have been very innocently
punished. And now are they all at work in removing the

two surviving unhappy wretches; who, on their being
moved, died also, and then I was courteously entreated
by their father to go to his house; which, as thinking
myself to be altogether unsafe till I had again joined my
own party, I did not think fit to do; therefore I went
directly in quest of them.

Now am I, after conjuring the conjurer, again breathing for some short time in Mequinez, and where is soon
about to be acted by the tyrant the most bloody tragedy
you ever before heard of; and though I was, during the
time of the transaction of the first part of this story, with
the caravan on the coast of Guinea, yet (as I had it from
so many undoubted reports) I shall here venture to set it
down for fact, and therefore I will tell it you from the
beginning, together with all its circumstances.   The tyrant
having amongst his soldiery a particular troop of brave
men, to the number of about eight hundred, commanded
by one Musa Jerrory * (one Eli Bendoobash † being his
lieutenant), who had of a long time behaved after the
bravest manner, and, like the veteran Janissaries in the
armies of the Grand Turk, bearing down all before them;
but talking a little too freely and openly touching the
tyrant's most unwarrantable bloody actions amongst his
subjects, which coming to his ears, he was thereat so
disturbed that he was thoroughly resolved to get rid of
them, could he tell how—and which, indeed, as standing
in very great fear of them, he could not for some time
contrive how to bring about.

However, his old friend the Devil soon put it into his
head, ordering them in a friendly manner to repair forthwith to the river Draugh, there to receive and bring to
him to Mequinez their respective tributes, though he at
the same time very well knew there was none due to him

* Moosa El Djerâri.   † Ali ben Doobash.

from them, they being, on account of their furnishing him
with a certain number of horsemen for his wars, exempted
from all other impositions whatsoever; and he knew, should
they be any further pressed, they would no doubt soon fall
on this small number and cut them to pieces. Nevertheless,
lest they might not do it so soon as he expected, he took
special care to preadvise them how they should behave to
them, viz. (for certain reasons of state, as then to himself only known), to put them all to the sword ; for should
he at that time go about to do justice upon them at home,
it might chance, as his affairs then stood, to prove to
him of very ill consequence; therefore, as he was in
danger of his life through their means, he humbly hoped
they would rid him of them as soon as they found a fit
opportunity.

And now are these daring lions, like innocent sheep,
hurrying on to their slaughter apace, their number being
now reduced to six hundred, the rest of them being slain in
several former battles ; though on their arrival, and for
several months after, they were treated after a seeming
friendly manner, giving them every day fair promises, still
drilling them on to meet with (if they could on their side)
a careless opportunity whereby they might, with the less
danger to themselves, perform their so bloody order. But
Jerrory kept his small number in so good order, that they
could not even at the last find an opportunity to their
minds.

This vigilance of these few troops not a little disturbing
them, they now order, for the better execution of the
bloody tragedy, great numbers of armed men to be with
the greatest privacy raised in several places, and in the
night-time those several troops to march and join at a
certain place in one body; and which, though they were
in all thirty thousand men, was managed with so much

secrecy, that had not Jerrory kept a good look out, they
had no doubt so surrounded him as to have performed
their orders to a tittle. But he having some small time
to rally his little army, put himself into as good a posture
as he could to receive them after the most advantageous
manner, his troops behaving like gallant soldiers, and in a
very short time killing thousands of the enemy.

But alas ! poor men, what could they do against so much
odds? To conquer was even impossible, and to save their
lives by flight very hazardous and uncertain ; however,
either that was to be attempted, or death must inevitably
attend them ; therefore, after he had of his six hundred lost
almost two-thirds, he turned his horse and cried aloud,
" Follow me ! " cutting himself a passage through the
enemy, and with two hundred and two, besides himself and
his lieutenant, in spite of all they could do, got off to
Mequinez. Which, indeed, was no more than too truly an
escape out of the frying-pan into the fire, or the sheep
running to the old wolves to tell that they would not suffer
their young ones to worry them ; though had they known
the threads of their lives to be so near being cut by the
accursed treachery of a bloody tyrant, they had no doubt
sold their lives at a much dearer rate.

Immediately on their arrival into the city, even before they
could of themselves have the power to appear before the
tyrant, the two commanders were ordered before him, he
demanding of them in an angry tone if they had brought
him what he had sent them for. They told him no ; for that
the Draughians, after receiving them in seeming friendship, and for a long time putting them off, and drilling
them on with fair promises, had basely and treacherously
fallen upon them with thirty thousand men, and that they
only, with about two hundred more, were miraculously
escaped to tell him the most unhappy news. " News,"

said he, "you dogs, of what?" "Why, sir," said Jerrory, "that they fell upon us all at once with thirty thousand men." "Very well," said he, "and I don't in the least doubt but that you, like dastardly cowards, ran away without fighting, to the utter disgrace of me, only for the sake of living a little longer and coming home to die by the sword of justice; and which," said he, swearing by the life of Mahomet, "you shall do this same hour." They told him that they hoped he would first inquire better into the merits of their actions, telling him that they had first killed their thousands. "Your thousands," said he, "you dogs! Pray why had not you stood it to the last and killed your ten thousands?" When drawing his sword, Bendoo-bash cried out for mercy; at which Jerrory told him that after so many brave actions he had seen him to perform, he thought it beneath him and a disgrace to beg his life of such a damnable villain; for that he then, though too late, saw the traitor, who, he said, had as good take his life then as at another time; for that he would, no doubt, at last murder all his loyal subjects, unless he was by the true sword of justice prevented, and therefore he scorned to beg his life on any terms of such a bloodthirsty damnable villain. On which the tyrant at one blow struck off his head, and that of Bendoobash at another.

Then he asked for the remainder of their men, and being told they were all on horseback without the gate, waiting their commanders' orders where to set up, after giving his guards secret instructions, he with a good body of them went directly out to them; and after telling them, after his deceitful manner, that he was glad to see them come home safe again, that they had had of it a very troublesome time, that their horses looked very thin, and the like, he ordered them to alight, in order to their being sent to his stables; when they answered him that they would, if

14

he pleased, ride them thither themselves. "No, no, poor hearts," said he, "get off, that I may see how you can stand on your own legs;" at the same time ordering them to deliver their arms and draw up into one rank; which they instantly obeying, and he riding forward and backward as if the better to view them, they were all on a sudden and in a moment shot by his guards, saving one only, who, seeing through the tyrant's intentions at his ordering them to alight, rode off to one of their churches. The tyrant, lest the victims might not be dead enough, ordered his guards to prepare to give them a second round, which, before they could make ready, the tyrant standing pretty near the fallen victims, one of them being still in a capacity of rising, and having about him a long knife, got so near him, that had not a lad standing by very unluckily perceived it, he had no doubt therewith given him his just reward by ending his days.

They were then again all shot at, and all their heads being cut of, the bodies laid on their backs, and the head of each man laid on his breast, they were for ten days (as none daring to carry them off) exposed in the open street to public view, and at last stunk to that degree that none could endure to come near them; but the smell even reaching the tyrant's apartments, they were all at last, saving what the dogs had eaten, carried by his order into the fields and buried. And so ended this so horrid and barbarous murder, which I was a witness of; though the first part, as I said before, I being then on the coast of Guinea, is only hearsay, which even as then sounded but harshly to his credit, and was soon after, by the Black Army in general —most of the late victims being their countrymen—in a great measure revenged, by driving him out.

Immediately after the perpetration of this so horrid and premeditated murder, I was with my comrades sent to the

castle of Boossacran,* distant from Mequinez about four
leagues; where I had, as to my own particular part, little
else to do than to hunt, fish, and fowl for myself and
comrades, having free toleration from the Emperor,
making amongst us a very good hand of it. Several
of us chiefly employed our time that way, and killing
great plenty of game, to our general satisfaction, though
not to be supposed in any way equal to that of the
Emperor. We went out, I say, but a few of us together,
without any dogs, and him with a great many, and several
hawks, as having at the least, though never a hunter, a
hundred greyhounds, or long-dogs, and on horseback and
on foot as many moors and negroes, by way of starters,
with their long poles in their hands, spreading abreast,
still beating the cover as they went on. Thus the game
sheltering therein were either on foot or on wing, it being
almost impossible for any, saving very young birds or
leverets lying very close, to escape them, having very often
on foot together four or five hares, and on wing twice as
many partridges, and dogs and hawks all at one and the
same time at work; and with the very great speed and
force the dogs ran, they being divided into as many parties
as were hares on foot, and often meeting on the turn,
struck against one another to that degree that they at
the best became useless, and many times fell quite dead
on the spot. After the Emperor spent the forenoon in
those exercises, and his stomach putting him in mind of
his dinner, he generally rode off to a pleasure-house he
had about a mile or two off, according to the part of the
country he was then in, to his dinner, though when the
maggot bit him he had it brought him into the field.

Near the walls of our castle ran a very fine river, and
plentifully stocked with many sorts of very excellent fish,

* Bou Sacran.

and as I for two reasons very much admired fishing, as first for the amusement, and next the gratifying myself and comrades with the fruits, seldom a day passed without my taking little or more.

One day, as I and one of my comrades (a Frenchman) were fishing, he with a casting-net and myself with a rod, and had between us both taken a large basketful, the Emperor with one of his brothers, before we saw them, were on our backs, and instead of giving us any discontent, he in a seeming pleasing way asked if we had taken any fish. I told him yes, showing him to the basket; and after he had looked at them for some time, he told us that he had not to his mind of a long time seen finer, ordering us to carry them directly to his pleasure-house—and which, it being from the place we were then at no more than a mile, we did in a very little time; and just as we were entering, the Emperor and his brother alighted at the gate, and very unexpectedly gave us twenty gold ducats, which cheerfully carried us back again to the river, and we again filled our basket, and went home to our castle as rich as emperors.

About this time the Emperor having two or three expresses on the back of one another from Itewoossey,* about four days' journey from Mequinez, intimating that a great body of malecontents were there gathered, behaving after a most insolent manner, and that they were still increasing their numbers, he ordered all the light horse he could pick up to be in readiness to go with him in person to correct them, and in three days and one night we got to the foot of the mountain wherein they had sheltered themselves, ourselves and horses sufficiently tired, before the rebels were apprised of our coming. However, after some short refreshment, we marched on

* Aït Wassou, a Berber tribe?

foot up to their nests, though of the birds we found but
few, most of them, on notice of our coming up the
mountain, being flown. Yet, we there found some,
and some of them we took by pursuit; but their ways
being in a manner past finding out to those therewith
unacquainted, it would have been altogether as dangerous
as in vain for us to follow them any further. Therefore,
after two days' pursuit, we again returned to their nests,
stripped them of all their furniture and provision, then set
them on fire, and taking with us all their cattle returned
again down to our horses, where, after two days' refreshment, and disposing of the cattle, &c., for what we could
get, we in four days followed the Emperor to Mequinez,
to which he, being mounted on the finest mare I ever
saw, rode without any attendant in the space of twelve
hours, being 140 miles from the place where we then were.
This mare was about fifteen hands in height, and she was
all over (except her eyes, which were of a fiery red, and
eyelids, which were red hairs pinked) as white as snow;
and notwithstanding the Emperor knew himself to be as
hated by his subjects as a serpent, yet did he put so much
confidence in this mare as not to fear when he was on her
back for any to come after him, for he often rode by
himself in this manner.

Now am I, after this short tour, again at Boossacran,
and every day employed in shooting, fishing, or hunting,
either for the Emperor or ourselves; and as he had
allotted us round the castle sufficient quantities of land,
with oxen, husbandry implements, and seed corn, many
of our company set themselves at work, ploughed the
ground, tilled it, and had plentiful crops. Though, as to
my own part, I being never in that way instructed, and
having others to work for me, I never troubled my head
about it, but acted by general consent as a purveyor

during the time of tillage, weeding, or harvest; and at all
intervals from our farming affairs, excepting those of
mounting the guard, we were generally all hands on the
game. And this was, I think, except my intervals at
Tamnsnah, the most agreeable of all the time of my living
in Barbary; though during this, scarce a day passed without seriously reflecting with myself on escape, which I then
found to be very hazardous. Therefore, as I found the
ruin of the country every day more apparently approaching,
and plainly foresaw that it could not be long e'er the
tyrant was driven out, and that all would be in the
utmost confusion, I for the time lived as comfortably as
I could, and with Christian patience waited the event.

CHAPTER IX.

The truce between England and Morocco broken by the Sallee men capturing an English ship—A Jewish interpreter burnt for daring to advise the Emperor—Mr. Pellow meets with an old school-fellow in misfortune like himself—The flight of Muley Abdallah to Tarudant—Another reverse in the fortunes of war—Muley Ali deposed and Muley Abdallah again Emperor—The fate of a rebellious chief—How the Fez deputation was treated by Abdallah, and how the blind man spared utilized his freedom—Our author once more meditates escape in the confusion of the civil war—A native fortune-teller prophecies fair things for the future—He, at last, makes a burst for freedom.

ABOUT this time was the truce again broken between the English and the Moors on the following occasion : The Moors having, as they thought, strongly provided themselves with shipping, sent to sea the following four, viz., *Anjour*, their Admiral, carrying twenty-four guns; *Cassam Benisha*,* a new ship never before at sea, carrying twenty ditto, *Elle Ouad*,† of twenty ditto, and *Absolem Candeel*,‡ of sixteen ditto ; and Candeel falling in with Captain Shelley, of Plymouth, then commander of an English ship, though freighted by the Portuguese, he having on board seventy Portuguese passengers, and amongst them six friars, made prize of him, and carried him into Mamora. Of which complaint being made to the British Consul then at Sallee, he immediately thereon made

---

* Kassem ben Isha.   † El Wad.   ‡ 'Abd-es-Slam Kandel.

application to Candeel, to set them again at liberty; and which, finding he could not do according to his hope there, they being sent all prisoners to Mequinez, he was thither resolved to follow them, in order to make his complaint to the Emperor. And thither indeed he went, taking with one Solomon Namias, a Jew, as his interpreter, and was soon introduced to the tyrant, who asked him what he would have. To which he answered by the Jew, that he was come to acquaint his Excellency with the breach of the truce which had so lately been punctually concluded on both sides between his subjects and them of his royal master; who, he said, intended nothing less than giving him or any of them the least uneasiness, by way of any hostilities, as Candeel had very lately done on him and his; therefore he humbly hoped that his Highness would be pleased to order the ship and prisoners to be again restored. To which the tyrant told him, that the prisoners were subjects to the King of Portugal, his bitter enemy, and not to the King of Great Britain, his master, and therefore lawful prize. When the Jew told him that he thought it very hard that the English should not be allowed to carry in their own ships passengers of any nation in peace with them; however, he humbly hoped that if he was not then disposed to set the Portuguese at liberty, he would at least set at liberty all the English and their ship.

But Candeel being present, he asked the tyrant if he knew with whom he had been so long talking. "Talking with," said he, "with an Englishman." "No, sir," said Candeel, "but with a Jew." "Indeed!" said he, "with a Jew!" and calling aloud to his guards, "Here," said he, "take away Mr. Jew and burn him directly;" and then the soldiers laying hold on him, he cried out to the Emperor to save his life, and he would give him two hundred cantles of silver; nay, that he would give it only to be admitted to speak a few words. " No, thou dog," said the tyrant, " all the silver in Barbary shall not excuse thee; therefore, I say, take him away and burn him; " which they instantly did, laying him flat on his belly, heaping in a most cruel manner the wood upon him alive, and in a little time he, with grievous shrieks, and no doubt in very great agonies, expired. His house was afterwards ransacked of an immense sum of money, and other riches. On which the consul, seeing no likelihood of better success, departed, as I was informed, for England. However, I know he was back again in a little time, and met with better success, as you shall by and by hear.

Not long after Shelley's captivity, the piratical villains being all hands at sea in taking and making prize of all Christian nations, there were brought to Mequinez the men which belonged to four other English ships; and I having information of their coming, and liberty when I pleased to go to the city, I set out from my castle very early in the morning to see if any of them belonged to or near Falmouth; and a little before sunrising, I within a league of the city met with a great many of the foremost of them. Inquiring of them what parts of England they were of, and if any one of them belonged to or near the above-said place, they told me yes, there was one coming up, named George Davies, of Flushing, a small seaport town within that harbour; and with whom I soon joined, asking him if he knew me. He told me no. " Why," said I, " you and I were once schoolfellows together at the church-town of Milor." "Indeed!" said he, "I cannot imagine who you should be, unless you are Thomas Pellow, who I have of a long time heard was in his childhood carried with his uncle into Barbary." "Indeed," said I, "I am that un- happy person," telling him I was very glad to see him again, though very sorry it should be in that part of the world, under such unhappy circumstances. He told me it was his hard fate, but he must endeavour, as well as I had done before him, to bear it with patience.

And after they were all entered the city, and according to custom carried before the Emperor, and sent to the Canute, I went to him, and cheered him up in the best manner I could, and afterwards visited him as often as opportunity would permit, he being with the rest of his comrades put to hard labour, and so kept for the space of three or four months; when the consul returned from England again with the character of ambassador, and full power to treat with the tyrant for the redemption of all the English slaves ; which, notwithstanding his so late ill success, and no doubt no little fright at the barbarous usage of the Jew, he managed so well, that he procure their freedom in a very little time, being in all 148 in number ; and they were by him and old Hammet Benelly * conducted to Tetuan, there to be kept till better security should be given for their ransoms, though they were at last, on the ambassador's offering himself to remain there for them as an hostage till it arrived, all by the Bashaw's consent shipped off.

And happy indeed was it for them, for they had but a short time departed before the tyrant was driven out by the Black Army, and Muley Aly set up in his room, and a peremptory order sent by him to Tetuan to send them all back again to Mequinez. These released slaves, on their marching off from Mequinez, had leave (for the better performance of their march to Tetuan) to refresh themselves for eight days at Cassavah-hartan,† where, at their request, I undertook to carry them some brandy, and got thither for the first time in safety with several gallons in bullocks' bladders : and they desiring me to come again the next day with some more, I told them it was a very

* Hamid Ben Ali.   † Kasbah Hartan.

dangerous undertaking. However, to oblige them, I would try what I could do, and had accordingly got my bladders again filled and tied up round my waist within my blanket. But alas! in going without the city, I was very unhappily surprised by some of the Emperor's people; who, on their finding the bladders about me, laid hold on me and committed me to close prison in irons; though not altogether, I believe, so much on account of the brandy, as of a jealousy they had (as I was so great with my countrymen) of my endeavouring an escape with them. So that in all likelihood (unless they were by some Jews going to Hartan, who knew how it was with me, informed to the contrary) my countrymen, no doubt, thought that I did not use them kindly; but whether it was one or the other, I know that I suffered by it very severely, insomuch that had not Muley Abdallah, through his so frequent ill usage of his subjects, been every moment in danger and fear of being driven out, I should in all likelihood have there taken up my quarters for a much longer time; but I was, at the end of twelve days, again set at liberty.

Now might you hear, even in all places, the Blacks threatening, "A new master, a new master, or none!" being the general cry; which, and on certain advices of a great body of them gathered at Shoarumlah, about two days' march from Mequinez, and that they were soon about to pay him a visit, put him into such a fright, that he, by way of sugar-plum, sent them 220,000 ducats of silver; and whilst they were disputing about their respective dividends, he packed up all the rest of his treasure and fled with twelve thousand horse; but he was in a short time to that degree forsaken by them, that before he reached Morocco he had not more than five hundred of them remaining. Yet, notwithstanding their daily falling off from him, he still took special care to destroy all the

stores of corn as he went on, so as the Blacks might not
be the better for it; and which, as they followed him,
they too soon found, to their very great dissatisfaction.
However, they still hurried on the pursuit, till they came
up within two days' march of him; of which being acquainted by his spies (after being at Morocco ten days), he
with his small number hurried thence four days' long
journey by a round-about way towards Sallee, and settled
at a place called Bolowan, where he had also vast stores
of grain laid up, all which he freely gave to the inhabitants,
with liberty to carry off at their discretion anywhere
but to the enemy. And here, as I could not yet venture
on escape, and foreseeing the scale would soon again turn
to his side, notwithstanding his cruel and bloody nature,
I, only by myself, joined him; and which proved, indeed,
according to my own sentiments, of two evils to be choosing
the best.

The second day after my joining him, on notice from his
spies that the Black Army were again within two days'
march of him, he with his small number (which was
then reduced to four hundred horse, excluding his beasts
of carriage) moved thence three days' smart journey to
Shishrah; where, on certain notice of the Blacks not
following him, we settled sixteen days, and at the end of
which, on hearing they were again within two days' march
of us, he moved also thence, and in three days' and one
night's tedious journey we got to the mountain of Iminta-
noot; and there falling all that night a very heavy snow,
we were by the morning almost dead with cold. However,
we were soon after daybreak, by way of warming our
blood, attacked by a great body of mountaineers, who
killed several of our small number, and of the mules laden
with Muley Abdallah's treasure they took and carried off
at least forty. All which, notwithstanding our few could

have beat them, did we (as fearing a far greater danger
to be at our heels) think ourselves obliged to suffer, and
to hurry on till we thought ourselves to be better secured
from their rage. And that evening we got to Immintackcamost, between two huge mountains, ourselves and cattle
almost spent, where we rested till midnight, and afterwards
travelled on between the mountains till daybreak, and till
four o'clock that afternoon; at which time we got to
Umcest Elcashib,* at the foot of another very high mountain, called Bebown,† settling there that night, and the
next day over this high mountain to Terrident, where he
was most kindly received by the inhabitants, and directly by
them put in possession of a strong castle; where the Black
Army, as thinking their families at home to be greatly
exposed in their absence amidst such distracting commo-
tions, did not think proper to follow him.

Now is the tyrant again breathing in security, remaining
here about eighteen months, though not altogether in
peace; for, notwithstanding all our neighbouring districts
(saving that only that of Howorrah) on his summons came
in to his assistance, yet they being a pack of daring
thieves, living all together on the spoil of their neighbours,
would not on any terms obey him, but plainly told his
messengers, that whereas they had so long depended on
their own strength, they were then so resolved to continue,
and not to submit themselves to him, or anybody else, be
the consequence what it would, and that they cared not
for him a rush.

Now is the tyrant, notwithstanding his haughty and
cruel nature, at a stand how to behave, such affronts being
never before put upon him. However, as his affairs now

---

* Umseet el-Kashib.

† Bibaouan, or Bitoutouan, where there is a pass across the Atlas
about 4,200 ft. high.

stood, he thought himself obliged to temporise and win them to his party, if he could, they being about six thousand daring fellows ; and his own army being so very small, he knew if he could by fair persuasions get them over to him, it would be, as his desperate fortune then stood, of very great advantage to him ; and therefore he sent to them again, though he was answered to the same purpose, gaining nothing but a more fancy confirmation of their insolence, which nettled him to that degree, that he was resolved to watch all opportunities to be up with them. He being also solicited by the honest party (to whom these thieves had of a long time been a grievous nuisance) to correct them, he went out against them with two thousand horse and four thousand foot, marching directly to Umcederrah, a little walled town, where many of their chiefs resided, and where there was then about six hundred of them ; who shutting the gates against us, in an insolent manner bid us defiance.

The main body of them was then abroad on the plunder. And now, on my seeing many of our people to have raised themselves on the top of the wall, and not being willing to be behind any of them, I was soon wounded by two musket shots in my left shoulder and the small of my left leg, and by some of my comrades holpen off the wall, many others of them soon sharing the same fate, and were with me carried off to our camp. There we were by far in the better situation, for as they were carrying us thither, we saw the main body of the rebels coming back to the relief of their town and comrades ; and our main body being between the town and them, there was soon betwixt them a smart engagement, our people receiving their first fire, and then instantly falling on them sword in hand ; which way of fighting they not at all liking, like dastardly villains turned their backs and

fled. However, their flight was not so prosperous, but that
we slackened the pace of a great many of them, killing at
least two thousand; and our party, saving about a thousand, who were sent to plunder and burn the town, returned
with fifteen hundred of their heads to Terrident, to the
very great joy of the inhabitants, and with the loss only
on our side of about one hundred and fifty men, and about
sixty wounded.

Now is the tyrant, after subduing those insolent thieves,
in very high esteem at Terrident, and treated by the
country round as their Emperor indeed, heaping in their
presents upon him in great abundance; and those who
were not thereof so mindful as he thought they ought to
be, he failed not to quicken their memories by a party of
horse; though, in short, he had no very great occasion of
using hostilities, all (or at least the much greater part of
them) readily conforming to his demands, and his army,
very much to his satisfaction, by the end of eighteen
months was increased to eight thousand brave soldiers.
At which time, on advice from his mother of the Blacks
being also highly disgusted with the proceedings of Muley
Ali, and that she had again gained the greatest part of
them to his interest and restoration to the throne, and that
she would have him to hasten with all diligence to Mequinez,
he with his army left Terrident, and in twenty four days
arrived at and sat down before Tedlah, where the Alcaydes
Mulootjibbilly and Mahomet Belchouse were with four
thousand soldiers closely shut up, and denied him entrance
after a most insolent manner, which to that degree nettled
him, that he was thoroughly resolved to get in by force, or
not to give out so long as he saw any probability remaining. And there was for three days very hot work on both
sides, when the rebels finding they could not with all their
strength keep him from entering, they gave us up the town

in possession, and retired into the castle, where they held us at bay for the space of thirty-three days, and then, though they had not all this while killed of us above a hundred, they surrendered themselves to the Emperor's mercy.

Now are they ordered to march out, and thirty-seven of their chiefs (but without Mulootjibbilly) instantly appearing, they were by the Emperor (who was then sitting on horseback on the other side of a river which ran between him and the town, out of musket shot) commanded before him, asking them in a furious manner if they did not think themselves to be very insolent fellows, not only to deny their sovereign entrance into his own town, but impudently to murder his body-guards before his face, as no doubt they would him had it been in their power; that he thought they might think it enough for him to be driven from his own, and to make such hard shift as he had done for the last two years, to content them for all the injuries he had ever done them, for that he had undergone a very hard and unjust exile. Yet had fortune again put it in his power to revenge his own injuries, and that they should be the first sacrifices to his just rage.

Then looking at them very fiercely, he commanded of them aloud where was Jibilly. They told him, that as he had been for some time before in his dishabille, he was then, in order to appear with the greater decency before his sovereign, putting on his clothes. "A dog," said he, "has he a mind to die in state!" looking at our people. "Go," said he, "bring the dog before me!" but hearing soon after, as all thought, the report of a musket, a messenger came to tell him that he had shot himself with a pistol. "A dastardly dog," said he, "shot himself! Go run, fly, bear his body to the top of the walls, throw it down, and drag it hither;" which was instantly

done, and his head as their grand ringleader cut off, and
after his, those of all the rest, and their bodies thrown into
the river; when he also ordered to be brought before him
all Jibilly's servants, in number thirty-seven, who were all
used after the same manner; and all the heads were set
up on a little watch-tower, just within the drawbridge;
after which he pardoned all the rest, and then we were
again at liberty to refresh ourselves.

However, as our army was by this time very much
increased from Mequinez and divers other places, he did
not think fit to go into the town, but encamped with
them on the further side of the river, where he had
before received the victims; and where in a very short
time after, came to him Howmead Losmee,* and with
him six thousand Blacks, to acquaint him from the Black
Army in general, that they were all again entirely in
his interest, and that he was come by their orders to
reconduct him to his former possessions. To which he
answered, that as he had so lately received at their hands
such ill usage, it was very much to be doubted if their
hearts and tongues wagged together, for that he had
through their means already undergone most unspeakable
hardships, therefore he hoped they could not take it ill
(considering it to be very natural for a burnt child to dread
the fire) for him to insist on nine of their principals to be
first delivered into his hands, as a pledge of their sincerity,
and after naming who they should be, as first Selam Ducullee,† their head Bashaw, and four of his sons, Elly ‡ Ducullee
their kinsman, Abderheem,§ Coddoorlasseree,‖ and Abdallah Bememsoddeel; ¶ on which Howmead Losmee went
directly back again to Mequinez, and at the end of ten days

* Hamid Losmee.   † Sâlem Eddoukkali.   ‡ Ali.
§ 'Abd-el-krim.   ‖ Kadoor Lasiree.
¶ 'Abd-Allah Ben-es-Soddeel.

again returned with them, when he, notwithstanding his slippery footing, ordered four of them, viz., the two elder Ducullees, Adberheem, and Coddoorlasseree to be instantly on the spot beheaded ; and the four sons after beholding the deaths of their fathers, to be with Bememsoddeel conducted by the army to Mequinez, where the tyrant at the head of his old army and the so scarcely reconciled blacks intermixed, got safe in six easy days' march ; and, after his long absence of twenty-two months, again in possession of the empire; though by the blacks, nor they by him, no further trusted, than one enemy might another.

Now is Muley Abdallah, notwithstanding his so late and grievous exile, again about Mequinez, beginning again to butcher his subjects,* sending the five surviving hostages in chains to Boossacran, where the four brothers were in a very short time strangled, and Bememsoddel (to show the tyrant's very extraordinary clemency) pardoned, and sent back again to Mequinez to rejoice with his friends. The tyrant, not content with murdering his subjects, treated the poor Christians at Boossacran after a most grievous and cruel manner, setting them at work in digging a deep and wide ditch through a hard rock round his pleasure-house, himself with his severe eye being their overseer. One day came thither, with their presents and excuses for not waiting on him at Tedlah, twenty-five of the principal inhabitants of old Fez, telling him in great humility, that notwithstanding they had not waited on him there, yet were they nevertheless his Majesty's most dutiful and obedient servants altogether as much as those that had, and that he might be assured that it should in all their future actions be made most evidently appear. At which the tyrant, smiling, answered, " My most rebellious Fasees, I mean my masters and governors, or at least I know it

* *Note* 25.

would be were it in your power, which I am resolved shall never be."

Then calling to his guards, " Here, take these dogs and call the headsman," who instantly appearing, he ordered him to cut off all their heads ; and the victims being placed in a row, he struck off twenty-four of them, at as many strokes, and then the tyrant ordered him to hold his hand, for that he had taken notice of the survivor to be blind in one eye, and therefore as he could then see more than all the rest, he would send him back to his fellow-citizens to reform their errors, and to tell them if they did not he would not in a very short time leave a head upon the shoulders of any one of them. Although in that, indeed, he was very much mistaken, he being himself in a very little time after, by the Black Army and then of Fez, through the instigation of this narrow-escaped blink-ard, a second time driven out, and Mahomet Woolderriva (one of his brothers)* set up in his room. And now the tyrant wanting money, horses, arms, &c., I am, with Bashaw Cossam Bereezom † and several thousand others, sent to Belearge's old garrison of Stant (or rather, indeed, my own), I being after his death put in possession of it by old Muley Smine.‡ Then the inhabitants were directly ordered to bring in all they had, and which I believe many of them did, and others were about to do, as they would no doubt all done, had not the tyrant fled with a few into the mountains, sending a letter to the Bashaw at Stant for him to follow him with all his people, for that on him was his sole dependence, and therefore as his affairs were then at the lowest ebb, he desired that he would be as expe-ditious in it as possible he could ; yet notwithstanding he was very inclinable thereto, and used all possible arguments with his people, he could not prevail with more (though

* *Note* 26.   † Kassam Bereezoon.   ‡ *Note* 27.

our whole army then was in all 15,000) than 800 to go
with him. And as to my own part, I thought I had followed
him and his evil genius too far before, and therefore as I
saw a likely prospect for escape, was resolved to follow him
no further, but with all my might to pursue it; and in
order thereto I directly went back in company of 14,000
of my fellow-soldiers to Mequinez, and went directly to the
Black Army, where we found Mahomet Woolderriva as
Emperor at their head, offering him our service, and directly
joining them, and as at that time our number, by way of
falling from one party and joining the other, was very considerable, we were by him most courteously received.

Now before I can bring my marks to bear, I find myself
obliged to make a short tour or two, and after my so long
and many good services in the armies of the tyrant, am
now about to fight against him, as indeed I could always
(and especially after his cruel usage of my deliverer from
the bloody knife at Assamoor) have found in my heart to
have done; for notwithstanding I followed him and his evil
genius so long, yet did I always hate him, and now to that
degree, that I was resolved to hazard the last drop of my
own blood to sacrifice that of the tyrant to Simmo Hamet's
ghost. And in order thereunto I am now one in an army of
100,000 well-appointed soldiers following him with a zealous
resolution of revenge into the mountains, and though we
made all imaginable speed and searched the lurking-places
as hunters for their game for the continuance of three
days, yet could not we light on him; therefore as the
weather was excessive cold, the snow prodigious deep, and
still more falling, we by the general consent for that time,
and till a more convenient season, left him there with his
few attendants to cool his ungovernable passions, and
returned almost dead with cold to Mequinez.*

* *Note* 28.

Now am I again all on fire for escape, and notwithstanding my former miscarriages and miraculous preservations that way, why might not I once be so lucky to get clear? I was twice before within an ace of it; and therefore, why might not my chance the third time turn up that ace also? However, I thought it highly necessary, that before an affair of that nature was again to be undertaken, it ought to be with myself seriously debated, and therefore I seriously considered thereof, and proposed several ways to myself. As first, that notwithstanding my so narrow escape, on failure of escaping at Marcegongue, why might not I now be by that way successful? To which I was by myself soon answered, Remember the murdering knife at Assamoore how narrowly I missed it, and that my deliverer was then dead, and very probably many of my cruel persecutors still living; why might I not fall again into their hands?" And therefore it was a most hazardous and dangerous undertaking. "Then," said I, "why may not I get off from Sallee?" I was again by myself answered, "Consider the story of the sloop, and Alcayde Ambork Foolan, the Black Governor." "That," said I, "can be no obstacle to my designs, he being to my knowledge long since dead; and as to the Moors, they knew nothing of the matter;" and therefore set it down in probability number one.

And next came in question, that in case I could not succeed there to my mind, what likelihood might there be by way of Santa Cruz? To which I was again by myself answered, that Santa Cruz was a very long and dangerous journey; however, if I took care to manage with caution, it might be the most likely of the two. So I for the time, without settling my resolutions, left it to hang between them both till the morning, and so well as I could settled myself for the night to sleep, and I being therein very much disturbed by dreams, as how I should get up and be going, &c. I

at my awaking made a thorough resolution with myself to
go first to Sallee, and if I could not there perform to my
mind, to proceed for the latter place.

My resolutions thus settled, I made all the necessary
preparations in my power for my departure; and then,
to my very great dissatisfaction. I was, on some advices
brought to Mequinez from the mountain Ceedehamsoe,
directly again summoned to arms, and with the army
(consisting of one hundred thousand Blacks and fifty
thousand Moors) obliged to march thither; for that Muley
Abdallah was there, and that he had there about him
a vast army of the mountaineers, which indeed we soon
found far to exceed our numbers. But the weather
being exceeding wet, as we had almost continual rains for
sixteen days, we could not, so soon as we would, attack
them; however, at last the rains ceasing, we fell upon them
sword in hand, and after a shrewd skirmish, wherein many
thousands were slain on both sides, we put them to flight,
the tyrant (soon after the commencement of the engagement) with a few showing the rest the way. And as they
were well acquainted with those secret haunts, and we on
the other hand altogether unacquainted, we thought it by
no means proper to follow them, but returned again to
Mequinez; and though we had of it for two months a very
hard time, and lost a great many thousands of our men,
yet I am, thank God, as to my own part, to my very great
satisfaction unwounded, and which did (thank the Divine
Majesty) in a wonderful manner confirm my former resolutions; and on the eighth day following I set out. But
before I proceed, I shall first beg leave to acquaint you,
that on the seventh day, or day before my departure, I
happening to be in company with two of my old acquaintance, a German and a Spaniard, there came in a black
woman, who looked very hard at me, desiring I would give

her a blankeel. " A blankeel! " said I. " Yes," said she,
" and then I will tell you all the secrets of your heart."
I told her I would with all my heart give her a blankeel ;
but as to my fortune, as being no doubt but a foolish whim,
I had much rather it should be left alone, and therefore she
should not trouble her head any further about it. " Foh,"
said she ; " but I must, that you may (when you are got
off safe to your own country) think upon me." " To my
own country! " said I, in a seeming surprise. " What in
God's name can you mean by that ? Prithee talk no more
of such impossibilities." " Oh, no, no," said she ; " it is
not impossible, and that you will soon find."

Then putting one end of a piece of green cane she
had in her right hand into the fire, taking it out, and
therewith crossing the palm of her left hand, she told
me my real fortune indeed ; as how I had of a long
time, and was then resolved within myself on escape,
that I had more than once before endeavoured it, though
without success, even to the hazard of my life. However, I should not then fear, for I should actually be
successful. " Therefore," said she, " let not your courage
be cast down, for you shall, though with much toil
and many hazards, get safe home, and find your
father and mother (who have for many years suffered a
great deal on your account) still living." " Oh," said I,
" you are in that very much mistaken, my father and
mother having for many years ago been in their graves ;
and had they, as you say, been still living, they would
never have been by me seen more. Therefore," said I,
" pray talk no further on this subject, for if it should be
carried any further, it might be taken for fact, and prove
to me of very dangerous consequence." " No, no," said
she, " keep but a good heart and your own secrets, and all
the devils in Barbary shall not have power to frustrate your

intentions, for to Christian land are you bound, and thither again are you destined to go."

To lean on, or to give any credit to such fopperies as these, was what I could never before chime in with; yet, as she had so far told me my intentions hitherto, I could not but entertain of what was to come more than a common notion, and that Enseph Haunsel's magic doings heretofore at Mequinez were more than imaginary; and therefore I was very much encouraged herewith. And now am I about to lay me down for the last time to sleep in Mequinez, where I had so often before had an aching heart; and as I could not now take any rest, I seriously reflected with myself how wonderfully I had been hitherto (through the goodness of God) preserved from so many perils and dangers, how many thousands I had seen slain in the field of battle, and why it might not have been my unhappy fate as well as theirs; then humbly offering up my most unfeigned thanks to God for all His mercies hitherto received, and earnestly imploring His future protection, got me up, and soon with an eager resolution set myself in order for my march. And as all my transactions under any of their emperors end here, I shall (and I think very properly) call the following part of my history my wonderful escape and happy return.

CHAPTER X.

On the road to freedom—At Sallee the fugitive meets with Muley
El Mustadi, afterwards Emperor of Morocco—He is suspected and
arrested, but is permitted to go—Leaves for Mequinez as a blind,
but actually makes for Tedla—Meets a band of conjurers, and, as
the result of being in bad company, is robbed by a rival gang—
Falls in with two Spanish quack doctors, and takes up their trade
—He meets an old friend, and practises physic with indifferent
success—Fish without fish-hooks—In peril from wild beasts—
Food without lodgings—How a Moorish highway robber is
chowsed—Arrives in Morocco city, and is succoured by a friend—
Sets out for Santa Cruz—Doctoring on the way.

NOW, after my so long and grievous captivity, cruel
hardships, wonderful and miraculous preservations
in the wars of the Infidels, &c., I am, you see, again fully
bent on escape. In which, as all was then in the utmost
confusion, and I was so very well acquainted with the
country, I flattered myself with a pleasing prospect of
success; though you will find my travels to be attended
with many grievous troubles and hazardous incidents; and
which, could I have foreseen, would no doubt in a great
measure have frustrated my designs. However, as these
afflictions happened to me unlooked for, I no doubt bore
them with a braver and more steadfast resolution.

Now am I soon about to encounter with this so hazardous
and painful undertaking; and at the end of the eighth day,
after my return to Mequinez from pursuing Muley Abdallah

the second time into the mountains, I set out thence about midnight with myself only for Sallee. There in three days, and the latter part of that night, I safely arrived, and notwithstanding I made all diligent inquiry after a ship, yet could I not there to my mind find any for my purpose in three days, and therefore I was resolved to push my way for Santa Cruz so well as I could; and the next day, at my going out of the town, I was surprised by some soldiers, who laid hold on me, and carried me before Muley Mataddy,* the Governor, and brother to the then Emperor, who asked them who I was, and for what reason brought before him. To which he was answered that they could not tell. "No!" said he; "are you not then very pretty fellows to stop a man for you not what?" asking me who I was, and whither I was going. I told him I was one of his brother's soldiers, and that as I very lately returned to Mequinez from following Muley Abdallah a second time into the mountains, and correcting the mountaineers gathered there in his favour, I was by his brother's permission come thither to visit my old acquaintance, and that I was then again going back to Mequinez; on which he gave the soldiers orders to set me at liberty. Yet did they thus treat me a second and a third time, at my going out of the town, still carrying me before him, telling him at last that I was a Christian, and that I was about to make my escape to Christian Land. "To Christian Land!" said he, staring me in the face. "Sir," said I, "as to that they may say as they please; however, before your Excellency gives any credit to it, I humbly desire you will ask them their reasons for suspecting me;" and they being able to give none, he told them that they were a pack of insolent fellows, that they should let me go, and if to Christian Land, what was that to them?

* *Note* 29.

Now am I again at liberty, and, as a blind, again on my road towards Mequinez, but out of which I soon turned towards Tedlah, wherein I had not travelled very far before I fell in company with one of their noted conjurers, having with him about four hundred of the poor credulous inhabitants, going also that way. But his conjurations did not find out my intentions, as to whither I was travelling, no more than that himself and followers should be that evening by a greater party plundered and stripped, as indeed they were, together with myself, to our skins; which, though a grievous misfortune, I was with Christian patience obliged to bear, and to travel on in this condition full three days in very cold weather, before I could get any thing even to cover my nakedness, and then I was so happy to get, through very great chance, a piece of old matting; and afterwards in that condition suffering extreme cold and hunger, it was eight days before I reached Tedlah, though there I did not enter, but directly crossed the river running at the foot of the high mountain Summough, and where I most opportunely met two Spaniards straggling the country, by way of deceiving the credulous inhabitants with their quack medicines.

However, be that as it will, it was for them good enough, and the same Spaniards were to me very kind and true friends in necessity, giving me a piece of an old blanket, filling my belly with such as they had, giving me friendly advice, six blankeels, several of their medicines, and an old lancet and burning iron, to set up for myself; and which indeed I, the better to conceal my intentions in my travels through the country, directly put in practice. And now am I asking every one I meet, if they had any work for the doctor; and the day after my parting from my benefactors, I happened to see a woman standing at the entrance of a tent, of whom (after giving her the country salute) I asked if she had any occasion or business for the doctor. " Yes," said she, " I have, and more I doubt than you are able to perform," calling to her daughter to help her father forth to the light; and which, whilst the girl was about, the good wife asked me what I did with those things in my hand; and where, indeed, as I had no pocket, I was obliged to carry them. " Do with them?" said I, looking her full in the face; " the one is for letting blood, and the other used in many distempers for burning, they being in my way of business two of the most necessary instruments." " Oh, then," said she, " I suppose you are an experienced doctor?" " Yes," said I, "instead of a better." " Alas!" said she, " I wish with all my heart you may cure my husband, for he is so very drowsy, that I fear he will die in his sleep." By this time his daughter had brought him forth to the door of the tent. " Now, doctor," said the wife, " is he not a sad object?" " Indeed," said I, " he is, and I could wish with all my heart I had for all our sakes seen him sooner, for that his distemper was then gone very far, and his condition very dangerous; however, I would try what I could do on him, there being but two ways of saving his life, and if one of them (which was bleeding) would not do, I must be also obliged to practice the other, which was burning."

So I went directly to work in binding up his arm, and to that degree tied it with a strong hempen cord, that he complained of it very much. And now I am at a stand and a very great loss (had the instrument been never so well in order) how to perform, and in the condition it then was, much more so, for it was really very blunt, and extremely rusty; however, as I found myself obliged to make the best use I could of a bad market, I in or near the vein gave him a very hearty prick, asking him if he felt it. " Feel it!" said he, " yes, yes." " Well," said I, " best of all." And little or no blood appearing, I twice repeated it, and though I pricked him much deeper than at first, yet could not I for my life (though I made him twist like an eel) make him bleed; and then I told him that I feared I should also be obliged to burn him. "Burn me!" said he in a very great surprise. "Yes," said I, "burn you." "No, I hope not," said he. "Oh, but," said I, "I do not mean by putting you into the fire, but with a pretty little iron I have for that purpose, in the head." "And do you think, doctor, that will do me any good?" "That," said I, "I cannot tell; but if you will be conformable to my rules, either that will do you good, or nothing." "Oh, then, good doctor, burn me, burn me;" and which, indeed, after heating my iron red-hot, I did in three several places very smartly, till I made him (as well he might) to twist and cry out after a most piteous manner. "Well," said I, "you are, I think, considering your so very dangerous condition, a very faint-hearted soldier," desiring him to look, if he could, at my forehead, and to tell me if he did not think it to be much more burnt than I had burnt him. "Yes," said he, "and it was, no doubt, very painful to you." "Yes," said I, "that it was, and yet my doctor did not think so, nor that he had burnt me enough. But come," said I, "have a good heart, take this small paper of powders about ten o'clock at night, and if you cannot sleep, it will be as I desire. For as your distemper is what we call a lethargy, sleep will incessantly steal on you; and therefore, when you find yourself pretty much inclined to it, and your wounds are not painful enough to keep you waking, order the good woman to rub them up afresh with her fingers, and never mind the pain;" telling him further, that as I was obliged to go that night to a patient about a league off, I could for that time stay with him no longer, and that by the time I came back, I did not doubt but to hear of his being much easier." And after I had filled my belly with cuscassoe, and for my doctorship received six blankeels, as an earnest penny, and a cake of white bread, I left them to their prophet Mahomet, and their country doctors; and though I had the good fortune to go no more back to inquire into the success of the operations, yet had I an account of it by one of his sons soon after, to my very great surprise, as you will by and by hear.

Now am I again on the tramp; and that evening, instead of one league, I travelled five, ascending up to the top of a high mount called Itatteb, where I found several inhabited tents, but no admittance. However, I with much ado got out of one of them a pretty large billet of fire; and with which, after I had gathered good store of dry wood, and laid a good parcel of it in a heap, I kindled a fire, and before the darkness came on I had gathered wood enough, as I thought, to continue my fire all night; which no sooner approached, than I plainly heard a great many jackals coming yelping towards me, and still drawing nearer and nearer, which gave me sufficient reason to suppose I should be soon surrounded by far more dangerous companions, as indeed I soon was by lions, tigers, leopards, panthers, &c., in abundance, making such a hideous and frightful noise as was enough to terrify a more courageous man than myself.

Though I cannot say I was altogether void of fear, yet was I thoroughly persuaded with myself that, so long as my fire continued, they would not offer to approach me so near as to do me any harm, I almost continually holding a firebrand well-lighted at one end in my hand, twirling it round my head, and sometimes throwing it amongst them; and, at the approach of daylight, they, without taking their leave, like unmannerly guests left me, though I must confess I was much better pleased with their absence than with their company. I then began to set forward on my journey; and though I was very hungry, and had most of my cake still remaining, yet would not I venture to break my fast till I was got clear out of this mountain. And well was it for me, in all likelihood, that I did not, for in a very short time, as I, instead of eating, was with a watchful eye looking sharp round me, I saw a large tiger lying on his belly, with his legs under him in a proper posture for leaping, within twenty feet of the little path I was walking in; when I, instantly taking my eyes off him, passed nimbly by, so that I received from him no further hurt than the fright; and in less than half an hour after, I got up within thirty yards of the largest lion I had ever seen before, sitting on his breech just in my road—though this did not, I declare, in comparison with the tiger, at all terrify me, walking up towards him with a fierce look, hollowing at him, and threatening him all I could; at which he got him upon his legs, severely lashing his loins with his tail, and roaring after a most terrible manner, went out of my sight in a very little time, though I again met him a second and a third time, and then he, after like usage, left me entirely. And in an hour after I got to the foot of the mountain on the other side, where lived Alcayde Woldlattabbee,* one of Muley Abdallah's old soldiers, and my very particular friend, whither I went, and was by him most kindly received; and on his asking me what business had called me that way, I told him that I was in pursuit of our distressed master; and which, as the Blacks had most severely used me on his account, I could do no sooner; therefore I hoped that it was not then too late for me to be by him instructed how to proceed further. "That," said he, "I cannot very well tell, yet did I very lately hear a rumour as if he should be gone to

* Al Kaïd Oold-et-Tabee.

Santa Cruz." "That," said I, "I heard, and thither was resolved to follow, but first to call on you in my way, in order to its further confirmation." "Well, my old friend," said he, "but what need have you to be in so much hurry? Stay with me first three or four days to refresh yourself, during which we may chance to hear further of him." And this offer, indeed, I was very glad of, as well as that my story was so well taken. And on his asking me by what way I got thither, I told him, together with all the difficulties, hardships, and transactions I had gone through, as how I was plundered and stripped, how I was obliged to practice by way of doctor, how I had met with a sick, or rather indeed a dead man, for that all the doctors in the world could not cure him; however, with what I did for him he was so well pleased, that he ordered his wife to give me six blankeels, my bellyful of cuscassoe, and a cake of white bread to carry with me; how I had been all that night surrounded by wild beasts, and how I had met with in the morning a tiger and a lion, and what means I had made use of to escape them.

Then I consented to stay with him for two or three days. And the third day, a little before my departure, who should, to my very great surprise, happen to come there to tell the Alcayde that his father was dead, but one of my old lethargic patient's sons? "Dead!" said the Alcayde. "Pray of what distemper?" "That, sir," said he, "I cannot tell, though one of the straggling doctors told him when I was from home that it was a letchery; and notwithstanding he had six blankeels, his bellyful of cuscassoe, and a huge great cake of white bread to carry with him for his pains, yet did he letcher him out of his life." "Poor man!" said the Alcayde, "then our old friend is actually dead at last!" "Yes, sir," said he, "he is, for my brothers and

I threw him into his grave." " Well, my friend," said the Alcayde, " that was the last good office you could do him, and as he was so long languishing under such torments, it was by far the best place for him." "As to that," said the young man, " we cannot' tell : not that I believe he could by course of nature have lived much longer, yet no doubt the doctor hastened his end, for he cut him and burnt him to that degree, that he never enjoyed one moment's ease after the operation ; and could I light on him, I would soon spoil his doctorship."

All this did I with my ears hear, and with my eyes often saw the Alcayde tipping me the wink, insomuch that I could not be easy any longer there ; but soon after finding an opportunity to take my leave, I took my way thence for the river Tennet;* and as I travelled all night, I got the next morning to the foot of the mountain Dimminet,† a very plentiful part of the country, the mountains round being in the seasonable times of the year plentifully stored with many sorts of delicious fruits, and especially grapes in abundance, yielding great store of very excellent wine. It was, before I could get free of these parts, full sixteen days ; during which I sold a great many of my medicines, such as small papers of bitter apples powdered, of which were in these woods great plenty, and are a prodigious purgative ; white dog's date, ellebore, and red pepper mixed, by way of clearing the brain and eyes, and which made them to weep and sneeze gallantly ; and with my pretty little iron I burnt a good number, one of them in particular in the belly for a dropsy ; and, to the very great content of himself and wife, I took thereout a very large quantity of yellow water, and received for it a gold ducat. On which I, with a Spaniard I had there procured to go with me, hurried

---

* Wad Teççaout?　　　　　† Demnát.

thence twelve leagues to the river of Tessout, still further on towards Morocco; and as we travelled all that night, we got the next evening to the riverside in good season, so as we had time enough before night to catch a dish of fish for our suppers.

But alas! how could we catch any without tackle? We had neither hook nor line. However, we were through great chance and a good deal of trouble soon furnished with the latter through means of some hairs we got from a horse's tail. But now what must we do for a hook? When it came into my mind, if I could get a needle it might soon be turned into the like shape; but as to my own part, I very well knew I had none. However, I asked my comrade, who, to my very great satisfaction, happened to have a great many; and in turning the first of them, as not very well understanding the temper of the metal, I snapped it off in the middle, as indeed I did a second. But now, considering within myself, that as they had been hardened by throwing them red hot into a seasoning liquid, unless I should again reduce them by fire to their natural temper, I should soon break all the rest. Therefore, whilst I was making my line, my comrade having gathered some wood and kindled a fire (as fully intending to take up our quarters there for that night), I put two of them between two coals, made them red-hot, and after they were cold enough to put my fingers to, I turned them into what shape I pleased, so as I made two tolerable good hooks; and then again laying them between the coals and making them red-hot, I threw them into water, and taking them out again, to work I went, and in a little time caught a tolerable dish of fish, broiled them on the coals, and with some green figs, of which there were abundance there, we made a very good supper.

Now, perceiving the night to draw on apace, are we busy

at work in laying on and getting more fuel, so as in a very short time we had raised a huge fire, and fuel enough, by way of reserve, to continue it for the night ; when I told my comrade that I in a little time expected more company, but such I feared as he would not by any means like. However, I would not have him to be over afraid, for that as we had wood sufficient to continue our fire all night, they would not dare to approach so nigh as to do us any harm, I having very lately sufficiently tried the experiment. "Experiment!" said he; "of what?" "Of what?" said I; "of our fire preserving us from the wild beasts." "Lord!" said he. What, are there any of them in these parts?" "Yes, yes," said I; "and that you will quickly both hear and see." And, indeed, in less than half an hour after, we plainly heard a great many of the forerunners coming yelping towards us. "Pray," said he, "what are they?" "They," said I, "are jackals, and the lions, tigers, &c., are not far off, and will no doubt be soon here ;" as indeed they were, roaring and growling after a terrible manner.

Upon which I ordered my comrade to take a large firebrand in his hand, and to keep twirling it round his head, and now and then to throw it amongst them. This did he (being not a little terrified) continue to do all that night, our furious guests sometimes approaching so near us as we could plainly distinguish them as to their species, and many times see them engaged with one another; insomuch that, had not an old stately lion, to whom all the rest seemed to be under subjection, decided their quarrels, there had no doubt been bloody work amongst them; but wherever he interfered, they submitted to him in seeming obedience, instantly giving him place, and, in short, all that quarter of the fire to himself. As to my comrade, notwithstanding his being seized with

so very great fear, yet did he seldom or never cease to
twirl his firebrand, unless when he was disposed to throw
it amongst them, and to take up a fresh one out of the
fire; insomuch that, after our unwelcome companions had
at the approach of daylight left us, he all that day complained of a grievous pain in his shoulders; though which,
he said, he was exceedingly well pleased to compound with,
for rather than run the hazard of such another night he
should be glad to endure the loss of a leg or an arm.   And
now are we, indeed, both better pleased; for, to be plain,
I did not care for their company no more than he did.

Now, after recovering ourselves of our fright, we cheerfully travelled on, though guilty, I think, of a very great
omission, and to ourselves very much wanting, for
though we were so very near the river and had nothing
for our breakfast, yet we did not stay to catch any fish,
which no doubt we might have done in a very little time;
but depending on our meeting with something better on
the road, we, instead thereof, were for that day obliged to
fast and to content ourselves without any the least refreshment.   However, we travelled on with courage, and,
without anything else remarkable, we got that night,
exceeding hungry, to Ceedeachall,* directing our course to
some inhabited tent, where we at the least promised
ourselves some small refreshment.   But alas! to our very
great dissatisfaction, we could get none, unless than being
admitted to lodge in one of them; and with which, notwithstanding my hunger, I thought myself by far better
off than I did the night before, and though I saw the dogs
eating cuscassoe before my face, yet could not I, notwithstanding I offered to pay for it, and my stomach was in
an uproar, get one pellet of it, and which was quite the
reverse of the Moorish manners of all I had ever seen

* Sidi Ra'hal.

before. Therefore we very early in the morning, being bravely refreshed by moderate sleep, set out towards Morocco to seek our breakfast, and which being but six leagues, and travelling at a good pace, we had by sunrising got over three of them, when we met a very well-dressed genteel Moor, accoutered in martial order, having by his side a very fine scimitar, and in his belt a pair of pistols. He in a haughty manner demanded who we were, from whence we came, whither bound, our business, &c. I told him we came that morning from Ceedeachall, were going to Morocco, and that we were by profession Chyrurgeons. "Chyrurgeons!" said he, "what do you mean by that?" "That, sir," said I, "is as much as to say surgeons, or, if you please, doctors." "Very well," said he, "and do you think you can cure my eyes?" Which indeed seemed to be very much inflamed. "Cure them," said I, "yes to be sure, though I really think them to be very far gone, and therefore I hope you won't take it ill if we ask your honour how much you are willing to give us?" "Give you?" said he; "a very handsome fee if you cure me: if not, nothing, unless it be to cut your throats." "So then," said I, "I find you are for no purchase no pay, or rather, indeed, what is a great deal worse; however, I dare venture it."

To be plain, I knew if I could but once get a little of my powders into his eyes, it would be sufficiently arming me against him and his weapons, had they been never so many; but to be too eager upon him for the operation I thought might not be so proper, therefore I left him alone to make the first advance. "Well, well, then," said he, "since I must be doctored by you, I desire to see first if you have any money about you," feeling and peering into our tattered garments, and rummaging a little knapsack the Spaniards had to carry a few medicines in; and though I had therein, at the bottom of one of my pots of famous ointment, a gold ducat and several blankeels, yet had he only his labour for his pains, telling us " that he thought our doctorship had been to us, so far as he could see, of but very little advantage hitherto; but if it had been otherwise, and which for our sakes he should have been glad of, notwithstanding what he had done to satisfy his curiosity, he had no design of taking anything from us." "Alas! sir," said I, " you cannot, I hope, suppose we could be under any such apprehensions. What! to be under any apprehension of that nature from a gentleman of your presence!" "No, no," said he, "I hope not."

Now am I to contrive how to be up with him. However, it soon came into my noddle, telling my comrade in Spanish (and which I knew the Moor, as having before tried him, did not understand) that he should be sure to be very observant of all I told him; and then I told this knight of the road (as being, no doubt, one of those who make their fortunes on the ruin of others) Anglice, a highwayman, that we were sent for in all haste to visit some patients at Morocco, and thither we were obliged to hasten, and therefore I wished him well, and his eyes a better doctor. " A better doctor!" said he in a very great passion; " a better doctor! Pray what do you mean by that? Did not you say you would cure me? and I expect you do, or I will soon spoil your doctorship." " Cure you, sir," said I; " how can that be, when you will not give me leave to apply my medicines?" " You dog," said he, " I never told you so," laying his hand upon one of his pistols. " Good sir," said I, " be not offended, for I am ready, when you please, to perform the operation and to use the best of my skill." "But do you think my eyes are not past cure?" "Why, sir," said I, "as to that,

I will engage to make on you a most sudden alteration, or I·will give you leave to shoot me with one of your pistols through the head." "Then," said he, "you dog, why don't you do it, or by God, if you will not, you shall have both." "Sir," said I, "with all my heart."

Then I opened the knapsack, and after I had taken out of it a paper of the powder of elebore and cod-pepper mixed, and therewith filled two quills, giving one of them to the Spaniard, I ordered my gentleman to sit down on the ground; when I told the Spaniard, that when I had got fast hold on one of his eyelids, he should be sure to take fast hold of the other and hold it open, blow in his quill of powder with all his might. And when we were both ready I gave the word "Blow," which he readily observing, and I blowing also at the very instant, we to that degree filled both his eyes as had our knapsack been full of gold ducats we might have given him leave to peer therein. The powders performed to admiration, he rubbing with both his hands, twisting and turning, and from his eyes flowed a little fountain of water. When I asked him how he did, "Do," said he, "you dogs, you've blown out my eyes!" "See now," said I, "how men be abused for their good will." "Oh, burn your good will!" said he. "Very well, sir," said I, "be that as it will, I am thoroughly resolved to extend it a little further." Then laying hold on his sword and pistols, after giving him two or three very hearty cuts by way of bleeding, I left him, and with my comrade in all possible haste travelled on, and about noon got to Morocco, where, would his present circumstance have permitted him, I thought he dared not to come after us.

Now am I, after two months' very hazardous and painful travel from Mequinez, safely arrived at Morocco, where, though I had a great many acquaintances, yet would I not venture to trust more than one of them; and finding my comrade did not care to encounter with any more suchlike adventures, and he had also there many friends, we, after his giving me the knapsack and medicines, and after most courteously bidding each other farewell, and having on both sides agreed with ourselves what friends to call upon, separated.   And then I directly went to my friend's house, and very luckily found him at home, and I met with a kind reception; and he asking me what business I was come upon, and if I thought it to be in his power to do me any service, desiring I would not be upon the reserve, for that I was to him very heartily welcome, and that he would serve me even to the hazard of his life, I with a small alteration told him the old story, as how that since Muley Abdallah's second driving out (who, said I, you know was very cruel, yet, between you and I, I think there is altogether as bad come in his room, the Blacks being become so insolent that they persuade him even to what they please) I was between them both really in a very great strait, and therefore I was come thither to consult him how to act.   " Indeed, my friend," said he, " I am as well as you in this affair at a very great loss ; however, between friends, I know not which barrel of the two is the better herring, and therefore, as you are now got so far out of the power of them both, was your case mine, I would depend on neither of them no longer, but take care of myself so well as I could."   " Indeed," said I, " that is a very natural case, and so would I also do, could I tell how ; for, to be more plain, I as little esteem them as you do, yet I cannot deny but it has been in my mind to follow Muley Abdallah, and so I told my old friend, Alcayde Woldlattabbee, in my way hither, with whom I stayed three days."   " As to that," said he, " you did not amiss ; but what said the Alcayde to it ? "   " Why," said I, " when I

had told him my inclination, and asked him which way he
would advise me to proceed, he told me that a rumour very
lately ran thereabout that the tyrant was actually gone to
Santa Cruz."

To which I answered him, that I had heard the same,
and that I was thither resolved to follow him. "Very
well," said he, "and let your intentions be what they
would, I think you answered him very well; and once
more, my old friend, I cannot help telling you, that was
it my own case, and you were therein sincere, I would
not follow him one step further." "Indeed," said I,
"the Alcayde did not so plainly tell me to do it, neither
did he, my friend, give me any great encouragement,
though he in a friendly manner told me that I need not be
in so great a hurry, for that I should first stay with him
three or four days to refresh myself; and which, indeed, I
did, and found myself thereby, after the many misfortunes
I met with in my journey thither, very much refreshed."
"Well, my friend," said he, " I am very glad the Alcayde
was so very kind to you, and that you so prudently
behaved with him; for give me leave to tell you, the times
are now so ticklish that a man cannot tell who to trust,
and in some cases it is altogether unsafe for a man to lay
himself open even to his own brother; therefore I shall be
no further inquisitive with you, and be your intentions
what they will, you are to me very sincerely welcome.
And now," said he, "I think it is high time to ask you
how your stomach may agree with a dinner." I told him
as to that he need not fear our falling out, for that as I
had not ate anything all that day, nor the day before, it
would be to me, next himself, the best friend I could meet
with, and therefore I did not care how soon I was at it;
when he called to his wives (as having, though a Spaniard,
no less than three) to order up the cuscassoe, and come

and take part with us : "for," said he, "though it is not
the country custom, yet, as this is my brother, I hope you
will so far oblige me ; " which, I assure you, was a very
extraordinary favour.

Then our dinner was by the three good wives directly
ushered in and set in the middle of the floor, which we
soon surrounded and fell to it ; and, as to my own part,
I in a very short time made good my leeward way, and
made an excellent dinner indeed. And after the women
were gone off, my friend brought in a bottle of excellent
good wine to wash it down, desiring me not to spare it,
for that that bottle had a great many fellows, and therefore he hoped I would be as merry as he wished me.
"Alas ! my friend," said I, " how can a man be merry
under my unhappy circumstances ?   However, I will force
my inclinations to be as merry as I can."   And indeed
we passed the evening in taking our glass and talking
over old stories, without on either side mentioning anything touching my future intentions ; and as I was with my
journey somewhat weary, we, at my request, separated for
the night to our rest.

Very early in the morning he came into my apartment, asking me how I had taken my rest, and telling
me that I had forgot the last night to go to supper.
"That," said I, " as you were so often pleased to ask me,
was not yours, but my own fault."   "Well," said he,
"but can you, do you think, eat a piece of a sheep for
your breakfast ? "   "Yes," said I, " with all my heart ; "
on which he brought me in a very little time a good piece
of a leg broiled on the coals, and after we had finished he
desired I would give him an account of my journey, and
how long I had been on it. "Do you mean," said I,
"after a methodical manner ? "   "Yes," said he, " if you
don't think it too tedious for you."   "Alas ! my friend,"

said I, "I hope you do not think there can be anything in my power too tedious for me to oblige you in." Then I, from Mequinez to my burnt and scarified patient, gave him a very particular account, and when I came to him I seemed a little to mince the matter; however, as I had promised him to tell him the truth, so I did, and when I came to the torturing part he asked me how I could be so cruel. "Cruel," said I, "just so (were it in my power) I would use most of the Moors in Barbary." " Ha, ha," said he, " now do I, without your telling me plainly, see through your intentions; but go on."

Then I told him what a terrible fright I was in on one of his sons coming to the Alcayde's house, whilst I was there, to tell him his father was dead, that the doctor had killed him, and that could he catch him he would soon spoil his doctorship; which made him laugh very heartily. And when I was come to my taking up my quarters amongst the wild beasts, he altogether as heartily mourned my condition; however, I soon put him again in good humour by my telling him the dialogue between me and my scour-road sore-eyed patient, and which really pleased him very much, laughing as though he had been tickled (though I told him then never a word of my bringing off his sword and pistols), telling me that by the description I gave of him he must be actually the same who had infested the roads for a long time back, insomuch as very few travellers escaped him. " But," said he, " did not the villain cry out ?" " Yes, yes," said I, " so well as he could; and now, sir, give me leave to ask you what you, through your very great clemency, would have done by him had it been your own case." " Done by him ? " said he; " with his own sword cut his throat." " Indeed, sir," said I, "that is what you might soon have done, it being actually a very good one, and the pistols not at all inferior to it; and which, if you will not believe me, be your own eyes the judge," taking them from underneath my old blanket.

At which he said he was very much surprised, for that he had not, to his mind, of a long time seen finer, and that he thought them to be of considerable value. I told him that I was very glad he liked them so well, and that if he was pleased to accept of anything which formerly belonged to a highwayman, they were very heartily at his service; and as to their late masters finding them upon him, he needed not to be under the least apprehension. With much ado he took them as his own, though first indeed he, by way of old friendship, compelled me to accept of three gold ducats, and which, he said, he was determined to give me had he not seen the sword and pistols at all. And after dinner, and drinking a hearty bottle, I told him, just as I was going to lie down, that I would not by any means have him to take it ill, for that I was fully determined with myself to pursue my journey early in the morning; and getting up accordingly I (after a good breakfast, and receiving from him three cakes of bread, some snuff, and very friendly advice, telling me he was fully apprised of my intentions, that he sincerely wished me well to my own country, and that God would be to me therein aiding and assisting, taking me in his arms, and giving me a very hearty and I dare say sincere kiss, which I without any further answer as sincerely returning) departed; and as I travelled at a pretty smart rate I got that forenoon about ten of the clock to Tamslaught,* where I rested me so long as to eat a few grapes with some of my bread for my dinner, and, travelling on, I got about one that afternoon to a part of the river Waddenfeeze, where I sat me down again, and began to consult myself if I should go directly on or stay there so long as to catch a few fishes; for notwithstanding

* Tamsaloaht, a village about 10¼ miles S.S.W. of the city.

I had so lately dined, yet methought I could (as the grapes
had but whetted my stomach) find in my heart to make
another dinner. Therefore I went to work, and caught a
brace of tolerable size in a very short time, and on my
seeing some Moors coming to the riverside I hailed one of
them (as being loath to be too profuse of my tinder), and
asked him if he could help me to a coal of fire; and which,
whilst he was fetching from one of their tents, I had
gathered a few dry sticks and laid them in order, and
whilst I was cleaning my fish he came with the fire and
kindled the wood, and then I laid my fish thereon and
made a very hearty meal, and some to spare to my
attendant.

And I being surrounded by this time with several other
Moors, they were soon very inquisitive with me to know
the guts of my knapsack. Alas! thinks I, these are
not, I hope, some of the under-strappers of my late sore-
eyed patient; but indeed I was soon given to understand
the contrary, for on my being asked a second time I told
them medicines for curing the sick; when I was asked by
one of them if I could cure sore eyes. " Sore eyes ? " said
I; " yes, I think I have hitherto cured a great many, and a
gentleman in particular, about three days ago, of a very
great inflammation therein." " An inflammation," said
he; "pray what do you mean by that ?" " Why," said I,
" that is when the eyes are attended with a hot scalding
pain, and look of a very red colour." " Then as sure as
daylight," said he, " my brother's are just so." " And so
are my sister's," said another. " And my wife's," said
another. " But," said they, " do you really think you can
cure them ?" " That," said I, " I cannot say; first let me
see them, and then I will tell you more of my mind, for the
gentleman the other day was also very inquisitive, and
asked me much the same questions, and notwithstanding

his eyes were really very much inflamed, yet did I make on him so great an alteration as to leave him quite another man in a very little time." " Will you then, doctor, be pleased to go with us to yonder tents ? " said they. " Yes," said I, " if you please, with all my heart ; " and at our coming up were brought out of two of them a man and two women, having in their eyes what I had often heard in my childhood called amongst the old women in England a " blast."

" Alas ! " said I, " how came you to suffer this inveterate disease to reign on you so long ? " " Indeed, doctor," said they, " to tell you the truth, we thought (as well as a great many of our neighbours who had the same distemper) to be well again in a very little time, as indeed they were in less than a fortnight." " Why," said I, " yours, or I am very much mistaken, has been coming on you more than a month." " Yes, doctor," said the man, " more than six weeks." " Very well," said I, " and are you resolved to make trial of my medicines, or suffer it to run on longer ? If you are resolved to put yourselves under my care, tell me directly, for I am obliged to go this evening, or to-morrow early, to a patient about two leagues off, and, as far as I can tell, when I come back it may be too late. However, as to that, as your eyes are your own, you may do as you please by them." " Good doctor," said they, " don't be uneasy, for you shall try your skill on us before you go." " Very well," said I, " but before I meddle with your eyes I design to give you a small matter of my purging powders, the better to prepare you for the operations ; and as the eyes are at this time of day very dangerous to meddle with, I will give you the physic directly, and take in hand your eyes in the morning, for, to be plain with you, in many cases of the eyes the light cannot, no more than our tempers, be too calm and serene." " That," said they, " doctor, you know better than we do, and therefore we are very willing to conform ourselves to your rules." " Very well," said I (as having a very great mind to a good supper), " and have you then in either of your tents any fresh mutton? In short, if you have not, you must look out for some; " when a messenger was sent to a neighbouring tent, and soon returned with a fore-quarter, asking me how I would have it dressed. "Dressed," said I; "I suppose now you think I ordered this only for myself; be that as it will, I heartily thank you, and set the pot over directly, for I shall want the broth for working the physic; but," said I, " be sure you put in all the meat, for the stronger it is I think it will be far the better."

So when I saw the mutton under sail I gave to each of them a small dose of my bitter apples in some honey, which I knew to be sufficient, and that it could in no wise hurt them, charging them to keep continually walking and stirring their bodies; and whilst the physic was performing its several parts came in a woman, to whom the people of the family spoke very courteously, asking her how she did. " Do," said she, " neighbours, very bad, and really I think very bad indeed." " Alas! poor woman," said they, "pray how long have you been so, and what may your distemper be, for we have observed you ailing for a long time?" " That," said she, " is what I cannot very well tell, though I am almost persuaded by some people that it is what the doctors call a dropsy. It has been coming on me now almost twelve months, and is, instead of the least appearance of amendment, I think still growing worse and worse, insomuch that I am to that degree swelled that my skin is ready to burst; but neighbours, I am told you have a doctor in the house, and to whom I am come to ask him if he can do me any good."

Then one of the family told her there was the doctor, pointing at me—of which I seemed to take no notice, though you may suppose I heard every word they said; neither did I till she came to me so well as she could, and asked me if I thought I could do her any good. "Any good," said I, looking her full in the face, "pray what ails you?" "Ail me," said she, "enough I think." "Pray," said I, "give me your hand," and after I had felt her pulse, and looked at her legs, felt her chest, &c., I told her that I thought it a most unaccountable thing that people should be so very careless of their health, and only for the sake of saving a little money to suffer such inveterate distempers to reign so long upon them; which, said I, is just the same with breaking your necks only for the humour of trying the skill of the doctor to set it. "However," said I, "I will do for you all in my power." "All in your power," said she. "Yes," said I, "all in my power. You would not have me to promise you further than I think may be performed by second means; and that, I say, I am ready, if you please, to put in practice." "Pray," said she, "what do you think my distemper to be?" "To be?" said I; "a dropsy, an old, confirmed, inveterate dropsy." "Indeed!" said she, "and so I did suppose it." "Why," said I, "I warrant it has been coming on you now more than twelve months." "Why really, doctor," said she, "you are very much in the right of it; and was I as sure of a cure as that you have hit my distemper, I would with all my heart give you twenty gold ducats." "Well," said I, "have a good heart, take this evening, by way of preparing the body, a small paper of my purging powder, and to-morrow morning early I will take from you some water, of which, let me tell you, you have in your body not a little." So I gave her a paper of my powders, ordered her to go home and take it in a little honey, and to work it

with water gruel, for that broth was by no means fit for
her.

And then indeed my stomach put me in mind of my
own supper, and after my patients had pretty well thrown
off their physic, and the mutton was fully boiled, I ordered
each of them a large dish of the broth, when I also fell at
it myself, and between the broth and the meat I soon made
a very hearty supper; and then I told my patients they
might also eat a little of the meat if they would, and that
they should immediately after it go to their rest, for that I
intended to rouse them very early in the morning, and that
in order thereto I would, if they pleased, also lay me down
and take a nap. And at daybreak I got up and went to my
dropsy patient, asking her how she did, and if she found
herself, after her physic, for the better or the worse. "As
to that," said she, "it has made on me no great matter of
alteration; however, I am fully satisfied it has done me no
harm." "Very well," said I, "and as I am just now
obliged to be going away, I desire you will tell me if you
are willing I should touch you first in two or three places
in the stomach with a hot iron." "Good doctor," said
she, "cannot you cure me by any other means?" "No,"
said I, "there is no other means that I know of, unless you
will give me leave to make a large hole in your stomach
and put in a tap." "Well," said she, "burning will no
doubt be very painful to me; however, I had rather suffer
that than the boring a hole through my belly." "Very
well," said I, "and I think you are very much in the right
of it, for I would have you to consider if it is not better for
you to smart once than always to ache; besides, you know
very well that a desperate disease must have a desperate
cure." "Indeed, doctor," said she, "all you say is very
true, therefore do by me just as you please."

Then I put my iron into the fire, made it hot, and burnt
17

her in the stomach in three several places, and there actually
came out a great deal of yellow water, and after I had given
her a piece of my plaster, and directed her how to use it, I
told her I must be going, and that if she would spare me a
small matter of money to defray my expenses till I came
back I shou'd think myself very much obliged to her.
"Pray," said she, "how long do you think you may be
wanting?" "Really," said I, "that I cannot very well
tell; it may be one, two, or three days, according to the
condition I find my patients in." "Alas!" said she, "and
what shall I do in your absence?" "Do!" said I, "was
I here I could do no more for you for three or four days
than keep drawing plasters to the burnt part, and that you
may do, or anybody else for you, as you may see occasion
to change them, and by the time I come back I do not
doubt but there will be on you a very great alteration."
Then she gave me a gold ducat, with which, after bidding
her for the time farewell, I went directly to my sore-eyed
gentry, who were all waiting my coming, and ready to
undergo the operations; however, before I took them in
hand, as not thinking it convenient for me to stay there
any longer after I had doctored them, and having, before I
left them, a very great mind to a good breakfast, I asked
them if they had ate anything for the morning. They told
me no, for that notwithstanding they were after their
physic extremely hungry, yet would they not venture to eat
anything till I came. "Very well," said I, "as to that I
cannot blame you; however, if you have any cold meat
left, I would by all means have you to eat a little before I
take you in hand, for, to be plain with you, you will not
for some time after the operation be able to see so well how
to go about it."

Then the remains of our last night's supper was directly
brought forth, and when I had filled my belly I told them

I was ready as soon as they pleased. They directly left eating, and according to order sat themselves all down on the floor, and then I, in a little time (it being my masterpiece, and I having several quills of my powders ready at my hands), filled all their eyes to that degree as to set them a wallowing and getting upon their legs, capering and dancing like so many fairies; when I told them that they must have patience, for that the violent smarting would soon pass off, and that as I was obliged, as I told them the last night, to go to a patient about two leagues off, I could then tarry with them no longer; therefore, said I, if you will be pleased to help me to a little money to bear out my expenses till I return you will very much oblige me; and if I did not at my return make on them a perfect cure, I would on my honour give it them back again. Then they ordered one of the women to give me a gold ducat; and which, indeed, they could not do themselves, they being by that time on the rubbing and twisting order, and such abundance of tears falling from their eyes, that had it been by way of a natural cause, and in contrition for their past sins, it must, no doubt, have been accounted a very happy introduction to their future repentance.[*]

[*] *Note* 80.

CHAPTER XI.

On the road to liberty—Another old friend—An awkward meeting, but a former enemy is luckily not recognized—Robbed of everything, Mr. Pellow reaches Tarudant in a woeful plight—Re-equipped, he arrives at Santa Cruz, and as a measure of precaution takes up his quarters in a cave, where he meets with strange company—Dreams, and their interpretation—Enters into a new partnership—Takes to duck killing for a livelihood—A new partner of the faint-hearted order—Being again stripped, he "borrows a point of the law" in order to exist—He takes refuge in the Kasbah of Ali ben-Hamedûsh at the Tensift River—At Willadia he falls in with an old schoolfellow, and, worse luck, meets the mother of Muley Abdallah—Plays the courier, escapes from robbers, and passes the night in a tree, surrounded by wild beasts.

NOW I am again on the tramp, and in pocket (or at least tied up in one corner of my blanket, at the bottom of one of my pots of ointment) six gold ducats, and in blankeels to the value of two more. So travelling merrily on at a good rate, I got that evening to the foot of the mountain Mosmeeth * where on a former expedition we left our horses, whilst we travelled on foot up the mountain, and returned there from subduing the castle of Ehiah Embelide, † and the four little towns on the top of the mountain, as is before mentioned; and where I called now on Tolbhammet Mesmeesey,‡ who very courteously received me, and asked me after a very friendly manner what wind

* Amsmiz ?   † Note 81.
‡ Taleb (Interpreter of the Law) Hamid Ams-mizi.

had blown me thither ; when I answered him with the old
story. In answer to which he told me that, so far as he
could learn thitherto, Muley Abdallah was at Taffilet.
"Sir," said I, "you are certainly therein very much imposed on, for I am credibly informed he is at Terrident, and
I am thither fully determined with myself to follow him,
for I shall not be at peace with myself till I have found
him, or at least heard a further certainty where he is."
"Very well," said he, "but I would have you to tarry here
first some time with me, to refresh yourself, during which
we may chance to hear of him further." I told him that I
was very much obliged to him for his civility, and that as
he was pleased to be so very kind as to offer me so great a
favour in my distress, I was ready with all my heart (as I
was through my great travel very much harassed) to accept
of it ; and, in short, I stayed with him three days, during
which (he being very inquisitive after my journey) I gave
him an account of it, so far as I thought proper to let him
know, and practised on several patients by his permission,
and amongst them all rose to the value of twenty shillings
English.

The third following morning very early (I having over-
night acquainted him with my intentions, and received
from him a gold ducat to help me forward, and his most
hearty, and, as he said, sincere obedience and good wishes
for Muley Abdallah, all which he desired me to make acceptable to him, so far as it might be in my power) I took
my departure thence, and travelled up the mountain as fast
as I could, though seriously considering with myself if it
might be proper or not for me to rest myself at the castle
of Ehiah Embelide, where I had been before to the then
inhabitants a very bitter enemy. Therefore I had with
myself a very great debate for some time concerning it ; as
how (many years having since passed) they might be all

then dead, thence removed, or their remembrance of me
quite worn out; to which I was by myself answered, what
occasion had I to run any such hazard? For that I was
then fresh, and very well able to perform without it; and
therefore I agreed to give the castle the go by, and to travel
on till I had gained the height; and I climbed up as fast as
I could, till I had got within sight of the four little towns
we had formerly destroyed, together with all the men inhabitants; when I had again with myself for some short
time another debate, if it might not be hazardous for me to
pass through them.

However (on considering the men then there to be
all strangers, or at least to be grown up during my
absence, those formerly there being all to my knowledge
dead, that the children then spared there did not exceed
ten years of age, and that the women who were then
also spared must no doubt be then under so grievous
and terrifying a consternation as not to be capable of
taking any notice of faces, by way of their making future
reprisals, or of my sweet phiz in particular), I passed
through without saluting any of the inhabitants, no further
than my asking a lad whom I saw there with some almonds
and raisins in a basket, how he sold them, and buying a
halfpennyworth of them, I travelled on down the mountain
on the other side, and about sunset got clear of it, getting
to another part of the river Waddonfeese, where I was for
the night tolerably well entertained in a Moor's tent, though
I had from him a very deplorable account concerning the
very late state of that neighbourhood, as how the country
was to that degree destroyed, and in such confusion, that
they and they only who happened to be of the strongest
party were accounted the happy people, and of whom I
soon found he had been so happy to be one. "Then," said
I, "it is no doubt very dangerous for a stranger to be

SALLEE AND RABAT IN 1760.

amongst you." "That indeed," said he, "is according to his behaviour, and the nature of his business which calleth him thither, or which party he sides with." "Why, sir," said I, "as to my part I have no further business here than to sell a few medicines amongst you, if I can, for the benefit of you all, without meddling with your quarrels on either side." "Why really," said he, "you say very well, and I wish you success with all my heart; but, to be plain with you, we have been of late so far involved in a civil war, that one parish was up against another in arms, destroying the fruit of each other's labour, and cutting one another's throats so fast as they could." "Alas!" said I, "a very unhappy case indeed!" To which he answered me, that I should not be under any uneasiness at it, but endeavour to compose myself, for that he would in the morning put me into the best method he could.

However, I could not (notwithstanding his fair promises, and though I was prodigious weary) take any rest for the first part of the night, still wishing myself further off; when I told myself, that as it was my chance to come there, it would be in vain for me to vex myself, but endeavour to get thence again as well as I could. So I fell into a sound sleep, and slept till sunrising; then I got up, and saluting my host with a good-morrow, and telling him that I thought myself very much obliged to him for my kind welcome, and if he was pleased to accept of any of my medicines, they were very heartily at his service. "No, no," said he, "you are very welcome to what you have had here; and as to physic, I never took any in my life, and unless I may happen to have more occasion for it than I have had hitherto, I never will take any. But what makes you in so much hurry? If I want none, there are those amongst us to my knowledge that do, and who, no doubt, when they hear you are come, will be very glad of it; and as to your safety amongst us (as our civil dissensions are now at an end) here is my hand," giving it in a very friendly manner into mine, and asking me where I intended to go.

"As to that, sir," said I, "I am not very well determined whether to Terrident or Taffilet." "Then," said he, "I tell you on my honour that both those roads are very unsafe, and dangerous to travel in at present, for after our several conflicts in these parts, they are now, by our example, acting the same in them : therefore stay with me till those bickerings are over, till which you shall be very welcome in my house to such as I have." "Sir," said I, "I most humbly thank you," and which, indeed, I was obliged to accept of ; for that very day came thither repeated advices that there was in and throughout both those provinces (which are much the same with our counties) very grievous doings, insomuch that they were killing and plundering all they could lay their hands on. So that I was obliged to take up my quarters with this hospitable infidel during the space of twenty-four days ; during which I had several patients, and amongst them all got about forty shillings sterling, acting after a most cautious manner, in giving such small doses of my purging powder as I knew could do them no harm ; and as I was so lucky to perform nothing by way of curing the eyes, I gave general satisfaction. In short, got amongst them so famous a name, as I presume none of the quack fraternity had ever done before me. They really had so good an opinion of me, that on another of the fraternity's coming one day there, and though he might, for anything as I knew to the contrary, have been a very able man, yet did they (on my seeming indifference of him) directly drive him thence, threatening him, that in case they ever caught him there again, they would cut off his ears.

Now am I, by the general approbation and consent, on

promise of my being back again in three weeks, and on
their hearing the roads were again passable, permitted to
depart, taking my way for Arhallah, in the plain of Souz;
and without anything remarkable, I arrived the second
following evening at a place called in their language Rosselelwad, or the head of the old river, thoroughly resolving
to get that night, if I could, to Terrident. And which,
indeed, had not that part of the journey proved most unfortunate to me, I should have reached before the gates
were shut, I being about ten o'clock at night within half a
mile of it; when I was surprised by three ruffian Moors,
knocked down, plundered, and, in short, deprived of everything I had in the world, stripping me quite naked; and
rummaging into my blanket, they soon found my blankeels,
which, as the moon was then at the full, and the horizon
very clear, I saw to my very great dissatisfaction.

When I saw them ransacking my knapsack, I was really
terrified a great deal more, I having hid all my gold at the
bottom of one of my pots of ointment, in all to the value of
six pounds sterling. But I had so far the presence of
mind as to tell them that they could not be anything the
better for the few medicines I had in it, but (as they did
not know how to use them) rather the worse, though they
would be to me, by way of my getting a small matter for
my subsistence, of very great service. And as my life depended thereon, I hoped they would be pleased to give me
my blanket, knapsack, and few medicines back again,
which, as they had taken from me all my money, would in
all likelihood keep me from starving. "No, no," said
they, "you have got your life, and go therewith about
your business." Then I very much complained of the cold,
and of the many wounds I had about me, desiring them
that if they would not give me back my medicines, they
would at least give me a pot of my ointment. "No, no,"

said they, " for if your ointment is so very excellent for your wounds, pray why is it not for ours ? "   " However," said one of them, " here take your blanket, and be packing about your business, or you will oblige us to be very angry with you."   To which another of them added, that I was an unconscionable dog, and if I said another word, he would take my blanket from me again.   " Then pray, gentlemen," said I, " if you will not give me a whole pot, give me a small matter of the ointment at the bottom of one of them."   "You dog," said they, "you shall have none ; and if you dare speak another word, we will cut off your ears." At which they went directly from me, and without speaking another word on either side, left me to consider the folly of heaping up riches, as not knowing who shall gather them.

And now am I obliged to travel empty away for Terrident, as you may suppose, in a very disconsolate manner ; and in walking but a slow pace, I got in half an hour's time to the gates of the city, which I found to be shut, and all within very silent, therefore I found myself obliged to lay me down in one of their burying-places, amongst the graves, where I continued till daylight, reflecting on my so late misfortune.   Then I got me up, and kept walking till the sun was up, and the gates were opened, when I marched in, and went directly to a friend's house, a Frenchman, we being formerly fellow-soldiers, and always very intimate with one another.   I was directly admitted entrance, and very courteously received by him, telling me that he was very glad to see me, but to see me there at that time very sorry.   "Why," said I, " what is the matter?   I hope there are not more evils soon about to befall me ; if so, I think it will be a very unhappy time indeed," telling him of my so late misfortunes.   " Alas ! my friend," said he, " that is what I did not dream of, and I am sincerely sorry for you ; but what I meant by saying

so, was tending to matters of another nature, and which is
indeed quite different." "Pray," said I, "what may it
be ? " "Be ? " said he ; " you must know that here is now
in the town Abdallah Mahomet, one of old Muley Smine's
natural sons, who hath lately gained to his interest at least
one hundred thousand of the mountaineers, and was with
them about two months ago at Santa Cruz, took it, and,
with a good part of the country round, brought it under his
subjection, and is now forcing all able-bodied men, who will
not voluntarily come into his service. Therefore I think
it (till he is departed hence) highly necessary for you to
remain secretly in my house ; for should he or any of his
people happen to see you, you would no doubt be obliged
to follow him." "And whither," said I, " does he design
to go, or what may be his intentions ? " "That indeed,"
said he, "I cannot particularly tell you, but first you may
suppose he will strengthen his party all he can, and then
most likely make a bold push against Mahommet Wolderriva, and the Black Army, for the Empire." "Indeed ! "
said I ; " then I find my wishes are still every day more and
more coming about, for if natural sons thus presume, where
there are so many born under wedlock, there will be no
doubt amongst them all (as they are so many hundreds)
rare work in a very little time. Therefore all I shall say
further to it for the present is, ' May God increase their
animosities, and send me from amongst them.' " "Indeed, my friend," said he, " happy are those who are out of
it ; and as to us, we have already acted our parts very sufficiently in their bloody enterprises."

Then I returned again to my late misfortune, telling
my friend, that in regard to my future proceedings, I
thought the loss of my knapsack and medicines to be
(amongst all my losses) the greatest. "Well," said he,
"I suppose I guess what you mean, and it shall go

very hard, if I do not in a very little time procure you some other," which indeed he did the next day, and then he also told me that he had been credibly informed that morning, that Abdallah Mahomet was fully determined to march the day after with all his people for Morocco." "Very well," said I, "and I the next for Santa Cruz." "Prithee," said he, "don't be so very hasty ; we may not perhaps see one another again of a long time, therefore pray oblige me with your company now as long as you can." "Very well," said I, "and so I will ; " as indeed I did till the third morning, when, after our taking our leave of each other, I departed with my knapsack, a few medicines, and six blankeels. And it being a very dangerous part of the country to travel through, I travelled on all day without intermission, and got about sunset to Terroost, a village in the parish of Gisseemah, near the river Souz, about three leagues short of Santa Cruz, where luckily meeting with two of my old acquaintance, I was entertained by them very friendly all that night ; and setting out thence very early the next morning, I about ten o'clock that forenoon got well to Santa Cruz, where being before well acquainted, I was kindly received by the inhabitants, and treated for two days after a most friendly manner. Yet I did not think fit to lodge in the town, but retired at nights to a cave about a musket-shot without, where I had several Moors and two Blacks for my companions ; and returning again at sunrising into the town, where, as not altogether caring to rely myself on my friends, I sought out an employ, and was hired by a baker to carry his bread round the town to his customers, through which means I got a sufficient subsistence, all this time looking sharp out for a vessel ; and though I found several, yet could I not meet with any so Christian-like commander as on any terms to carry me with him.

However, I did not despair, for notwithstanding my present state, and no hopes of a vessel at that time, yet did my mind daily tell me that my captivity was running out apace, and my nocturnal imaginations were sufficiently stuffed with foolish idle fancies and dreams about it, insomuch that I was not a little afraid that I should thereby let my companions know my designs. For they often told me how I cried out in my sleep, and mentioned Gibraltar (where, indeed, there was scarce a night passed without my dreaming of my being safely landed); and as at my awaking I very particularly remembered it, and took notice that my comrades began to prate amongst themselves concerning it, therefore I one day, as it were accidentally, began the following discourse with them. " Pray, gentlemen," said I, " is any one of you a good interpreter of dreams ? " " Not I," said one ; " Nor I," said another ; and, in short, so said they all. "However, lay them before us," said they, " for if we cannot come up to the true interpretation, it will be still doing no harm."

And I having before duly considered my story, I told them that I had for several nights past been strangely hurried in my sleep by dreams, as how that Muley Abdallah should be fled to Gibraltar, that he was there kindly received by the Christians, and that we were all going with Mahomet Wolderriva to bring him back. Nay, further, that we went, and that at our arrival we were met by one of the most stately lions I had ever seen before, and by him driven back again, threatening Mahomet after a high rate, that in case he ever caught him or the Spaniard there again, he would send them in chains to his royal master, to be exposed to public view amongst the other outlandish monsters in the Tower of London. This, I hope, though altogether false, my readers will not impute to my love for romance, and disregard for truth, when they have duly

weighed the circumstances that induced me to it, but
consider it, as it was really intended, to take off the edge
of those inquisitive wretches from talking any further
about what I talked in my sleep; and having told them this
strange fiction, they said they could not tell what to make
of it, and could not but allow it to be a very extraordinary
and most unaccountable dream.

Now, being still without any likelihood of meeting with
a ship, I am thoroughly resolved to forsake my cave, and
seek farther, telling my comrades that as I was somewhat
apprehensive I had worn out my welcome at Santa Cruz,
I would first go thither to thank them for all past favours,
and then travel farther by way of serving the country with
my medicines. The second following morning, meeting
there in the street a German, one of the quack fraternity,
I soon insinuated myself so far into his favours as to get
him to promise me to go with me; and the next morning
we accordingly set out, and travelled back the three leagues
to Terroost, on the river Souz, where I lodged the night
before I came into Santa Cruz. Now we begun to open
the many strange and wonderful cures we had performed
by way of our doctorship, insomuch that we had at the
village of Terroost, and up and down the parish of Gisseemah, great business for a week's time. But, alas! what
could all that avail me. Indeed, it was with much hazard,
present bread. But on my duly considering the many
hazards and difficulties I had undergone to get thither, and
that my former practices that way were altogether on
account of the better concealing my escape, and that as
I had behaved with so much caution in my travels through
so many dangerous and roundabout tiresome ways, insomuch that I was obliged from Mequinez to Santa Cruz to
make of it more than six months' journey. Whereas I might
by travelling the direct road have performed it in thrice as

many days, and all for the better keeping my intentions
from suspicion therefore as I had thereby so far accomplished my desired ends, I really thought my business now
to be of a quite different nature than practising physic, and
that notwithstanding there was no ship for my purpose
whilst I was at Santa Cruz, yet I could not tell how soon
there might.

I had been from thence a week, during which there
might happen to come in several, therefore I plainly
told myself that where I was then I had no business,
and therefore it was by no means consistent with
my unhappy condition, and that I ought to make the
best of my way to Santa Cruz again, or some other seaport. However, on my seeing vast troops of wild-fowl on
the river, I thought if I could get a few of them they might
be to my friends at Santa Cruz a very acceptable present.
But how to get them was the chief point. Gun nor ammunition I had none, nor where to get any I did not know.
However, I was through very great luck provided with them
both in a very little time, and that night I went to the
riverside, and as the moon shone very bright, I saw a vast
number of them swimming on the water in a still part of
the river; and levelling amongst them as well as I could,
I fired and killed four couple of ducks. Then, throwing off
my blanket, I threw myself into the river, and soon brought
them out, and I retired for the night to my rest, and
lay me down by my comrade, telling him of my success,
and that I designed in the morning to present them to my
friends at Santa Cruz, and that if he would go with me
I would dare engage to make him very welcome. " No,"
said he, "I am fully determined in the morning to go
another way, and as I find you are designed to leave me,
I wish you very well." And after taking a short nap, and
the daylight appearing, we started up and set out, he to

seek after fresh patients one way, and I another to Santa Cruz with my ducks ; where I was very kindly received by the merchants, and handsomely rewarded for my fowl, but finding no ship for my purpose, I returned again to the river, killed more fowl, carried them to Santa Cruz, and sold them at a good rate. And after I had recruited my ammunition, I went back again, and so continued in going and coming for several weeks, by which time the winter was pretty well past—though all this time, to my very great dissatisfaction, no ship.

This trade of duck-killing I found to turn to a much better account than my former business, and to kill them, rather than the Moors, much the safer way ; though it was attended with some hardships and very severe cold, yet as my present condition was so very unhappy in the general, I thought myself very well off in it.

Now is the spring approaching apace ; therefore, as I had been so long in and out about Santa Cruz, looking out after a vessel, and all to no purpose, I was fully determined with myself to try what might be done that way at Saphee, and in case I could not be there successful to travel on to the Willadea. And meeting soon after a Spaniard, one of my old acquaintance, I thought if I could get him to go with me it might not be amiss ; but he in very little time saved me that trouble, telling me that in case he had not happened to meet me there, he should have been at that time at least a league on his way. "On your way," said I ; "pray whither may you be going to ?" "Going to?" said he ; "a long journey, and as I hear a very troublesome one." "Pray," said I, " to what part of the country ?" "Why," said he, "to Saphee." "To Saphee," said I ; " that is a place I have had very great inclination to see for some time, therefore, had I any business there, or was I sure to get by it but one single blankeel, I would go with you. "Why, said he, "if you are in good earnest, and your business will permit you, I will bear out your expenses on the road, and be helpful to you in everything else that I can." "Very well," said I, "have a care I don't take you at your word; for to be plain with you, you don't know how far you have brought me in the mind of it, and as I have very little to do here, a very little further persuasion may prevail." "Well then," said he, " we will first go to my friend's house, and take a bottle upon it, and by the time we have finished it, your resolutions may be better settled." As indeed they were, before our bottle was half out, giving him my word to go with him; at which he seemed, and was I dare say, very glad, telling me that as it was so far onward in the afternoon, he thought it would be the best way for us to set up there for the night, and so set out early in the morning. Then he ordered for a good supper, after which we drank two bottles more, and went to our rest.

Now am I really better pleased than I had been of a long time before, and as soon as the morning light appeared, I got up; and by the time I had stepped to the door to look at the weather and in again, my comrade was up also, and after making a good breakfast, and taking with us about six pounds of bread, we set forward together, and got that evening without any disaster to Agroot, the little fishing-coves before mentioned, in my travel with the caravan to Guinea, where we met two Moors just arrived before us from Hahah, a parish about a day's journey in our way farther on towards Saphee,* and which we must be obliged to pass through the next day, who told us that the inhabitants of a neighbouring parish to them were up in arms against them, and proving much too strong for their parish they were obliged to fly

* Note 81.

18

for their lives, the greatest part of them being destroyed,
and that throughout all that province were the like doings.

This so terrified my comrade that, notwithstanding his so
very great hurry for Saphee, and my cheering him all in
my power, yet could not I persuade him to go with me but
very little farther. However, I so far prevailed with him
as to continue with me there for that night, and then I
thought it high time to look about me for something for
supper; but there being nothing to be had, we took out our
bread and fell at it, and whilst we were eating a Moor
came up to us, desiring us to look at his eyes. " Your
eyes," said I, " pray what ails them ? " and laying one of
my fingers on one of his eyelids. " So, so," said I, " you
are coming blind apace; but," said I, " I cannot see
what encouragement travellers can have to do any good,
where nothing is to be had to keep them from starving."
"Nothing!" said he; " notwithstanding my eyes are so
very bad, I see you have got very good bread." " Yes,"
said I, " and so we have, but without any thanks to you or
any of your neighbours, for we brought it with us from
Santa Cruz." " Indeed ! " said he; " then I will tell you
for your comfort, if you will look at my eyes, and help me
all in your power, I will give you a dried haike and some
very good oil." " Very well," said I; " you speak like an
honest man, and therefore pray hasten and show yourself
so, and after supper we will do somewhat for you."

And which, indeed, he did in good earnest, bringing
us a middling haike, and about a pint of oil, and making us
a fire broiled the fish, and we soon made a very hearty
supper on it; when we gave him a paper of our purging
powders to prepare his body against the morning, and lay
us down under a fig-tree in the court for the night. At
daybreak we got up, and without doing any further
mischief to our last night's benefactor, we set out and

travelled on farther together about two leagues, which brought us to the foot of the mountain Gorrasurnee, where the Spaniard's heart failing him, he told me plainly that he would not for that time travel on any farther in that road, was he sure to get by it a hundred ducats, but that he was resolved to return again to his house at Terrident, till the country was again a little better settled, and if I would go with him I should on his honour be very heartily welcome. I told him that I altogether as heartily thanked him, but as I was got over my journey so far I was thoroughly resolved to see it out, be the consequence what it would. So after sharing our little bread and few medicines we parted, him back towards Terrident, and I forwards towards Saphee, travelling up the mountain as fast as I could, though before I had got quite at the top of it, I very unhappily met with four ruffian Moors armed with muskets, and long murdering knives, who immediately, without asking me any the least question, fell to rifling me, stripped me quite naked, and were going off with my knapsack and blanket, when I earnestly intreated them to give me them back again, for that I had nothing else to depend on for a livelihood but a few medicines I had therein, and nothing to cover me from the inclemency of the air but that old garment. "You lie, you rascal," said one of them, "it is a very good one, and therefore you shall not have it." "Pray then, sir," said I, "let me have my knapsack." "Ay, ay," says another, "let him have it, for it can be of no benefit to us, and may very likely keep him from starving."

So through the means of a conscientious thief I had my knapsack and few medicines back again. I then travelled on quite naked till I had got two leagues farther up the mountain, where I, to my great satisfaction, came to three houses, out of one of which came an old woman, who seemed to pity my condition very much, and gave me a piece of an old blanket, a dish of buttermilk, and some " jerrodes " or locusts, with which they are visited once in six or seven years to that degree, swarming in from seaward upon them in incredible multitudes, as even to darken the air, and at once overspreading a province, eat up every green leaf and herb, so that the fields and trees look all one as they do in the bleakest winter. These insects are not only innumerable, but of a large size, some of them at least two inches long, and about the bigness of a man's thumb. They are really good eating, and in taste most like shrimps, and are by the inhabitants, first purging them with water and salt, boiled in new pickle, and then laid up in dry salt by way of reserve.

After this good woman had thus kindly used me, and given me some more of the jerrodes to carry with me, one of her neighbours happening to come by, and taking also some pity on me, gave me a piece of another old blanket, so as I was between them both pretty well covered again, and really thought myself well off, travelling cheerfully on to the house of an old acquaintance, by trade a shoemaker, who made me very welcome, took off from me my old rags, and gave me a very good blanket; and as he knew I fully intended to stay with him for the night, he ordered his wife to get ready some cuscassoe for my supper, and in the morning for my breakfast some " Zumineeta," * which is barley roasted in a pan over the fire, much in like nature of coffee, then it is ground down by a hand-mill, and after it is clean from the bran it is mixed with water, and is very often carried with them in a little bag to their labour or on a journey, and when they are disposed to refresh themselves, they take out some of

* Zesomeeta, or Zummeeta.

this zumineeta into a little cup they generally carry with
them for that purpose, mix it with some water, and drink
it off, being much after the Scotch fashion—with this only
difference, that being plain oatmeal, this, barley roasted;
and on this I travelled all that day, getting towards night
to the parish of Idogurt,* where I very luckily happened
to meet with a very friendly and hospitable house, getting a
good supper and lodging, and the next morning a good
breakfast. I travelled merrily on all that day, and without
any accident got before night to Shedemah, which I found
to be engaged in quarrel with Abdah, a neighbouring
parish, and here I am obliged, on account of those civil
dissensions, to lie by for sixteen days, and really a good
part of it in a miserable condition, being obliged, as provisions were scarce, to borrow a point of the law or starve,
living altogether on raw carrots; though indeed I had
them for the first three days with permission, but wearing
out my welcome, I was afterwards obliged to go into the
gardens at nights, and take them after a clandestine
manner.

And this should I have been obliged to have continued longer, had I not very accidentally happened to
meet a Moor who had seen me somewhere before selling
my medicines, who earnestly entreated me to go with him
to his house to see his wife, who, he said, was very much
indisposed; as indeed she really was, for at my coming I
found her to be in a high fever, being in a dry burning
heat and very restless. And now was I at a stand for some
time how to manage, for as this was what I had never
practised before in, I knew not for some time what to do
with her, especially as I had lost my lancet and burning
iron. However, I thought myself obliged to do something,
and therefore I was resolved to put her to sleep, in order

* District of Ida (properly *Aït*, or tribe) ou Gort.

to which I desired the man to send somebody directly to gather some poppy flowers, which being soon brought in, I boiled a handful of them in water, strained it off, sweetened it with honey, and gave her about half a pint of it to drink, which threw her in a very little time into a great sweat, and sound sleep; when her husband and I fell at a good bowl of cuscassoe, filled our bellies, and went to sleep also.

Early in the morning my patient and I happened to wake much about the same time, which was indeed very much to my satisfaction, for to be plain, I thought she would have slept much longer. However, be that as it will, she was revived to a very great degree, and grew perfectly well in a few days, praying for the doctor, and nothing she had was too good for him. At my request she, after giving me two gold ducats, desired her husband to convey me safe thence to the castle of Allalben-Hammedush,* where I was obliged, on account of a report there of a great party of the mountaineers having been very troublesome a few days before at Saphee, getting over the walls, and killing the sentinels, &c., to remain seven days; during which I was, through means of some old acquaintance I met with there, well taken care of, and never failed of my belly full thrice every day; and there being a very dangerous wood to travel through between that and Saphee, it being the general rendezvous of a gang of merciless thieves, who generally stripped and murdered all that came in their way, insomuch that it was even impracticable for any going single, or but a few together, to escape them, therefore when any of the people had occasion to go that way, they gave timely notice round the neighbourhood, so that they might muster up a party well armed. This wood is plentifully stored with certain trees called argon, growing

* *Note* 86.

to a very large size, and their branches spreading a vast circumference, which are full of long prickles, much in like
nature of a thorn, bearing great plenty of a fruit—if it
may be properly so called—much like a peach in shape
and smell, though none can eat of them; however, when
they are ripe and fallen off the trees, the inhabitants carefully gather them off the ground, and make thereof—that
is to say, of certain small stones growing in the middle,
the outer part being no other than a shell or husk—a very
good sort of oil, by grinding them small, by which means
an oil comes forth, which is used in most of their eating,
and esteemed amongst them by far preferable to that of
their olives.

And now am I about to beat up the quarters of these
desperate outlaws; for on the eighth day, very early in
the morning, I set out in company with about thirty
Moors well armed, having with them several camels
and mules laden with their merchandise, as argon oil,
Barbary skins, &c., for Saphee, passing on till we got over
the better half of this wood without anything remarkable;
when we came up with seven Moors, *viz.*, four men and
three women, three of the men just expiring, and the
fourth with the women, very much wounded, lying quite
naked on the ground, being, they said, thus used by a
party of the mountaineers about an hour before we came
up with them, and that on notice of our approach they in
a very great hurry left them. This put our merchants
into a great fright, and they consulted amongst themselves
for a long time if it would be best for them to proceed or
to go back again; to which I answered that as we were
got over the better half of our journey, it would be altogether as great, nay, the greater hazard of the two, to go
backward than forward, for that they might depend the
villains were nearer to us than they imagined; and should

we offer to go back it would but show our fear, and then they would, no doubt, soon become the more bold; whereas if we continued our march boldly on, and kept a good look out, they would not dare to approach us, as by their running away at our approach seemed to me to be very plain.

On which it was agreed by all to travel on; and after taking up the three women and the wounded man—the other three being then dead—we proceeded, and got without any other hindrance, about two of the clock in the afternoon, to Saphee, where I passed for a day or two for one of the people belonging to the caravan; and, as you may suppose, I looked sharp out for a vessel, but could not find any one to my mind. Not but here were two, and one belonging to Joshua Bawden, of Flushing, my first cousin, we being sisters' children. However, though I met him twice, and my blood boiled in my veins at the sight of him, yet did we not speak on either side, which was no doubt a very great misfortune to me; for had he known who I was, he would, I am well satisfied, have carried me with him, and thereby have prevented me from many troublesome and imminent dangers which happened to me during the time that I was obliged to stay longer in Barbary through this omission. My abode at Saphee was no more than sixteen days, during which I often frequented the house of Monsieur Pedro Pollee,* a French merchant, who was extremely kind to me, and with whom I always met with a very friendly entertainment, and I had amongst his servants, though they were poor enough, twelve blankeels, over and above the master's liberality, and they otherwise did me all the good offices in their power.

However, notwithstanding all this kind treatment, I was more down in the mouth now than I had been from my

* *Note* 81.

first setting out from Mequinez, reflecting on the many
hardships and dangers I had thitherto undergone, and still
no manner of appearance of an alteration, when who
should happen to come into my mind but the black
prophetess, whom I met with at Mequinez the day before
my setting out, and very particularly how she had told me
that I should meet with a great many difficulties before I
got off; which, indeed, I knew so far, to my very great
discomfort, to be true, and therefore I was resolved with
patience to wait the event of what was to come. That
night, on my lying down to my rest, and reflecting on my
dreams in the cave at Santa Cruz, I was, on my falling
into a slumber, again hurried after a very surprising
manner, my black prophetess, to my seeming, taking me
by the hand, and telling me with a smiling aspect, looking
me full in the face, that I was a very faint-hearted soldier,
for that I could not thitherto charge her with anything she
had told me concerning my escape more than I had found
to be true; for notwithstanding I had thitherto suffered a
great deal, yet was I still out of the hands of the enemy.

Therefore, as she had told me before to keep a good
heart and my own secrets, so must I continue to do, and
my redemption would soon be accomplished; and for me to
abide where I then was any longer would be altogether out
of my way, for that was not the place for me to find a ship
for my purpose, I having yet many more difficulties to
undergo. However, I should continue my resolutions, and
all would end well to my satisfaction. Then, to my
seeming, she was going off, and I, struggling to detain her
longer, started up and found all this to be no more than a
dream; and after reflecting thereon for some short time,
I fell again into a doze, and again dreamt the same, and
further that I should hasten to the Willadea, and there I
should find things more to my content. As soon as the

daylight appeared I got up to consult myself about the journey, and in a very little time I was fully resolved thereon. However, I considered that it might be very proper, if I could, to procure me some company; but though I looked out very sharp, yet could I not all that day meet with any to my mind. However, I the next day met with a mulatto, one of my old soldiers, and after telling him that I was very glad to see him, I asked him what business had called him thither; to which he answered me, " None further than my own curiosity." " Then, old friend," said I, " you had as well go with me to Willadea, hence about twelve leagues." To which he readily consented, and as readily travelled on with me, and got that evening into the middle of a large wood, where we found half a dozen inhabited tents, and in one of them got our supper and lodging.

Setting out early the next morning, we got about noon to Willadea, off Marcegongue, the Portuguese garrison, about fifteen leagues. Here I found two brigantines and a sloop; and of one of the former John Simmons of Penryn, one of my old schoolfellows, happened to be commander; with whom I soon renewed my acquaintance, and found him and his people extremely civil to me. But he being, poor man, very sick, departed this life in a few weeks after, which was a very great disappointment to me, and I was really very much troubled at it. Now, finding provisions to be very dear here, through means of the Moorish butchers and bakers imposing upon the Christians, selling their beef at threepence per pound, and bread in proportion, I, at the request of the ships' masters, went to the markets or fairs in the province of Ducallah, about five, or sometimes seven leagues off, and bought bullocks and sheep according as they wanted, driving them to the waterside, where the sailors conveyed them on board, and

neatly butchered them; and reckoning all charges, the
meat did not come to more than three farthings a pound,
a middling bullock costing in the market about thirty
shillings, and a very large sheep six. After which I lived
altogether on shipboard, and the merchants, &c., were
extremely kind to me.

One day I being on shore as a linguist, two of the
Moorish merchants came to me, viz., Elhash Mahomet
Benino, and Elhash Absolom Benino, being uncle and
nephew (the word Elhash* signifying as much as if they
had been at Mecca to visit the tomb of their prophet
Mahomet; after which Elhash is added to their former
names), desiring me to do them a favour. I told them I
would with all my heart, so far as it might be in my
power; which, indeed, as they had been before so very
kind to me, I thought I could not in gratitude refuse,
though I must confess I thought it to be something of
another nature, relating to the ships' masters, or the like;
when they, to my very great surprise, told me that I must
go to Santa Cruz with some letters; and as I had given
them my word before to serve them all in my power, I
took the letters, and after they had given me money to
defray my expense on the road, I went directly out of the
town, and as I travelled very hard, I got that evening to
Saphee, though indeed I happened to be very ill received
there, very unluckily meeting there Muley Abdallah's
mother, and with her a strong guard, going in quest of
him, who demanded of me whence I came and whither I
was going to.

To which I answered them, that I did not know.
"Then," said they, "what business have you here?
and" (as knowing me before) "why don't you follow
your old master?" "Follow him!" said I, "I wish

* *Note* 82.

any of you would be so good to direct me how to
proceed, for I have hitherto travelled many a wearisome
and dangerous step in seeking him, and, by all I can
find, I am still as far off from my desired end as ever."
" Why," said he, " he is actually at Tessout, and thither
are we directly going to him, and you shall also go with
us, for you seem to be bound another course." " Really,
gentlemen," said I, " I cannot imagine what can induce
you to entertain such a notion of me, which I am well
satisfied our royal master would not, for he cannot but
remember, when he was first driven out by the Blacks, in
favour of Muley Aly, how I joined him and his small
number at Bolowan, following him and his hard fortune
to Terrident, and brought him back again to his former
right and dignity, and now you say I am about to desert
him. No, no, gentlemen, had I not a sincere regard for
him, what could have hindered my kind reception with
Mahomet Wolderriva. I hope you think me as good a
soldier as any of you, and that I dare do as much for my
Emperor ; and all this, I say, he very well knows, as
having very sufficiently tried me." " Indeed," said one of
them, " you talk very big ; " " and faith," says another,
so he does ; for my part I don't think but what he has
money about him."

On this they felt the corners of my blanket, found
all my money, and took it every penny from me, though
they did not find the letters ; and then they kept me
under a strong guard till about midnight, by which
time (they having laid out all my money in brandy)
they were drunk enough, and all snoring one against
another ; when I, taking up one of their muskets, ammunition, and scimitar, gave them the slip, and travelled on
all the remainder of that night (avoiding that dangerous
wood) and the next day, till I got me to the province of

Shademah; where, as I had no money, I made bold to
sell the musket and ammunition. And after I had refreshed
myself I travelled on, and in four days more (without
any other misfortune on the road) I got with my scimitar
to Santa Cruz, and safely delivered the letters to Absolom
Tooby, a Moorish merchant, as directed. During the two
days he was in preparing his answers, I visited my old
acquaintance, and sold the scimitar, thinking my old
knapsack and a few worthless medicines to be by far the
better arms for me; and finding there no shipping, I got
the answers to my letters, some bread, and a small matter
of money, and therewith directly went out of the town and
back for the Willadea, as fast as I could. And as it was
then full four o'clock in the afternoon, I could get no
farther that night than to the river Tammorot, where I
had the company of some travellers also resting there
with their camels, and in the morning I travelled on with
them, and kept them company as far as Hahah, where I
met with an old acquaintance, and lodged with him that
night.

Very early the next morning I set merrily forward
towards Segosule till about noon; when, having got
within half a mile of it, I saw a Moor lying quite naked
in my road, with his throat cut, breathing his last;
which soon damped my mirth, and in less than half an
hour after I met the murderers, and stood more than a
fair chance of sharing the same fate, they coming directly
upon me, stripping me quite naked, and taking from me
all but my life. This I earnestly implored them to spare,
for that I was a poor miserable wretch travelling the
country for my subsistence by way of carrying letters
from one merchant to another, and that I had no other
way whereby to get my bread, and that I should think
myself to be for ever obliged to them if they would give

me my letters back again, for that they could not be of
any service to them, but to those to whom directed, most
likely of a great deal; which, after much intreaty, they
consented to give me, together with my life, and sent me
away in a miserable condition, though indeed I expected
a great deal worse, and therefore I was very glad with the
loss of my blanket and knapsack to compound for my
life.

And now am I travelling on quite naked for the
mountain Idoworseern, which indeed was but hurrying
myself from one bad evil into a worse, for on my gaining
about two-thirds of the height, I was at once surrounded
by about six thousand horse and foot, and strictly examined what I was, whence I came, whither going, my
business, &c. I told them that I was a letter-carrier,
come from Santa Cruz, and going to the Willadea.
"Very likely," said one of them to the rest of his companions, "for I see the letters in his hand." "But,"
said another of them, "how came you to be naked?" I
told him that I happened to meet that forenoon some
gentlemen on the road, who had taken my blanket from
me. However, they were so civil as to give me the letters
back again. "As to the letters," said he, "they could be
of no service, but I think they were very great fools they
had not cut your throat, for in short, you dog, you are
a spy, and come to take notice of our strength and
actions." "Alas, gentlemen," said I, "I am a most
unfit person for a spy, neither did I ever hear of any such
troops to be gathered hereabouts." And therefore I humbly
entreated they would be so good as to let me go about my
business; but instead of this they soon laid hold on my
arms and throat, and had there not been one amongst
them who knew me formerly at Mequinez, they would no
doubt have soon hauled me in piecemeals, but he, stepping

forth, desired them not be in a hurry to take away my
life, for that he believed me innocent, and if they were
willing of it, he would carry me for that night to his tent,
and if in the morning they thought me worthy of death,
I should be executed in sight of the women.

Which being agreed to, he ordered me to follow him,
and conducted me safe home in a very little time,
telling me in a most friendly manner not to be afraid,
for that he would warrant to protect me from their
rage, and that after I had refreshed me by a good
supper, he would set me again at liberty. "But here,"
said he, "first take this old blanket, which is better
than none, and put it about you." And whilst the
cuscassoe was making ready for our supper, I asked
him what those people were, and what might be their
intentions in gathering into such a body? "Why,
really," said he, "I am almost ashamed to tell you, and
much more that I should happen to be amongst them;
for notwithstanding they are my countrymen, yet do I
think their actions to be most unwarrantable. However,
I am constrained for the present to come into the
measures with them; not but could they be contented
to labour but a very little they might live very well on
the fruits of it, as having land sufficient to employ a far
greater number, allotted them by old Muley Smine on
his first settling them here; and as they increased in
number, so did he also increase their territories."
"Pray," said I, "how long have they been here, and for
what reason were they brought." "Why," said he, "you
must know they were no more at first than five hundred
of both sexes, being inhabitants of the deserts, and
nearly allied to one of Muley Smine's wives (they being,
as they term themselves, a better sort of Laurbs), and
were here brought in the beginning of his reign, behaving

in his lifetime tolerably well, though soon after his death, the breed being very much increased, they grew as rebellious as you please, and after Muley Abdallah's being driven out a second time, I (to shun a greater evil) joined them; not that I am any way related to any of them, I being born in Mequinez, though indeed of Laurbish parents." * But the cuscassoe being brought before us, he left off that discourse, desiring me to fall to and feed hearty, which indeed (my condition considered), I did, and made a good supper in little time; when he told me he doubted some of his neighbours would come to look after me, and therefore he would show me out into the mountain. And after giving me all friendly instructions, and telling me he would answer to his comrades for my escape, he left me to shift for myself.

I climbed up the mountain as fast as I could; however, though I was destitute of company then, I had not gone but very little farther before I had company enough, and, indeed, more than I desired; but on my hearing the jackals coming yelping towards me, I betook myself to a tree, where I had not been but a very short time before my tree was surrounded by a vast number of wild beasts, making a frightful noise, and so continued till daybreak. However, as I knew myself to be out of their reach, I thought myself far better off than to be amongst my last night's Laurbish gentry; and as the day came on, they got them away to their dens, when I came down from the tree and scrambled up the mountain as fast as I could, till I gained the height, and quite down on the other side, without seeing any of my last night's companions, save only two tigers, which I passed without receiving any hurt from them.

* *Note* 85.

CHAPTER XII.

Mr. Pellow keeps north—Gets to the Tensift River and again takes shelter in the castle of Ali ben Hammidùh—Back to Saffi—He finds it necessary to try a Cornish hug with a robber on the road —At Willadia, where he meets with English ships—Engages himself as interpreter, when he frustrates a plot of a Moorish merchant to get quit of his obligations—The vessel on which he is on board of is plundered by the knavish officials—The hard way in which ship captains had to transact their business in those days—Mr. Pellow has to keep concealed, as the Moors suspect him —Sails for Sallee—More trouble, which determined the captain to take French leave—As a precaution the Jews and Moors are put under hatches.

NOW am I, to my very great satisfaction, got clear out of the territories of my Laurbish enemies, and safely arrived near the walls of a well-built house; when, being excessive weary, and very drowsy, I laid me down in the sun and soon fell into a sound sleep, out of which I was as soon roused by the master of the house, asking me who I was, whence I came, and what business I had there. I told him from Santa Cruz, going to the Willadea, and that I was obliged all the last night to keep myself in a tree out of the reach of the wild beasts. "Very well," said he, "and a good shift too." Then I told him how, at my passing by such a place the evening before, I was surrounded by a vast number of armed men, and that I very narrowly escaped with my life, being really put in a very great fright. "Oh," said he, "if that was all, I

19

think you are very well off, for they are a pack of the vilest villains in Barbary, and generally murder all they meet with. I heard their fire yesterday—pray, was you there then?" I told him yes, and through what means I got out of their hands. " Get you up out of the sun," said he, " and lie you down in that shed in the shade." And when I had slept a good nap, he brought me out some butter-milk and cuscassoe for my breakfast; with which, being wonderfully refreshed, I, after returning him my most humble and hearty thanks, travelled briskly on, and got me that night to the province of Shademah, where at my going out I had sold my musket and ammunition, and here I slept that night. And setting out thence early in the morning, I happened to meet about ten of the clock that forenoon, at the foot of the mountain Jibbil Neddeed, or the mountain of iron, with five footpads, and from whom, thinking to get off to a little house hard by, I ran with all the speed I could. However, I was soon overtaken by a very speedy messenger, being wounded by a musket-shot in my right thigh, passing between my legs, and grazing about half an inch within the flesh, which slackened my pace to that degree that they were soon up with me, and gave me the most severe dry-beating I had ever met with before. But on some passengers coming by they made off as fast as they could, and I, making a bad shift (which is better than none), got with much pain to the house, where I got me some herbs and staunched the blood, of which I had really lost a great deal. Here I got a lodging for that night, and some cuscassoe for my supper, and, notwithstanding my wound, slept very well, and early the next morning went limping on, and got that day in some pain to the river Tensieft, near which stood a castle belonging to Elelbenhamedush,* one of their great

* *Note* 86.

men, and where I found residing a great many Jews, from
whom I had some remedies for my wound, and a good
supper, and very civil entertainment for the night. Early
in the morning, after getting a good breakfast and dressing
my wound, I travelled slowly on, still avoiding that
dangerous wood, and a little before night got to Saphee,
though I did not think it fit to go into the town, but
lodged in a little house without, where I got me some
cuscassoe amongst the family for my supper, and in a
very little time after I had filled my belly, I lay me down
to my rest.

But never was I more hurried by dreams as how I
should be at the Willadea, where methought I happened
to meet with a commander of a vessel, and who,
though I had never seen him before, yet did he in a
most Christianlike and courteous manner offer (without
my asking him) to carry me off with him at all hazards.
Thus, at my intervals from slumber, I could not all that
night put out of my head, but what it must be somewhat
more than imaginary, for to my mind I plainly saw him,
conversed with him, and found him in every point to be
a complete man. Then, getting up very early, I travelled
slowly on till about noon, when I met a single Moor, and
I not at all liking his countenance, as supposing him (as
indeed he really was) one of their footpads, I began to
consider with myself how to behave to him, and he seeing
me limping, gave him no doubt the greater assurance.
Therefore, coming directly to me with a pistol cocked in
his hand, and presenting it close to my breast, he in an
insolent manner demanded what I had about me. I told
him that I had nothing worth his acceptance, unless he
would be pleased to accept of my blanket. " Then, you
dog," said he, " why don't you take it off?" " That, sir,"
said I, "is soon done," slipping it directly off my shoulders

and in a seeming fright presenting it into his hand, and he not being very ready to take hold on it, I threw it at once over his head, and soon gave him to understand that I was a true Cornishman. For notwithstanding my wound, I clasped my right arm about his neck, stuck to him with my lame hip, and soon had him on his back on the ground, when I instantly decided the dispute who should have my old blanket. In short, as he had so much mind to it, I left it for him, taking his, and after giving him a farewell pounce, went off with his pistol and ammunition, and got that night into the middle of the wood, and lodged in the same tent I formerly did at my first going that way with the mulatto, and where I was again very kindly entertained, insomuch that I thought myself obliged to make a present to mine host of the pistol, of which he was not a little proud, and very early in the morning provided some cuscassoe for my breakfast.

After this I set merrily forward, and about noon got well to the Willadea, and safely delivered my merchants the answers to their letters. And before I had the power to give them an account of my miserable journey, I am hurried by the merchants on board a Genoese brig, telling me that Absolom Candeele was then in the town, and should he happen to see me, he would no doubt carry me with him. This brig was first commanded by Captain Wilson, an Englishman (who was about three months before unfortunately drowned at Saphee), and then by a Swede, his chief mate, with whom, as the brig was there before I went to Santa Cruz with the letters, I was before well acquainted, and with the rest of the crew; so I went directly on board, and was very courteously received by them, telling me that they were very glad to see me come back well, and that they had been at a very great loss, during my absence, for a linguist, asking me if I had

dined, and if I would eat any mullets. "Yes," said I,
"with all my heart;" when they directly ordered the cook
to fry some for me. Whilst they were frying, I asked the
mate what snow that was to windward of us; he told
me one Captain Toobin, of Dublin, who came in about four
days before, and that he had met with a great deal of
trouble by way of the Moorish merchants, on account of
his freight. "Indeed!" said I; "pray what manner of a
man is he?" "Why really," said he, "a very jolly, well-
discoursed man, so far as I have yet seen of him." "Pray,"
said I, "is he a man of a pretty big stature?" "Yes,"
said he, "he is a very lusty man." "Well," said I, "I
wish I could see him." "Why," said he, "that you may
soon do, for he is as well as us in a very great strait for a
linguist." When, on the cook's telling us that the fish
were ready, we went into the cabin to dinner, and before
we had finished, Captain Toobin came on board, and the
moment I saw him I was thoroughly persuaded with
myself that he was actually the same that I had so lately
seen in my dream at Saphee, and soon found him to be
under some distress; and on his understanding me to be
an Englishman, he asked me if I would go with him on
board his ship. I told him, "Yes (if he thought I might
be of any service to him there), with all my heart;" so I
stepped into the boat along with him, and we were soon
on board, carrying me directly into his cabin, and after
drinking a cheering cup of wine, he asked me how long I
had been in Barbary. I told him, ever since the commencement of the twelfth year of my age, it being then the
twenty-third year of my captivity. "Alas! poor man,"
said he, "a long captivity indeed! but could not you in all
this time find means to escape?"

I told him I had often endeavoured it, even to the
very great hazard of my life, but I was always so

unhappy to be intercepted, telling him of my several
disappointments that way, and what difficulties and
dangers I had undergone to get thither, and that though
I hanged off and on at Santa Cruz for three or four
months, and there were during that time several English
vessels, yet could I not meet with any so Christianlike
commander as to carry me off with him. "No!" said he,
" then they were a parcel of brutish fellows ; and I tell you
for your comfort, that you have met with a Christian at
last, and here's my hand" (giving it into mine) "to serve
you all in my power. Therefore don't despair, for I am fully
determined to carry you with me, even to the hazard of my
life, and be the consequence what it will." This he spoke
with so much sincerity of heart, and tender feeling of my
sad case, that he could not forbear weeping; which you may
suppose raised my joy to that degree at his so tender behaviour, that I could not forbear to keep him company.

Thus far is my dream come to pass, the captain telling
me further that, if I was anyways apprehensive of the least
danger of my appearing in public, he would keep me close
on board the vessel. I told him that I was at a loss in
what terms to express my gratitude; however, I did not
doubt but that time might put it in my power to make him
some recompense; but as I was then in more than ordinary
favour with the merchants, I thought there would be no
occasion for keeping myself close; however, I would be
frequently with him on board, and do him by way of
linguist all the most faithful services and good offices in
my power. For which, indeed, he had an occasion very
often after, for he had, as it were, but just mentioned his
merchant (who, he said, owed him four hundred ducats for
freight, and that he was under no little fear of losing it,
for that he did not like his frequent put-offs), but the boy
came down and told the captain he was coming on board ;

at which he stepped upon the deck, and received him at
the ship's side; and he, seeming to be in a great fright
and hurry, ordered me to tell the captain the following
terrifying lie, viz., that an order was just then come from
Muley Abdallah, by way of Torbo Hallusah, the governor
of Ducallah, to seize all the Christian vessels, to make
slaves of the men, and to apply all their cargoes to his
property. Therefore he should get the vessel in readiness
as soon as possibly he could, assist him in all his power in
carrying off part of the corn then on board the Genoese
brig, which was so deeply laden that she drew more
water than was on the bar to carry her over; but by taking
out one-half of it they might both get over very well.

All this I faithfully told him in English, desiring him not
to vex himself at it, for that I believed it to be a trick, only
to hurry him away and cheat him of his freight. However,
he directly ordered all hands at work, and early the second
following morning got alongside of the brig, and that day
took in half her lading, with some more from the shore,
which belonged to other proprietors, and hauled down the
next morning so fast as we could. And as the brig was
before us, she got well over the bar and clear off, as indeed
we might also have done, had not the proprietors of the
corn stopped us and kept us there some time at an anchor;
during which there came on a violent storm, which drove
our ship, anchor and all, quite back again into her old
berth, where we were again securely moored. And then I
was soon confirmed in my opinion of the merchant's
villainy, and that he not only intended to cheat the
captain of his former freight, but to run further into his
debt, and cheat the proprietors of their corn. For we had
but just done our business in securing the vessel, before
our roguish merchant came on board, ordering me to tell
the captain that he and some more of his comrades were

going to visit the governor of Ducallah to know the truth
of this report, and that if the captain would spare him an
English pistol, he knew it would be to the governor of all
things the most acceptable present. "Therefore," said he,
"pray ask him"; which I did, and it was as soon granted,
and he immediately departed with it, and (as we had after
very good reason to believe) went to the governor.

But though it was only one day's journey, we never saw
nor heard of him after, no further than in a sham way; for
the second following day came the governor of Ducallah,
and with him four hundred armed men, in seeming-wise to
inquire after him, they having no doubt agreed together
before to make use of Muley Abdallah's name, the better
to carry on their so villainous designs; and lest the then
governor of Willadea might be in any wise an obstacle to
them, he sent his brother the day before to secure him,
and for male practices to bring him to Ducallah before
him. And on his carrying him thither, he met the governor, his brother, on the road, who brought him back again,
and confined him close prisoner, under pretence of his
suffering three sail of ships belonging to the Christians to
depart without his permission. He then commanded his
brother, with a few more, on board our vessel, where our
captain made him very welcome, and he supped and took
up his quarters there all night, though indeed he had his
supper brought from the shore, which was a very large bowl
of cuscassoe, with half a sheep boiled to rags on the top of it,
and the other half roasted, brought on a huge long wooden
spit on a Moor's shoulder.

Yet though they were but three that sat at supper,
yet did our captain declare that he had never seen so
much eaten at one meal before by twenty men, though,
poor man, as to his own part (as not at all liking their
foul and ravenous way of eating, he did not eat any; how-

ever, I had a good piece of the meat and some cuscassoe sent me out, which I and my comrades soon despatched. As soon as the Moors had supped, I was ordered into the cabin, and asked by the governor's brother how I came there, and what was my business; and having an answer ready for him at my tongue's end, I told that I had been for some months past travelling up and down the country, exposed to many dangers, and very great want, in seeking Muley Abdallah, and all to no purpose; for that before I got thither, I could hear nothing of him.

However, I was then well satisfied that I might very likely accomplish my so long frustrated desires in a very little time, and therefore I was glad I had come so far; and as soon as I had gathered a little strength after my late hardships, I was fully determined to proceed further, and I hoped to better purpose; that the merchants there had been very kind to me, encouraging me all in their power, in way of a linguist, whereby I got my subsistence, to which end I was then on board the vessel. " Well," said he, " our people are going to him in a very little time with their presents, and then you may also go with them." " Indeed, sir," said I, " that may save me a great deal of trouble, for I have been almost ever since his last absence from Mequinez roaming up and down the country in seeking and inquiring after him, exposed to many hazards, and all, till I came hither, to no purpose." At which he seemed to pity me, being with my story very well satisfied. After he had drank about a gallon of tea,* he laid himself down to rest for the night, and getting up early in the morning, our people put him ashore in our boat; and after he had been some time with the governor, his brother, he returned again with him to the waterside, bringing with them two hundred armed men, peremptorily

* *Note* 88.

requiring Captain Toobin and I to come directly on shore before him.

Then I told the captain the merchant's rogueries would soon appear, and that I knew as well as any of them all, an English pistol to be an extraordinary present amongst them, and therefore I thought it not amiss to take one as a present to the governor, and if we found him not worthy of it, we could but bring it back with us again. "That, my friend," said he, "is what I would do with all my heart, was I sure I could be permitted to send a brace of bullets out of it though his brains." However, he gave me one, which I conveyed close under my blanket, and then we went directly on shore. The governor asking which was his linguist, and his brother pointing at me, all the mystery was directly unfolded, he ordering me to tell the captain that he would not have him to be under the least apprehension of danger, for that his orders from Muley Abdallah were only to take the effects out of the ships, and all the Christians on shore, in order to be sent to him, and afterwards to send the ships by Moorish sailors to Saphee, there to be ripped up.

All which I accordingly told him. "A very extraordinary favour indeed!" said he. "Pray ask him if he has any orders from Muley Abdallah for so doing." He told me yes. "Then," said I, "the captain desires you will let him see it, or at least that you will read it;" which indeed he did directly, and it was according to its true interpretation in English, after the following manner :

"*Alcaide Torbo Hallusah, my trusty and well-esteemed Governor of Ducallah.*

" On the complaint of some of my loyal subjects lately laid before me, relating to five sail of Salleeteens now lading corn at the Willadea to be carried either to Sallee or

Mammora, for the benefit of the Black Army, my utter
enemies; you are therefore on receiving this my peremptory order, for the preventing all future abuses of that
nature, directed to take all the said vessels and cargoes
into your custody, send all the Christians to me, reserve
the several cargoes to my proper use, and send all the
ships by Moorish sailors as soon as you can to Saphee,
there to be ripped up; and for so doing, this shall be your
warrant.—*Muley Abdallah Woold, the Kunnateer Binthebucker* " * (in English, a slave to God and son of Kunnateer
Binthebucker, who was his mother).

After this letter was read, and I had faithfully told its
contents to the captain, I told the governor that his
Majesty had not mentioned anything that these vessels were
freighted by the Salleeteens, or that they were English,
and that he very well knew that ever since the last truce,
and especially since his last exile, he and his few friends
had relief from them, and which if they had not, they
must in all likelihood have been starved long ago.
Therefore should they then go about to treat the English
after that manner, it would be a means of deterring all
others of that nation from coming thither for the future, and
which if they should do, before they had better informed
him concerning the truth of this affair, he would no doubt
be very angry with the transactors of it, and in all likelihood make then answer for it with the loss of their heads.
This put the governor to a stand, and then his brother
told him he thought it very likely to be true, for that as I
had been brought up with Muley Abdallah from a child, I
therefore knew his temper, so that he would have him take
great care how he acted therein; at which he ordered the

* Muley 'Abd Allah oold el Kunnateer [Lalla Khoneta] Bint el
Bukir.

captain to go again on board, and that he would follow in a very little time with a few of his friends to give him a visit.

At which I came close to him, and gave him the pistol, telling him that the captain had ordered me to give it him in his name, as a present; and to tell him, that he had reserved for him on board the vessel two bottles of superfine English powder.* "Indeed!" said he, "pray then let him keep it from the knowledge of the friends coming with me, or very likely they will desire to come in for their shares;" and just as I was stepping into the boat, to be going off, "Stay," said he, "let the captain go, and you shall follow him in a very little time, for I have ordered a couple of sheep for him." And whilst they were bringing to the waterside, he asked me if I knew anything of a skin of saffron to be on board. I told him no, for that I had never seen nor heard of any such thing. "Prithee," said he, "do me the favour to inquire amongst the ship's company, after the most secret manner you can, and let me know it when I come on board." "That, sir," said I, "you may depend on." And the sheep being brought by this time to the waterside, "Here," said he, "lay hold on them, and carry them to the captain with my service, and tell him that I shall be very glad if he think them worth his acceptance, and also that I fully intend, as I told him just now, to come off to see him in the afternoon." And then, as the saffron was running in my mind, I hailed the boat, and was aboard with the sheep in a very little time, and delivered them with my message to the captain; and then I told him how inquisitive the governor had been with me, concerning some saffron he should have then on board. "What, in the name of God," said he, "are they about to do by me now?" "That, indeed," said I, "I

* *Note* 34.

cannot tell, but that he made such inquiry is most certain." At which the captain knocks in the head of a little cagg, put something into it, headed it up again, and put it into the bottom of the flesh cask, laying all the meat upon it, and the pork in particular at the top. And in a very short time the governor came on board with twelve of his Moorish friends, the captain showing him directly into the cabin, where I was soon called as an interpreter ; and the first question he asked me was, if I had done as I promised him. I told him yes, and that I could not get intelligence of any such thing, and that he must certainly be imposed on. " Well," said he, " as to that, it will soon appear ; " and then he ordered me again upon deck, to discourse his friends ; and the first question they asked me was, if I could tell of any chests of loose clothes, or anything else belonging to the merchants, to be on board. I told them no, for that I had never heard of any such thing.

Then Captain Toobin came upon deck to acquaint them that the governor wanted their company down to drink a cup of tea in the cabin with him, and which, indeed, he was drinking ; however, he ordered for those inquisitive gentry a sufficient quantity of strong Malaga wine to be made very hot, well sugared, and brought in a tea-kettle; when they seemed to sip on at first, as if they did not know what it was, but in a very little time they began to like it, and swallowed it down as infants do their nurse's milk ; so that in an hour's time, or thereabout, they were all of them as merry as you please. Then the governor took his leave, taking with him his powder and his merry companions. By the time they were got to the shore, the tea operated into their noddles to that degree, that they were all (the governor excepted) together by the ears, and there was really between them a very hot combat, which soon made bloody work, they flourishing their scimitars, and cutting one another very severely, which the captain and I saw from the vessel. After they had cut one another very heartily, and very much blunted and gapped their scimitars, they were contented on all sides to give out; when one of them came again on board our vessel, with two of their scimitars, staring like a wild bullock, and reeling like a light ship in a great sea, desiring me, as well as he could speak, to grind them for him. " Yes, sir," said I, " I will with all my heart ; " and which I did to a very good edge indeed. " But pray, sir," said I, " how fell you out ? It is a great pity but what you had ground your swords before you went ashore." " What ? " said he. " I ask you, sir," said I, " how you fell out ? " " Indeed," said he, "I cannot tell, nor, as I believe, none of us all ; " and then he was again handed into the boat, and put on shore with his scimitars.

In a very little time after came off the governor of Ducallah's brother-in-law, bringing with him Sidi ben Raudee, the new governor of Willadea, to be kept there as a prisoner, in order to prevent his running away, for that he had suffered the Genoese brig to sail, contrary to order, saying to me in the Moorish language, " Tollahfee haddah Corran Astah Loggadah Sbaugh ; " *
in English, " Take care of this cuckold till to-morrow morning." So we put him into the ship's hold, and there lodged him on a piece of matting, on the corn. And the next morning he was again ordered on shore, aboard again at night, and the next morning on shore again: when they finding the bait would not take, he was again set at liberty, all this being no more than to try Captain Toobin's fidelity; for, in short, had he suffered him to make an escape, they would no doubt have made a great handle of it, and it would have been very

* T'halla fi had el curran hata Khrudda es-sbah.

much to his prejudice. However, they were disappointed
of their aim, and therefore, without forming any other
designs of that nature, they are now resolved to be more
open and bare-faced, the governor of Ducallah's brother,
and with him thirty men in two boats, coming the next
morning, requiring the captain to set his men at work
in hoisting out the corn; on which the captain ordered
me to ask him if he had any orders from the owners.
He told him no. " Then," said the captain, "I will not
give my consent to let any of it go; but if they would do
it after a forceable manner, it was what he could not help,
but as for any of his men, they should not hoist out one
grain of it, for that he very plainly perceived it was no
more than furnishing the merchants with a plausible
pretence to cheat him of his freight." At which they
offered to use him very rudely; but he bravely stood his
ground, and told them that unless they could produce
such an order he would not meddle in it.

On this the Moors broke open the hatches and fell to
work, and then the skin of saffron came again to be inquired after; and as they could not find it amongst the
corn, as they expected, they rummaged the ship very
strictly. And when they came to the flesh tub, and had
taken off the cover, and saw the pork, they fell a spauling
and spitting, shrinking up their faces, and swearing that
there was nothing in that tub but a salted devil, and ran
from it as if the devil had been in it indeed : and notwithstanding they could not find the saffron, they found the
corn, and carried it all off that day, without leaving us any
for the ship's use.

Now have we an empty ship, no merchant to talk with,
and therefore no further business for me by way of interpreter; so that I thought myself obliged to act very
cautiously, and to expose myself to the view of the Moors

as seldom as possible; though, at the request of the captain, I went to the governor of Ducallah, to tell him that all the ship's corn was taken out and carried away by his brother, without paying one penny freight: and then I told him also that the captain and his people were under very great distress for provision, having nothing on board but a tub of pork, which was so very fat that they could not eat it without bread. "Why," said he, "do you eat pork?" "I eat it," said I, "fah!" shrinking up my face; "however, if I did, I should not eat very much of theirs, they having very little further business for me. But really, sir," said I, "they are under very great distress, and if you do not send them some relief very speedily, they must starve, of course, for they have no money nor credit; insomuch, that I am very apprehensive of losing my little brokerage."

On which he sent the captain aboard two bags of wheat, containing about a quarter or eight bushels, and the next day four bags more, and one bag of beans, which was all we could get from him. And our captain having, on their taking out the corn, sent a letter by a Moor to Monsieur Pedro Pollee, at Saphee, to acquaint him of this hard usage, and to desire his answer how to behave under it, and Muley Abdallah's mother being then there, he directly applied to her. Then in consideration of a sum of money given her, he obtained her order to the governor of Ducallah, that on the ships' masters sending each of them a man to Saphee as hostages, for the better security of each of them paying her forty ducats, to let the ships go, and to hasten with them thither as fast as they could, where they should be new freighted; which was to the captain of a Genoese tartan * then there, as he had freight in before for another

* *Note* 89.

SANTA CRUZ OR AGADÍR IN 1760.

port, very heavy news. For that he could not by any means
stop at Saphee, neither should he be able to produce
the forty ducats, and therefore he earnestly desired that
Captain Toobin would pay it for him, which he would
repay him at Sallee, whither he said he was obliged to go,
and for which he would then give him his promissory
obligations; which was complied with, the obligation
given, and one of our people sent away by land, but none
from the Genoese. But on my telling the governor what
he had done, and that Captain Toobin had given his
honour to pay forty ducats for him, to which end he had
sent one of his people as a pledge before him, the tartan
was permitted to sail with us. And I going privately
aboard in the night, we set sail together, the Genoese for
Sallee, and us for Saphee, where we found our hostage.
During the time of our stay there I was kept close aboard;
however, I had a faithful account every night of what was
acting on shore, as how we were about to take in a new
freight for Sallee; how that our man was, on Captain
Toobin's paying the money for him and the Genoese, again
at liberty; and then our cargo was sent off, such as several
bales of Barbary skins, saltpetre, and in skins a good
quantity of Argon oil.

One evening our captain came on board and took me
into his cabin with him, telling me, poor man, in a very
troubled manner, though I dare say with a great deal of
sincerity, that Monsieur Pedro Pollee had told him that
I was actually on board of his ship. "Therefore, for
God's sake, Tom, take care that you don't let any of the
Moors see your face, for I told him you were not with me,
and that I wondered how any one could invent so base
a lie; that indeed you was with me in the Willadea, and
general on board my ship as a linguist. 'Then, captain,'
said he, 'there lies the mistake;' so that I hope he is

20

again by this time out of mind of it. However, I say, be
sure to keep yourself close, and I hope to be going hence
in a very little time."

The next morning after this discourse, came into the
road a Dutch frigate of twenty guns, who dropped her
anchor, hoisted Dutch colours, and a flag of truce, and
fired a gun with a signal for a boat to come off. However,
as none of the Moors would venture to trust him, Captain
Toobin went off, and found the commander to be one of
his old very intimate acquaintance, and brought ashore his
letters to Elhash Mahomet Wadnoonee,* the governor
of Saphee, relating to the releasement of some Dutch
prisoners lately taken out of another Dutch ship. To
which the captain was answered that they were then up
in the mountains with Muley Abdallah, and that they
knew not how to get at them. On which the Dutch skipper,
seeing he could not get any better satisfaction, sailed with
us the third following day, him to Markadore,† on the
wreck of a Portuguese ship, bound home from the Brazils,
taken by the Argaireens,‡ and by them cast away a little
to the northward of that port, and we for Sallee; where
we beat up in thirteen days, and came to an anchor in the
road, with thirteen Moorish passengers and three Jews on
board, being most of them concerned in the cargo, with
whom I soon got a very intimate acquaintance, telling
them that Captain Toobin had, through very much
entreaty, on account of my promising him to be his
linguist, been so very good as to give me my passage with
them; and then they desired me to be a faithful linguist
for them also. I told them I would with all my heart, if
my business would permit me to remain at Sallee so long,
insomuch that I really believe they took me for their friend

* Hajj Mohammed Wad Nûni.
† *Note 87.*   ‡ *Note 88.*

in good earnest, and that they were not in the least
apprehensive of my intentions.

Here we found the Genoese tartan; and Captain
Toobin desired me to step into our boat and go aboard
her with his service to the captain, and to desire him to
come with me on board his snow, for that as his people
were then very busy in taking out the cargo, he could not
by any means come to him, and to tell him he had
completed his affair with the governor at Saphee, for
which he had brought with him proper vouchers. But he
being then on shore at Sallee, I could not speak with him.
However, his mate told me that he had met with a great
deal of trouble with his merchants on account of his
freight, and that he was very likely to meet with a great
deal more : "therefore," said he, "tell your captain to take
a great deal of care how he behaves with his, for should
they once get him over the bar, they will no doubt use him
after the like manner." All which I faithfully carried back;
and then Captain Toobin sent a letter by one of his
passengers going ashore to an Irish merchant, residing at
Sallee, with the Genoese's promissory obligation and the
governor of Saphee's vouchers enclosed, to demand of
Captain Baptista, the commander of the Genoese tartan,
on his sight thereof, forty ducats to his proper use and
account; and on his payment thereof, to give him up his
obligation; and also another letter enclosed to Baptista
for his so doing. And though he, on his receiving this
order in the morning, acknowledged the debt and promised
to pay the money, yet did he in the afternoon again deny
it; upon which he was secured under safe custody, and
not permitted to go on board; and then he confessed the
debt again, and that he would go directly on board and
deliver to the value thereof in goods as a pledge, till such
time as he got to Gibraltar, and then he would again

redeem it. To which the captain's friend answered him, that as he had behaved so very much like a knave, he would not suffer him to stir thence, till such time as he had paidthe money.

But Baptista finding means to escape, got off to a Moorish justice, swore the debt quite off, and had a pass from him to go aboard his own vessel, which he forthwith did, and directly weighed his anchors, and set sail as fast as he could. All which Captain Toobin seeing, and he having an account from his friend how much like a villain he had behaved, desired me to go aboard him, and once more to demand the money of him ; and in case he still persisted in not paying it, to cut off his boat, and bring her to him.

On which, I taking with me seven other hands, eight muskets, and as many scimitars, went in our boat to the vessel's side, and delivered my message. To which Baptista answered, that the money was safe; which was all I could get from him. Then I ordered one of our hands to step into his boat, cut her off with his scimitar, and let her fall astern; on which, several Argaireen merchants being then on board, they having chiefly freighted her, stood up together with the Genoese sailors, the former with stones, and the latter with muskets in their hands, highly threatening us that in case we did not bring the boat on board again directly, they would knock us all on the head ; at which we also stood up with our muskets ready at our shoulders, presenting the muzzles directly at them; at sight of which they all fell flat on their bellies upon the deck, and notwithstanding they were more than double our number, and in close quarters, yet did we, notwithstanding, bring the boat quite off, without any of them daring so much as to fire one shot at us; but we safely brought her to Captain Toobin's snow.*

* *Note* 89.

It coming towards the evening, and some odd things being still on board, I, as a blind, stepped into a boat which was alongside, wherein were several of the Moorish merchants, just putting off for the shore, in seeming-wise to go with them; and when the merchants asked me where I was going to, I told them first for Sallee, and if I could not there better myself, anywhere else in the country, where I thought I might. " Why," said one of them, " I hope you will not leave us, till such time as we have taken out the small matters we have still remaining on board of the cargo, and if you will remain aboard the ship for the night, you shall be well rewarded for your trouble." " Why," said I, " I thought the cargo had been all out." " No," said he, " and our nephews and two Jews are still on board; and you will oblige us, if you will keep them company." " Very well, gentlemen," said I; " if you think I may be there of any further service to you, I will go aboard again, and remain with them there for the night with all my heart."

So I stepped with a great deal of pleasure into the ship again, at which the nephews, who were by their uncle's orders to remain there for the night with me, seemed to be very glad. Soon after the Moorish boat was gone with the merchants, the captain tipped me the wink to follow him into the cabin; and after he had shut the door close upon us, he began to discourse me after the following manner. " Now, Tom," said he, " you and I must seriously consult together, how I ought to act in this troublesome affair; for these Moorish merchants are, as sure as death, about to play the old one's game with me, and cheat me of my freight; for on my demanding it according to the contents of my charter part, which actually runs, and plainly specifies, that my freight should be every penny paid down at the mast, before they took out any of the cargo. For as I had been so sadly bit by the former villains, I thought it very natural for a burnt child to dread the fire, and therefore I would not before they had thus covenanted take it in; though I now plainly see, to my very great dissatisfaction, it had been all as well left alone; for to be plain with you, I know not whether their honour or bonds are the best, they being both, with men of their principle, where no justice is to be had, very paltry, and not worth one of their blankets. Therefore, happy are they who are got quite out of their country, and out of their hands. This, Tom, you may plainly see, as well as myself, and on my refusing to let any of the cargo go, before they had performed their covenant. You also saw how they broke open my hatches, went into the hold, and carried off almost all of it by force."

"Why, sir," said I, "don't you remember that on their taking out the skins of oil, one of them proving faulty, had leaked most of it out?" "Yes," said he; "what of that, pray?" "Why, sir," said I, "one of the Moors told another that it must be your fault, and that you should answer for it. To which the other replied, that when they had taken out all the cargo, the captain would no doubt be glad to come ashore for his freight, and then they would manage him well enough." "Indeed," said he, "that, Tom, is just as I expected; though, between you and I, it is, I hope, what will never be in their power; not but I am thoroughly persuaded with myself, should they once but get me into their clutches, they would make slaves of us all, and seize my vessel, and all I have in it, to their own vile uses; which, if I can avoid, shall never be in their power. Therefore Tom, what do you think of our putting too all for all, and going to sea this very night!" "Indeed sir," said I, "if you stay here but a very little longer, it will be entirely

out of your power." "And will you stand by me?" said
he. "Yes, sir," said I, "to the last drop of my blood."
"Then," said he, "what shall we do with the five Moors
and the two Jews, a married woman of about twenty-one
years of age, and a young man of about seventeen?" "As
to that, sir," said I, "I would not have you to be under
any the least concern : for I will engage only by myself to
secure them, so as you and your people shall have no more
to do than to weigh the anchors, trim the sails, and manage
the ship."

"Well then, Tom," said he, "I will also first consult
my men;" and after telling them the danger that he
thought himself and all of them in, he proposed his intentions to them, which they very well approved of, and
as readily came into, and fell to consulting the means
without any loss of time; and it was by all agreed on to
weigh our anchors at high water, and push our fortunes.
As we knew the tide would suit our purpose about ten at
night, we got our supper over in season, and every one,
except the watch for the night, seemingly to their rest,
lodging the five Moors, for our better securing them, in the
hold, and the two Jews in the steerage. And when our
appointed time was come, and our men all ready to weigh
the anchors, and trim the sails, Captain Toobin went to
the helm, and I to my post at the hatchway, armed with
a scimitar and two pair of pistols ; and hauling in the
cables, though with as little noise as possible, the Moors
were in a very great hurry, calling aloud to know what we
were doing. "Doing," said I, "about to new moor the
vessel." "New moor her," said they, "what occasion of
that, when she was in a very good berth before ? Therefore
we rather think you are about to run away with her, and to
carry us with you," endeavouring to get themselves upon
deck, when I told them to sing small, and that if any of

them all offered the least resistance, or presumed to stir from the place he was then in, or to make the least noise, I would directly shoot him.

"Therefore," said I, "take hold of the cable's end, and handsomely coil it away;" and which I compelled them to do, though no doubt sore against their inclinations, telling them that they should not be under the least concern or fear of danger, for that if they proved conformable to what they were commanded, I would dare engage to answer for their lives with my own. "But where," said they, "do you intend to carry us?" "Nay, as to that," said I, "I cannot as yet tell; but be that as it will, do you behave civilly and as contentedly as you can, and I will bring you everything you want : for in short there is no harm intended against you." And then I bolted the hatches upon them, and left them for a little while to condole with each other's misfortune; when we all took a cheering tiff to our voyage, and proceeding, pacified the Jews (who also by that time knew their misfortune) as well as we could.

CHAPTER XIII.

Compelled to anchor off Mamora, fresh troubles make their appearance
—Apprehension of an attack from the Moors—Arms are served
out; but a fair wind springing up, Mamora is left behind—Distress of an involuntary lady passenger—In passing Cape Spartel,
those who had never sailed through the Straits before, pay their
footing to those who have—A Jew objects, and what came of his
objection—Gibraltar is reached, and the slave, after twenty-three
years of captivity, is again a free man among his own countrymen—He is cross-questioned by the officials, and claimed as a
Moorish subject by the Emperor's agent—Governor Sabine speaks
a bit of his mind—He is well treated, and arrives in the Thames—
A painful meeting with William Johnson's sister, and a happy
arrival in his native town—The end.

NOW are we under sail with a tolerable leading gale of
wind and strong tide with us, being the 10th of July,
1738, a little after ten o'clock at night, though about daybreak, the wind slackening all at once, and a strong current
setting right in upon the shore, we were obliged to come to
an anchor off Mamora,* in five fathoms water, where we
were obliged to remain all that day, and till two o'clock
the next morning, still in expectation of some boats from
the shore, and which really caused some uneasiness amongst
us, though during this we were not idle, for we got our
arms upon deck, in all twenty-four muskets besides pistols
and scimitars, and put them in complete order, putting

* *Note* 40.

into every one of them a new flint, and charging it with
three musket-shot, keeping them ready on the deck in case
of any visitors coming aboard to salute them, for in short
rather than to be carried back again, we were all thoroughly
resolved to fight it out to the last man; but none of them
coming, they saved us that trouble, and we were through
that means, I think, by far the better off. About two in the
morning, as I said, a fine breeze of wind coming off shore,
we weighed our anchor, and before sunrising were carried
to seaward about five leagues; and then we did not much
fear any of their boats coming after us, and row-galleys we
knew they had none ready.

Now are we, notwithstanding so very little wind, in much
better temper than before, when Madam Luna—which was
the name of the woman—desired me to tell her where we
designed to carry her, and what we intended to do by her,
and if it was not then too late to set her on shore on the
Barbary coast. I told her yes, and that in case it was not,
yet would it be altogether inconsistent with our own safety,
and therefore she could not in reason expect any such
thing; "however, to satisfy you of our intentions, we are
bound for Gibraltar, where you will be better off than to go
back again to Barbary; for as you so very much deserve
your name, you will no doubt be there very well cared for."
"Alas!" said she, "had but I my little son with me (whom
she sent ashore at Sallee) I should not so much mind it!"
"Why really, madam," said I, "since things have so fallen
out, I think it would be acting the prudent part in you, to
forget him for a short time as much as you can, and to
consider that as he is among his friends he will be well
cared for, and very likely be better off than to be here. And
as to your own part, you need not fear of being as well
used where you are, your beauty being a very sufficient
protection." "But cannot you really," said she, "put me

on shore to Barbary." "Indeed, madam," said I, "it cannot be done; and if you will be pleased to step upon the deck, you will soon be convinced of the truth of it." Then she gave me her hand, and I lifted her up, and after she had taken a full prospect of the distance of the land, she seemed to be much better tempered.

Now are we sailing slowly on with very little wind till the beginning of the eleventh day, when we were got off of Cape Spartell; on sight of which, it being an old custom for those who had never before passed through the Straits Mouth to pay for the benefit of those who had, a bottle of brandy and a pound of sugar, or half a crown in money in lieu thereof,* we held a consultation thereon, and found all saving the two Jews to have done it before, and being resolved not to pass this custom by, the male Jew was required to pay it. "Pay it!" said he; "how can that be when I have no money? You should have told me this at Sallee, and then I would have taken care to have been better provided." "Indeed," said the sailors, "you are a very cunning fellow, and therefore answer us, will you pay it or will you not, or will the captain and Madam Luna, or either of them, pass their word for you?" which, by way of making more diversion, they seemed both to be very backward to do.

It was therefore agreed on all hands for him to undergo the usual discipline, which was, in case of refusal, to be hoisted up to the main-yard-arm, then to be let run amain into the sea, then hoisted up again, and repeated a third time; and then to have his face well daubed over with lampblack and tallow: in order to which a rope was tied about his waist, and the tackle hooked to it, which made him to look after a very piteous manner, as being no doubt sadly afraid he should be disciplined in good earnest.

* *Note* 41.

And being hoisted up about half way, the captain was so good as to pass his word for him; upon which he was let down again, though this did not very much please Madam Luna, she seeming to blame the captain very much for it. As to her own particular part, her bright beauty was to all of us a very sufficient cordial, and therefore it was by all allowed for her to go scot free.

This pastime being at an end, and passing most of that night in merry talk about, we about ten o'clock the next forenoon, being the 21st day of July, 1738, arrived safe in Gibraltar Bay, where my deliverer (for so must I now call him) and his people bid me very heartily, and I dare say most sincerely, welcome, when I fell to my knees, offering up my most hearty thanks to Almighty God for my so wonderful and miraculous deliverance and the sight once more of Christian land; being really as it were at a stand with myself if it were more than an imaginary dreaming in my cave at Santa Cruz, and I had really a debate with myself if I was well awake. However, I was soon confirmed in its reality, and that I was actually in sight of Gibraltar, and soon about to set my foot on shore in that garrison, where my deliverer, in order to prepare my way, went directly on shore, and after he had answered to the governor concerning his own affairs, he told him that he had a poor Christian slave aboard his vessel that was taken by the infidels and carried into Barbary in the twelfth year of his age, which was then more than twenty-two years ago; that I had undergone a great deal of hardship, and that had he not very accidentally and most opportunely happened to meet me there, he should not in all likelihood have been permitted to come from thence himself, so that our meeting on both sides was very extraordinarily providential.

Then the governor (as my deliverer told me) ordered

him to bring me ashore; however, as he lodged ashore
that night, I knew nothing of it till the next morning. About two hours after we were at an anchor, came
alongside of our vessel an English sailor with whom I
happened about a few months before to have some small
acquaintance at Santa Cruz; and on his seeing me on
the deck he came on board to bid me welcome to
Gibraltar; when I asked him if he could not give me
an account of the ships then there, and if he knew if any
of them belonged to Falmouth. He told me yes, there
was one Captain Pye, but that be was bound for Ham-
burgh, and whether he intended to call at Falmouth in
his way or not he could not tell. So that for my better
satisfaction I desired some of our people to go aboard his
vessel; but he being ashore at Gibraltar, I could not
hear any further of him that night.

Early the next morning (being Sunday) our mate went
ashore, and after he had spoken with my deliverer, came
directly off to fetch me; and after securing the Moors in
the hold, and taking my leave of Madam Luna, I stepped
into the boat with him. Here it is impossible for me (or
at least for anybody but myself) to describe the excessive
joy I felt during all the time of our rowing to the shore,
though all may suppose it, after my so long and grievous
servitude amongst the Barbarians, to be more than ordinary.
And now are we come to the landing-place at the Water
Port, where, offering to land, I was denied by the sentinels,
telling me that till they had orders for my so doing, they
would not suffer any Moor to land. "Moor," said I;
"you are very much mistaken in that, for I am as good
a Christian, though I am dressed in the Moorish garb, as
any of you all. Therefore, pray," said I, "suffer me
once more to set my foot on Christian land." "Indeed,"
said they, "we cannot, if you was our brother."

Then one of our people (for whom my deliverer had taken
a license the day before, and as no doubt he had done for
all the rest, and amongst whom I was most likely also
included) got out of the boat, ran to the office, and was
soon back again with a note for the sergeant of the guard,
on which I was directly permitted to land; when I fell
on my knees, and after the best and sincerest manner I
could, offered up my most humble and hearty thanks to
God for my deliverance and happy landing; being now
thoroughly convinced that I was at last delivered out of
the hands of the infidels, though I very soon after most
unexpectedly met with some small discontent through
their means, though which, as it happened, did not prove
of any great signification, as you will by and by hear.

Now is the sergeant of the guard very inquisitive with
me concerning my misfortunes; and when I had given
him a short account of them, and he had returned his
hearty congratulations for my deliverance, I passed
through three other sentries and got into the garrison;
and going directly with one of our people to my deliverer's lodgings (where I found him washing his face
and hands), he took me directly in his arms, embracing
me, and with a very hearty, and I dare say sincere, kiss
bid me welcome to Gibraltar. "But, Tom," said he,
"you were yesterday, on my coming ashore, demanded of
the governor as one of the Bashaw of Tangier's subjects."
"Indeed, sir," said I; "by whom, pray?" "Why,"
said he, "by one Abramico, a Jew, his linguist; but don't
you trouble yourself about it, for I dare engage to send
you safe home to England, in spite of all the Jews in
Barbary." "Indeed, my deliverer," said I, "you surprise me, for you may suppose I could not in the least
imagine any such thing." "Foh," said he, "never mind
it, for as you are a subject to the King of Great Britain,

I am very well assured the governor will not suffer you to go with him." "But pray, sir," said I, "does the governor know anything of it as yet?" "Yes," said he, "and when the Jew demanded you of him as one of the Bashaw's subjects, I heard him give him for answer that he could not imagine how that could be, asking the Jew what countryman you were. 'What countryman?' said the Jew; 'an Englishman.' 'An Englishman!' said the governor, 'and a subject to the Bashaw of Tangier! Pray, how can that be? I tell you he is a subject to the King of Great Britain, my royal master, and thither will I send him.' And so far, Tom, is actually true, therefore don't you trouble yourself in the least about it; for, in short, you have already got so tender a regard amongst the inhabitants here, on account of all your sufferings hitherto, without their hearing anything from your own mouth by way of confirmation, that you need not doubt of their most Christianlike assistance."

And then Mr. Cunningham, the minister, came in, and with him several of the head officers of the garrison, with whom my deliverer was before very well acquainted. There being amongst them one Mr. Beaver, a gentleman belonging to the virtualling-office, he asked me how long I had been in Barbary, with whom and when taken, and if I did not know Tom Osborne, of Fowey, there. I told him I had been there almost twenty-three years, that I was taken with John Pellow, my uncle, in the second year of the reign of King George the First, and that we found Tom Osborne at Mequinez, he being taken some short time before us, with Captain Richard Sampson,* of Fowey. To which Mr. Beaver answered, that all I had said was undoubtedly true, for that he knew Tom Osborne very

---

* Captain Sampson was, with twenty-four other commanders of ships, redeemed in the year 1721 by Commodore Stewart.

well, and that he had heard him, several times after his
releasement and return, to talk about me. On which the
minister and he gave me their words to stand my friends;
and which, indeed, they did after the most Christianlike
manner, advising me to present a petition to General
Sabine,* the governor, which the minister readily offered
me his service to present, and which my deliverer got
directly drawn, and was by the parson accordingly delivered. From the governor he brought me back two gold
ducats as his charity. Then I went to church and returned
thanks to Almighty God before the congregation for my
deliverance, and received the charity of several of them.
After which there was a general contribution; though I
did not stay there so long as to receive the whole of it, as
I shall mention hereafter.

The charity of these Christianlike people extended
even to the highest degree; for on my proposal of going
thence in a small vessel for Falmouth, they would not by
any means suffer it, but that I should wait for the opportunity of a ship of force bound home, or of a man-of-war
for Lisbon, whither they would send me well recommended
to the British Envoy, in order to my being by him sent
home to Falmouth in one of the packet boats; which,
though I waited there twenty odd days, did not happen.

The day after my landing Captain Pye came ashore,
with whom I had the pleasure of conversing for some short
time, as also with the boat's crew, and they were all of
them very civil to me; but as his vessel was of no force,
and my benefactors had before absolutely determined that
I should go in none but such as was, I did not urge it to
him. However, I humbly entreated that he or some other
of his people would, in case they touched at Falmouth,
inform my friends of my happy deliverance and escape

* *Note* 42.

thither out of the hands of the infidels, and that I believed I should be sent home by way of Lisbon, so that
they might expect me in one of the packet boats; which I
found, at my coming home, they were so very good to
remember. However, lest they might not touch at
Falmouth, my good friend Mr. Beaver was so kind to
write a very tender letter to his friend at Looe, in
Cornwall, to the same purport, and which was conveyed
by his friend to my friends in Penryn.

During my stay at Gibraltar I saw Mr. Abramico, the
Jew, generally every day, and whom I found had more
than an ordinary notion with himself of carrying me back
with him to Barbary, often threatening me behind my
back, as I had heard by several people, with the most
cruel death; whereat I was so exasperated that I really
shunned him all I could, lest I should let loose my rage
upon him and happen to do him some bodily mischief,
and thereby bring myself to further trouble—not that I
was, as he no doubt believed, under the least fear of him,
but really on account of my letting loose my rage upon
him. However, what could I do when I had every day
so many repeated accounts, by way of my friends, of his
insolence? Insomuch that I thought I could never forgive
myself if I did not give him some gentle correction;
which, on my discoursing one of my very good friends
immediately after, I was more absolutely determined in,
he being come but that very minute from the Jew, who,
he said, had been confirming his former sentence on me;
and I very soon after meeting him in the street, the first
salutation I gave him was a hearty box on the ear,
seconded by a Cornish tip, which brought him head-
foremost to the ground, and beat it against the stones very
severely; insomuch, that had not some of my friends
persuaded me to the contrary, I should certainly have

21

done him far greater mischief: though this, I think, did him no hurt in the main, but rather on the contrary a great deal of good, for he really took special care to bridle his tongue and keep himself out of my clutches for the future as much as he could. And now was this shrewd combat in everybody's mouth, as how I had corrected him very justly, and that he deserved a great deal more.

Now are the worthy gentlemen raising contributions for my benefit, and as the generality of the people were very charitably disposed, there was gathered, no doubt, some hundreds of dollars; but before the contributions were finished, the good ship *Euphrates*, Captain Peacock commander, from Turkey for London, mounting twenty-six guns, came to an anchor in the road, when my deliverer, and some other of my friends, went at my request directly on board, earnestly soliciting the captain in my favour for a passage; for that as I had undergone so long and grievous a captivity in Barbary, and was so fortunately escaped thither, they humbly hoped that he would not refuse me so Christianlike a kindness as to further me with him to my native country; or, if he should not happen to touch at Falmouth, or any other port in the west of England, to land me at London. Which, as my deliverer told me, Captain Peacock readily came into, and he as soon hastened on shore to me with the welcome news; and doubting lest my very great enemy, Abramico, might, by way of bribe or otherwise, induce anybody to show me some foul play, it was agreed by my friends, and thought highly necessary on all hands, for me to go on board directly; and which, indeed, as agreeing so very much with my own inclinations, after taking my leave of my deliverer and my worthy benefactors, I forthwith did, and was by the captain very kindly received.

On this my so sudden departure, I was obliged to leave most of my contribution money behind me; however, I had some, which was of very excellent service to me, by way of providing me some few necessaries, and sea stores; though I wished many times since, and especially on my poor reception on our arrival at London, that I had stayed there a little longer; which, as they were very considerable, would have been of no small benefit to my present unhappy circumstances. However, I am well satisfied that my worthy benefactors at Gibraltar are gentlemen of so much strict honour and goodness, as to remit it me on my petitioning them thereon.

And now am I on board the *Euphrates*, and under sail for my so long desired and longed-after island. But we met with very high and contrary winds, and, according to the season of the year, a very high and troubled sea; though our ship being in all points well provided (lodgings only excepted), I did not much mind it, she being so full between decks, and close stowed with cotton, that the people had but just room through it to their cabins or hammocks, which made it so very sultry hot that I could by no means bear it. Therefore, for my better breathing I generally took up at nights with the boat on the booms, where I lay me down to my rest covered over with an old sail; and as we had abundance of wet weather, scarce a night passed without my being sufficiently wetted, and standing more than an equal chance of my being washed overboard. However, I bore it with Christian patience, and as this part of my sufferings was in order to put an end to and sum up all the rest, I was not only contented, but well pleased therewith, rather than to suffer the smothering between decks; for I might have lodged between decks if I would, and therefore it was my own choice.

And now is it come to the twenty-fourth day of our

passage, when I heard called out aloud from aloft the very much pleasing and long-expected word "Land," and which proved to be the western Land's End of England, or Cape Cornwall; and the wind favouring to carry us up the Channel, we crowded a great sail, passed by Falmouth, and kept on all upon the same tack till we got off of the Bill of Portland; when, on account of one of our people falling overboard, we were obliged to bring to; and on our throwing out some empty kegs and rails of timber, he caught hold on one of them; then we hoisted out our boat, and had him well on board again. After this accident (which, I thank God, was the first and the last we met with during our passage from Gibraltar) we kept on with this favourable gale to the Downs, passed through, and cast anchor at the Nore, where Captain Peacock found his wife with her brother on board of a man-of-war (of which he was commander), waiting his coming. The next tide we got to Gravesend, and the next up the river Thames to Deptford, where our ship was to be disburthened of her cargo, it being the thirty-first day after our departure from Gibraltar.

Here, as being altogether unacquainted at London, I remained on board the ship seven days; during which, on some of the sailors publishing on shore of their bringing me home with them, and it reaching the ears of William Johnson's sister, she came on board to inquire after him, asking me if I had ever seen him in Barbary. " Seen him, madam!" said I; "yes, yes, to my sorrow; for had I not, it would in all likelihood have prevented me of many years' grievous captivity." " Lord!" said she, "what was the matter?" "Matter!" said I; "matter enough, I think; for he not only refused to embrace a most glorious and certain means of getting off himself, but (too much like the dog in the manger) treacherously,

and contrary to his oath, hindered those that would!"
"Why," said she, "I hear he is very much cut in the
face." "Yes, madam," said I, "and so he is, though, I
think, not half so much as he deserved." "Pray," said
she, "tell me how it happened, and what it was for."
And then I told her the story from the beginning to the
end, and that I was sorry I had not cut off his head. At
which the pretty girl wept. However, to comfort her
again, I told her that her brother was soon well of the
wounds I gave him, and set at liberty through my means,
and that unless it were his own fault, she might very
likely see him home again in a very little time. At which
her countenance began to clear up, and she seemed to
behave with much better temper, though she was, no
doubt, not a little displeased with me, and ready in her
heart to revenge, as she termed it, her brother's
injuries.

Now I went ashore at Deptford, and going directly to
church, returned public thanks to God for my safe arrival
in Old England, and received the charity of the minister
and parish clerk, staying in the town eight days longer;
during which I was very civilly entertained by Mr.
William James, a Cornishman, Captain Peacock's steward;
and amongst all the vessels bound down the river, finding
none bound for Falmouth, I asked my friend, Mr. James,
what course I had best to steer. He told me my most
likely way to get a passage would be for me to go to Beels'
Wharf, a little below London Bridge on the Southwark
side of the river, and there I might very likely find one or
more of the Cornish tin vessels, or some other bound for
Plymouth. So I went directly thither, and soon found, to
my very great satisfaction, three tin vessels, and on discoursing the people, I understood that the captains were
all on the other side of the water, and that I might have a

further account of them at the King's Head in Pudding
Lane, near the Monument.

Passing over London Bridge, I soon got to the house,
and luckily found one Captain Francis, of Penzance,
who was commander of one of them, named the *Truro*.
And after I had told him my name, he was extremely
civil to me, and readily offered me a passage in his
vessel with him down to Cornwall; which I most
heartily thanked him for, and with joy gladly accepted
of it, telling him I should depend thereon, and that I
would be sure to give my attendance accordingly. But
as I found he could not sail in ten days, I, through the
advice of some of my new acquaintance, went to the Navy
Office, praying the Commissioners' kind introducing me to
his Majesty; to which they, after they had discoursed me,
seemed to be pretty well inclined, ordering me to come to
them again, as indeed I did again and again, though all
I could get from them at the last was the very extraordinary
favour of a hammock on board of a man-of-war.

I told them that I was very much obliged to them, and if
I could not get a livelihood through other means on *terra
firma*, but must be again obliged to go to sea, that a man-of-
war should be my choice of all other ships; for as I had
never made but a piece of a voyage in a merchantman, and
that so very unfortunate, I did not care to encounter with a
second, which if I should, and again fall into the hands of
the Moors, it would soon be out of my power to encounter
with a third. Then I fully resolved with myself to give
these worthy gentlemen no further trouble, but to hasten
as fast as I could home to the place of my nativity, there
to get proper vouchers and recommendatory letters to
some worthy person, and return therewith, in order to his
introducing me and my petition.

At my going out of the office, I chanced to meet in the

street one of Elhash Abaulcodah Perez, the Morocco
ambassador's nephews,* and whom, as I had been so well
acquainted with him before in Barbary, you may suppose
I was very glad to see, even much more than ever I was to
see him in Barbary. He very earnestly entreating me to
go with him to visit his uncle and the rest of my old
acquaintance, I told him I fully intended to do it, if I had
not met him there. " However," said I, " it may now be
so much the better for me, through means of your introducing me." So I went directly with him, and was by the
old man very kindly received ; and after he had discoursed
me so far as he thought fit, as asking me how I got off,
and the like, he told me that he was very glad I was
delivered out of an unhappy country, and that he wished
himself in no happier condition than I was, charging his
people to make me very welcome, and if I was disposed to
take up with his house altogether as to my eating and
drinking, it would please him very much ; though this I
did not care much to accept of, neither did I, after a blunt
manner, refuse it, answering him with a low bow.

And after I had dined there that day on my favourite dish,
cuscassoe, and some English dishes, I returned to my lodgings in Pudding Lane ; where I had not been but a very little
time, before a gentleman came in, congratulating me on my
being so near to be introduced to his Majesty, and he was
soon seconded by several others. I humbly thanked them
(as supposing it only their pleasure to say so by way of
merriment), and that I wished it were true, though I very
much doubted the contrary, by reason I could get nobody to
introduce me. " No!" said they. " Why, it is actually in
the newspapers!" " Indeed!" said I. " Yes," said they,
" it is." On which the newspaper was directly brought
forth, and I read in it the following paragraph, viz., " A

* *Note* 48.

man is now in town, lately arrived from Gibraltar, in the *Euphrates*, Captain Peacock, escaping there from Barbary, where he had been a slave twenty-five years, being taken by the Moors in the tenth year of his age, and is to be presented to his Majesty one day this week." This I soon found to be one of Mr. Newswriter's truths; for which I told the printer that I thought him very much to blame, for that I had given him no such licence, neither could I, without asserting a very great falsity; and as to his Majesty, I believed he knew nothing of the matter.—After this I waited on the Morocco ambassador several times, and was always by him and his people kindly received.

Now is Captain Francis ready to fall down the river. The first tide we got to Gravesend, and the next to the Nore, and the third over the Flats and into the Downs, and thence with a favourable gale kept sailing till we got off the Start, where the wind taking us right ahead, and blowing very hard, we let go our anchor, and rid it out there two days, when we moved thence, and got that day off Plymouth, and the next, being Sunday, we got about four o'clock in the afternoon safe into Falmouth Pier; whence being to Penryn, the place of my nativity, no more than two miles, I got to the town in the evening.

And as my father's house was almost quite at the other end of the town—perhaps about half a mile—I was, before I could reach it, more than an hour; for notwithstanding it was almost quite dark, I was so crowded by the inhabitants that I could not pass through them without a great deal of difficulty—though this, I must own, was of a different and far more pleasing nature to me than my first entrance into Mequinez, every one, instead of boxing me and pulling my hair, saluting me, and after a most courteous manner bidding me welcome home, being all very inquisitive with me if I knew them. Which, indeed, I did not, for I was so very young at my departure, and my captivity and the long interval of time had made so very great an alteration on both sides, that I did not know my own father and mother, nor they me; and had we happened to meet at any other place without being pre-advised, whereby there might be an expectation or natural instinct interposing, we should no doubt have passed each other, unless my great beard might have induced them to inquire further after me.

And now is the so long lost sheep again restored to his owners, after his long straying and grievous hardships amongst those monsters and ravenous wolves of infidelity, and safely returned to his parents, in the town of his nativity, being the 15th day of October, 1738, and the twelfth year of the reign of our Sovereign Lord King George the Second.

To look back upon and seriously to consider the years of my captivity, is so frightful and amazing, that all must allow that nothing but the Almighty protection of a great, good, all-seeing, most-sufficient, and gracious God could have carried me through it or delivered me out of it. Therefore to Him be the glory, honour, and praise, and may He so order my heart as always to continue a lively remembrance thereof, and so order my ways to live up to His Divine precepts during the remainder of this mortal life, that after all these my sufferings ended here, I may be crowned with a glorious immortality in the kingdom of HEAVEN.

FINIS.

NOTES.

NOTES.

—–••—–

(1) *Sallee and the Journey to Mequinez,* pp. 50–53.—" Sallee is built on the banks of the Guerrou, which falls from the mountains of the Zaoyias, and divides it into two parts. That on the north side is called by the natives Sela [S'la], but by us Sallee. It is encompassed by good walls, about six fathoms high and two yards and a half thick, composed of clay, red sand and lime, worked together after the manner of the country. On the top of the walls are battlements flanked with good towers; the other part of the town which lies on the south side of the river is called Raval, and occupies a much larger compass than the former. Within the circumference of this town are abundance of gardens, and a large field, where they might sow corn enough to serve fifteen hundred men. Its walls are very ancient; the natives say they were built by the first Christians who were brought out of Europe by the generals of Jacob Almanzor, king of Arabia Felix, who conquered Spain. On the south-east quarter stands a high tower called Hasans, which serves as a land-mark for ships to come in. At the foot of this mountain are docks for building ships, and for them to winter in. The ascent of this hill is so gentle that a man may ride on horseback to the top.

" Sallee has at present two castles, the old and the new. The old one stands directly at the mouth of the river Guerrou, next to which its walls are built on rocks, and very lofty, sheltering the governor's house, which joins to them, from any cannon-shot. This castle is very irregular, being built according as the ground would permit. The walls fronting the river are for the most part of square stones, with several towers built by Muley Semein. Within this castle, and before its principal gate, is a high fort, which commands the town. Below, next the sea, on the point of the rock facing the bar, is a bastion, mounted with five pieces of cannon, to secure the vessels which come to·an anchor in the road, and cover the retreat of the Corsairs, when pursued by the Christians. The walls next the sea are low, and very easy to be scaled, heaps of dung and earth lying against them, almost of the same height. It is destitute of fresh water, except what they save in a large cistern, which receives all the rain falling on the flat roofs of the houses. There is also a well, but water is brackish, and serves only for the cattle. The new castle is situated on south-west side of the town. It was built by Muley Archy, is square, flanked with good towers, and has battlements like the walls of the town. There is a communication from one castle to the other by a high wall, flanked with two towers, and built upon arches, under which the people pass when they go to walk upon the strand. There are in this castle twelve pieces of brass cannon. On the west side, before the breach on the town wall, on the edge of the sea, stands another bastion on a rock, but neglected of late, which renders the taking of this part of Sallee very easy. The chief riches of this place consist in its piracies, the Sallee Rovers [the Salletines, or Slani, as they call themselves] being the most expert and daring of any on the Barbary coast."

This note is appended to the original edition of Pellow's work, and is evidently an accurate description of the place when he was so unfortunate as to visit it. The town as it at present exists is very well described by Mr. H. C. Browne in the *English Illustrated Magazine* for February, 1890, pp. 396–402. What Pellow and earlier writers call "Raval" or "Arraval" is now known as Rabat, and is still the side of the river on which the Europeans reside. M. Charant, a French merchant who lived in Morocco only a few years after the last of the Moors were driven out of Andalusia, confirms the belief that it was enlarged by the latter by arrangement with their African countrymen, who continued to inhabit Sallee in amity until in due time the two towns were at daggers drawn. The river "Guerrou" is the modern Bou-ragrag. But in former times it commonly bore

A Pirate Zebek of Sallee.

that name, the Bou-ragrag of which it is now regarded as a tributary (just as the Missouri is of the Mississippi) being then considered the less important stream. Lorshia seems to have been a mere country place or hamlet—or, as the word, written in corrupt Arabic (*Larsah*) might signify, a garden. It is evidently the same place by a stream called in the itinerary of the "Religieux de l'ordre de Notre-Dame-de-la-Mercy" (1724), "Larga." The forest of Sallee or Mamora is still in existence, a haunt of robbers and wild beasts—lions, it is said, among the number—and so dangerous that travellers hesitate to pass through it without a strong escort. When the refractory Zemmúr tribe are visited by the Sultan's tax-gatherers, they often retreat into its fastnesses. The river Teffilfílle is of course the Wad Tilfíl, and the Darmusultan the Dâr-es-Solt'âna ("House of the Sultana"—the mother of Muley Ismaïl), a now abandoned building, erected as a shelter for travellers. But though the political divisions of Morocco have been often changed, to describe the modern province of Beni-Hassan as "Wolelsager" must have arisen through some mistake. Can he have heard the Zemmúr, the Beni-Hassan, or other people through whose country he was passing, contemptuously spoken of as the "Woled saghir"—the "little tribe"—and imagined that this was the name of the province? Yet he must have traversed this region several times. The "Garnoe" (pp. 8, 18) who so frightened the Moors was Captain Delgarno (not "Delgardenoor"), who with his twenty-gun frigate exercised so wholesome a terror over the Sallee men that they never ventured over the bar when he was known to be in the vicinity. Moorish mothers used to frighten naughty children by threatening to "give them to Garnoe."

(2) *Mequinez* (Maknas of the Moors), p. 53.—"Mequinez," Windus wrote in 1720, " stands about twelve leagues westward of Fez, and was of small note before the Emperor chose to build his palace there ; though according to Leo Africanus, it was about two hundred years ago a place of considerable trade and riches, but since almost ruined by the civil wars, and different sorts of government that obtained in the country. It is situated in a delightful plain, having a very serene and clear air, which made the Emperor rather make it his place of

residence than Fez, and now it is in a more flourishing condition than ever, being the metropolis of a large empire, between two and three miles in circumference, and containing about 300,000 inhabitants, surrounded by an ordinary wall, and separated by a road from the negro town, so called from the Emperor's black troops (on which he principally depends) being quartered there. To which the Bashaws and Alcaydes resort with the tributes and presents every two or three years, according to the Emperor's pleasure. In the middle of the city live the Jews, having a place to themselves, the gates of which are locked at night, which privilege they also have in most of the cities of this Emperor's dominions. They have an alcayde to guard their gates, and protect them against the common people, who otherwise would plunder them; for they live in great subjection, it being death for them to curse or lift up a hand against the meanest Moor; so that the boys kick them about at their pleasure, against which they have no other remedy but to run away. They are obliged to pull off their shoes whenever they pass by a mosque, and to wear black clothes and caps; nor are they allowed the use of horses."

The city (containing about 40,000 people) is now one of the ordinary capitals or residences of the Sultan. It is also the treasure city of the empire, the vaults of the palace containing considerable quantities of coin and other valuables, though by no means so much as rumour affirms, civil war, and the necessity which the Sultan found, on fighting his way to the throne, of purchasing the goodwill of powerful personages, having kept the balance low. In those days Jews, in spite of the contumely with which they were treated, played a much more prominent part in the government of Morocco than they do at the present day. Many of them were farmers of the customs, Consular agents, or merchants to the Emperor, and they were almost the only interpreters to be had, a fact which these sharp-witted people were not slow to use to their own advantage. Some even had much influence about the palace. One of them was this Ben Hattar, or Benatar, treasurer of the court (p. 15), who figures prominently in the by-ways of diplomatic history. Windus tells an amusing story of him and a rival co-religionist.

"They have in this country," as they have still in another

form, or had until lately, " a most inhuman custom, viz., that any man has the liberty of buying another and all his effects, to do what he pleases with him, by giving a certain price to the Emperor, or the governor of the place he lives in. Which custom is practised all over the empire among the Moors and Jews; whereby the enjoyment of life or fortune is not only precarious, but a man is liable in an instant to fall into the extremest degree of misery, at the pleasure of any one who (prompted either by covetousness or malice) will be at the expense of buying another, and run the risk of being reimbursed out of the effects of the person he buys; in which case they go to the bashaw, alcayde, or governor of a province, and bargain with him (for so much money) to have the person they have a mind to; upon receipt of which the bashaw will deliver the wretch into the hands of the buyer, to do what he pleases with him. So that the bought man is frequently tortured in the cruellest manner to make him discover what money he has.

" One Memaran being formerly chief favourite, had the sole command of the Jews; but seeing Ben Hattar, another Jew, boldly push himself forward, and fearing a rival in the Emperor's favour, he endeavoured to destroy him, and offered the Emperor so many quintals of silver for his head. Upon which he sent for Ben Hattar, and telling him that a sum of money was bid for his head, he resolutely answered, that he would give twice as much for the person's who offered it. Then the Emperor, bringing them together, took the money from both, and told them they were a couple of fools, and bid them be friends. Which made Ben Hattar desire Memaran's daughter in marriage, who being granted to him, they now between them govern the Jews of his dominions with absolute authority."

A similar tale, often told in Morocco, is that of the conscientious Moorish gaoler who served two clients, and kept his word with both. Among the prisoners in his custody was a homicide, the son of a rich man, who, after the fashion of the country, offered the gaoler a handsome bribe to permit the murderer to escape. The bribe was duly accepted and a day fixed for his release. Meantime he went to the son of the murdered man, and received from him another fee for telling him when the first incident was to come off. He then conducted the prisoner outside, where he was promptly stabbed

22

by the avenger of blood. "I set him free," he explained to the expostulating father who just then arrived on the scene ; "surely it was his own business to take care of his life afterwards? In'êshallah !"   Muley Ismaïl was much helped by the Jews, and to the end of his life notably under their influence, while the chief advisers of Sidi Mohammed and many minor officials were Hebrews.

(8) *The Emperor's Palace*, p. 59.—Muley Ismaïl is said to have had, first and last during his long lifetime, "no less than eight thousand wives [or inmates of the harem], by whom he had nine hundred sons and about three hundred daughters. This prodigious number of children might pass for a fable was there not a certain proof of it, viz., the register of a particular tax which this province laid upon the Jews to be paid by way of presents on the birth of every one of his children, to wit, a pair of gold pendants, or ear-bobs, a pearl, and two thin plates of gold, on which were engraved some wishes or prayers in favour of the child and its mother.   The value of such a present amounted to about fifteen pounds for a son.   That which they were obliged to make on the birth of a daughter was not so considerable, the ear-bobs being only of silver, and the two plates of the same metal, and no pearl."   The number of sons has by other authorities been reduced to 520, and the ladies of the harem to four thousand, though these estimates are little better than guesses.   The palace of Sherrers as it existed early in the eighteenth century is fully described in Windus's "Journey to Mequinez," pp. 100–106, the long note appended to the original edition of Pellow's narrative being, like most of these addenda, taken from that volume.   This building, or collection of buildings—for it contained fifty palaces, each having its own baths and mosques, and independent of the main structure—comprised a stable or "Aroua" capable, according to Aboulqâsem ben Ahmed Ezziâni, of accommodating twelve thousand horses, including granaries and store-rooms.   This once noble imperial quarter is now a mass of ruins, very well described in M. de la Martiniere's recent volume.

(4) *Cruelties of Muley Ismaïl*, p. 68.—These and a host of

even more horrible tortures are described by many contemporary writers as practised by this savage monarch and his successors. The modern Moorish sovereigns are less addicted to cruelty, but curious tales are told of nails wrenched out by pinchers, of splinters driven in beyond the quick, of hands rotted off in raw-hide bags filled with quicklime and salt, mangling by wild beasts; of the " wooden jellabia," a box lined with sharp spikes into which a Kaïd unwilling to disgorge his wealth is placed, and even of burning, baking in ovens, and crucifixion having been occasionally followed in days not so very remote as not to be remembered by living men.

(5) *Commodore Stewart's Embassy*, pp. 65, 72.—In this embassy of Commodore Stewart's, Pellow had a certain share, though excluded from the good offices of the ambassador owing to his having "turned Moor"—all renegades being recognized as subjects of the Prince of True Believers, and therefore for their soul's sake not permitted to return among the infidels. For he was constantly about the Emperor's person during the stay of the mission in Mequinez. But he " passed it by in his journal" because, as he told the editor of his MS., " I have matter enough concerning my own adventures (over and above the small share I had in that), and such I hope (being the plain and natural truth, without the least mixture of romance or affectation) as will in no wise be unacceptable to the reader." The original editor of the narrative, however, thought fit to " pad " it out with a long extract from Windus's account of the mission,* which we have not considered it necessary to reprint. In all, the ambassador ransomed 296 English captives, " being what were left alive and had not turned Moors of those who had been taken in about seven years' war," including twenty-five commanders of ships. Among the latter was Captain Henry Boyd, who made the sketches of Alcazar, Mequinez, &c., engraved in " Several Voyages to Barbary " (1786).

(6) *Moorish Surgery*, p. 70.—Almost the only remedy practised

* " A Journey to Mequinez, the Residence of the present Emperor of Fez and Morocco, on the occasion of Commodore Stewart's Embassy thither for the Redemption of the British Captives in the year 1721 " (London : Printed by Jacob Tonson, 1725).

is the burning of different parts of the body with a red-hot iron. The Moorish doctor selling charms written on scraps of dirty paper for the cure of internal diseases, and with his "actual cautery" in the fire before him, ready to apply it with equal readiness to the horse and to his rider, is a familiar sight at any market in Morocco.

(7) *Henna*, p. 76.—This plant (*Lawsonia inermis*) is now grown all over Morocco as an article of commerce. The colour it imparts is, however, not black, but reddish orange.

(8) *Horses*, p. 88.—Most of these remarks about horses seem to have been interpolated by the editor from the information contained in his usual authority.

(9) *Wild Animals*, p. 84.—The "tygers" which so many old writers on Morocco mention, are not the Asiatic animals of that name ; they are leopards (Nemeur). Even Bruce talked of "tigers" in Africa. Jackals (Dib), hyænas (Debaâ), wild cats (El Cat el berranee) and foxes (Thaleb) are, however, sufficiently common. There is, indeed, a fox-hunting club at Tangier, and Major Gilbard informs us that in 1858 the Calpe Club hounds, in a meet they had on the African side of the Strait, "had a splendid run with a wolf—forty-seven minutes with only one check—the distance traversed being nine miles over a very rough country." But I do not know any species which inhabit Barbary, and in M. Lastate's "Etude" (*Actes de la Société Linnéenne de Bordeaux*, vol. xxxix. pp. 129–289), which gives a list of all the mammals of that region known up to the year 1885, no wolf is mentioned.

(10) *Province of Talgror*, p. 86.—This must be either a mistake or some obsolete designation, though I am not aware that any division of Dukkala (often as it has been broken up and reunited) was called by this name. Those of the other places, in spite of their primitive spelling, are not difficult to trace. "Cedeboazzo" is, for example, Sidi Bou Azza, "Mesmeath," Amezmiz, &c.

(11) *The Golden Globes of Morocco City* (Marakesch) p. 99.—

These globes on the top of the Kutubia Mosque (three in
number, not four, their size graduating from the undermost
to the uppermost), though often an object of cupidity to kings
in want of coin, remained *in situ* to early in this century,
mainly owing to the difficulty which their mode of fixation
offered to the plunderer, these failures giving rise to the story
that they were protected by "djinns," "afreets" (more correctly
jinoon and *afart*), or spirit - guards.   But they were finally
taken down, and either replaced by others, or, when their
true value was discovered, replaced by gilded facsimiles.
Another story is that their origin was due to the desire of
the Queen of Muley Abd El Mumin (1128–1162) to ornament
the mosque built by her husband, and that the gold they were
made of was derived from the jewels presented to her by the
King.   Captain John Smith, visiting Morocco in 1604, saw them
on what he calls the "Christian Church."   Against "these
golden Bals of Affrica," he tells us, "hath been shot many a
shot," though none ever hit them.   He gives their weight at
784 lbs., and repeats the tale he heard of their origin, which
was to the effect that the Prince of Morocco betrothed himself
to the "King's Daughter of Etheopea."   But he dying before
their marriage, " she caused those three golden Balls to be set
up for his Monument," while she herself remained single all her
life.   Jean Mocquet, " Garde du Cabinet des Singularités du
Roi, aux Tuileries," who reached Morocco the year after the
" Admirall of New England," tells much the same story with
other romantic incidents.   Monsieur Charant, a French merchant who visited the city some time between the years 1645
and 1670, also mentions them.   But by that period shots seem
to have taken effect, for these "golden apples, especially the
biggest, is banch'd in several places with the blows of musket
bullets which have been shot at it, and some places pierced
quite through them, for they are not massive, but only about
the thickness of a finger's breadth.   I wondered at it, and
asked some of the ancientest men, how they came to be so:
It was answer'd that souldiers of Jacob Elmansor (1168–1184)
when they took the city did it.   I reply'd why did they not
take them away?   O they durst not, said one, for they are
sacred."
The city is now only a large decaying town, half in ruins, civil

war and bad government having reduced its population to about 80,000 in ordinary, and perhaps double that number when the Emperor and his troops are there.

(12) *Robbery of Officials*, p. 105.—Without any alterations these words apply equally well to the extortions of all the officials. They buy their offices, receiving no pay, or a merely nominal salary; yet they usually enrich themselves by robbery until the evil time comes when they are invited to digorge, and unless they manage to satisfy the Sultan are thrown into a dreadful prison, or, after drinking tea with their sovereign, die in agony from a dose of arsenic. Poison in Morocco is a recognized instrument of diplomacy; it is what all men dread.

(13) *Lions, &c.*, p. 109.—Leopards are now rather scarce in Morocco, and lions are seldom seen in the northern parts of the empire, though they are by no means absent; yet men live for years in the country without catching a glimpse of one. But last century, and even at the beginning of this, they seem to have been common. Francis Brooks in 1681, and Thomas Phelps in 1685, while making to the coast after their escape from Mequinez, encountered several; and at a later date Dominique Busnot supplies a curious account of the boldness of these beasts, the semi-depopulation of the country during the wars of succession, and the absence of arms and provisions, having allowed them to multiply. The account Pellow gives of the way the Arabs treat a lion when they meet it unarmed is an exact description of their present *modus operandi.*

(14) *The March to Guzlan*, p. 112.—Most of the places named in this itinerary are as yet unknown to geographers. Swagtah is not, to my knowledge, the name of any large district in Morocco, far less of a province, though it may be the name applied in former times to one of the transmontane areas. Guzlan (or Ghrazlan?) is not a town which comes within my ken; but there is, in the region described, a province once known under the designation of Guezula, Gzoula, Gesula, or Guezzoula, all of which may be corruptions of the ancient Gaetulia. It must, however, be remembered, setting aside the

errors due to the author's failing memory, and the misapprehension of Arabic and Berber names, over which even the most educated of travellers make sad blunders, many of the places named were no more than kasbahs, or mud forts, which are apt not only to change their names with the various commandants, but to disappear before the wrath of the Sultan or of warlike tribes, or to melt away under the influence of the weather when from any reason they are deserted. It must also be remembered that the limits of the provinces have frequently varied according as they have been occupied by different tribes, the whim of the Sultan, or the convenience or interests of the hour, and that this variation of extent may have caused a variation of name. Most of the best-known provinces were originally, like the old provinces of France, small kingdoms perpetually at variance among themselves, till the present dynasty subdued and united them under one sovereign. In Chenier's day several of these divisions bore more than one name, and even yet it is seldom that two intelligent Moors agree in giving the list exactly the same, while no one pretends to define these provincial boundaries with more than approximate accuracy. Agoory, so frequently mentioned in Pellow's narrative, though not in any previous author's, is a little town which looks like a garden surrounded by walls. It is inhabited by the descendants of Renegades.

(15) *The Moorish Army*, p. 115.—This force is now much more efficient, being better armed and more scientifically drilled than in Pellow's day. But its commissariat is, as of old, organized plunder of the country through which it passes. The land is "eaten up" by it during a march, so that instead of any district petitioning after a fashion with which we are familiar in England for the sovereign to honour it with a visit, the people humbly beg his Shereefian Majesty to save them from this costly distinction, offering him in lieu of his intended purpose a sum of money. But in one respect the soldiers with whom Thomas Pellow marched were better situated than those who are led to victory by the gallant Kaïd Maclean, an English officer to whom the Moroccan troops owe a deep debt of gratitude. For while many of the latter are clothed, armed, and drilled something after the Eastern fashion, they have no longer a " German " or

any other surgeon to bind these wounds. These misfortunes of war are left to nature, or the blood is rudely staunched by native methods, such as dipping the stump into hot pitch, after the manner in vogue when Ambrose Paré was the most cunning leech of his day ; or, more frequently, the patient tribesmen die untended, refusing to risk entering into Paradise maimed by the hand of man. Yet they are eager enough to accept medical advice and medicine from any infidel doctor, and as all Europeans are supposed to belong more or less to the medical profession, a journey into the interior of Morocco is not without perils to the philanthrophic traveller who takes a pleasure in dispensing pills or potions with more zeal than knowledge. The Emperor has sometimes the services of a European physician at his disposal, preferring such a one to his native At'oubba, and of late years the presence of the French Military Commission with his army has enabled him to obtain the aid of the surgeon attached to it without the fear of being poisoned which constantly haunts the great ones of Maghreb-al-Aksa. The German surgeon in Pellow's force was doubtless a renegade slave. In those days the Sultan had a free choice of almost any professional or artistic skill from among the many captives always arriving. To them some of the so-called triumphs of old Moorish architecture are due. The buildings were, in reality, constructed by Christian slaves, just as so many in Grenada and Cordova reared during the Arab domination were the handiwork of Egyptian, Spanish, and Jewish craftsmen in the employment of the Moorish monarchs.

(16) *Wine Drinking,* p. 119.—The ease with which Pellow indulged in drinking bouts was due to the Jews, who to this day make great quantities of a Malaga-like wine from the native grapes, besides a peculiar (and particularly disagreeable) kind by boiling down the must. They also prepare a brandy from dates and figs and other fruits, though of late, owing to it having been introduced into the harems, their freedom of distillation has been somewhat curtailed. The Moors in Pellow's time seemed to have drunk wine more freely, or at least more openly, than now. In the coast towns a tipsy native is not an uncommon sight, though his escapade usually costs him dearly if the Bashaw—or Kaïd, for the word Bashaw is unknown to the

Arabic, being simply a corruption of Pasha, the Turkish term
applied to a high official by the Europeans—considers him worth
squeezing by means of a judicious course of imprisonment, or
of the stick. On Mogador Island there is a place of confinement
for Moors convicted of the offence, though the gossips of S'ouera
whisper that even there the obtaining of a supply of gin is
only a question of money paid to the guardian of the Retreat.
In the interior, however, it is much rarer ever to see drinking,
far less drunkenness, and at no banquet given by the great
officers of State, either to private individuals or to embassies, are
strong waters of any sort even offered. But it is affirmed that
though the Emperor is a strict observer of the law, some of his
ministers are, in the privacy of their own dining-rooms, by no
means so abstemious. Moreover, many of the more dissolute
Moors, besides smoking tobacco (which also is against the
Moorish interpretation of the Koran, and in 1887 was expressly
prohibited by Muley El Hassan, the present Sultan), are understood to be quite familiar with the flavour of brandy—anything
being lawful if only it is regarded as medicine ; while one or
two—the Grand Shereef of Wazan among the number—are
rumoured to have even discovered what bit of pig was pronounced accursed by the Prophet. As for the Berbers of
the Riff mountains, they drink wine and eat the wild boar
without the slightest compunction. In Muley Ismaïl's day
there was scarcely any concealment of the vice. The more
favoured Christian slaves, as in Algiers, were permitted not
only to distil spirit, but to make money by keeping taverns
in Fez and Mequinez, which enabled them to buy their
freedom. The renegades almost to a man indulged whenever
they had a chance, and "One Carr," a turn-coat Englishman,
who during Pellow's time had charge of the cannon foundries,
and by Captain Braithwaite's account seems to have been a bad
specimen of a bad type, not only got drunk at Mr. Russel the
English Envoy's dinner, but confessed that unless he shut himself up at times and took a "good dose of wine" melancholy
would have taken possession of him. The brothers of the
Bashaw of Tetuan used to enter the kitchen during Mr. Russel's
embassy, and threaten to murder the cook "if she did not give
them pudding and wine." But as one of the guards picked the
pocket of Mr. Windus as he stood beside the prince, afterwards the

Emperor Muley Abdallah, and the domestics at the palace were
so prone to cut the buttons off the ambassador's coat that he
generally appeared in his worst suit, this trait is not remarkable.
A renegade who kept the Sultan's garden sold "a cup of wine
on the sly;" a saint entertained the embassy with a "pleasant
drink" not unlike mead, and among the presents for the
Emperor Muley Ahmed IV. (Ed-dehèbi), the English Government of those days had, either through ignorance, or through
very accurate knowledge of the Imperial tastes, sent "four cases
of Florence." This his Shereefian Majesty, with the help of a
few boon-companions, finished in a couple of sittings, and was
so tipsy when the ambassador called upon him that all he could
say was that the Christians were to have all they wanted—
plenty of roast pig and wine. The former forbidden dainty the
Sultan also freely indulged in, though he preferred a roast fox.
Muley A'bd-el-Malik II. was assassinated in his tent by a French
Renegade named Chaban (not by "a discontented slave" as
Chenier has it) while he was sleeping off a bout of drunkenness.
Crom-el-Hajj was slain by his unwilling bride (who afterwards
married his son) on the wedding night while the king lay stupefied
by drugs she had dropped into his wine, and thus not only freed
herself from a distasteful alliance, but avenged the blood of her
family which had splashed the throne of the usurper. The
infamous Muley El Jezid was also an almost open drunkard. And
though it is not exactly history, we must all remember the case
bottles which Robinson Crusoe found on board the Sallee boat,
and the liberal use he and Xury made of their contents. To
this hour, the bacchanalian song of Muley Bou Shaïb, often sung
at feasts, celebrates the pleasures of grape juice. In short, nowadays, as in those of Sir John Maundevile, "Sùme sarrazines
drynken wyn prevyly."

(17) *Taffilet and the Imperial Family*, p. 120.—These data are
still accurate. The Sultan cannot provide for all of his family,
so that by this time thousands of people who are the poorest
labourers have some of the blood of Muley Ismaïl in their veins.
In the time of Sidi Mohammed (1747–1789) the surviving
male children occupied five hundred houses, in Taffilet, or
· Sidjilmasa, as Aboulqâsem calls it, indifferently. I have
even known second cousins of the present Emperor humbly

engaged as domestic servants to Europeans. As for descendants of the Prophet, they fill places in every grade of society; there are plenty of "Shereefs" begging their bread, and are doing very well at this business, which in Morocco is an excellent one, especially if the mendicant is of saintly character or illustrious lineage. Taffilet being the natal land of the Shereefs, and most of the inhabitants being descended from them—their distinguishing mark being a green turban—the country is known as Bled Shereef—that is, the Country of the Princes (descended from the Prophet). The entire territory is scattered with fortresses surrounded by walls of " tabia "—each containing three or four hundred families, who hold weekly markets.

(18) *Moors and Arabs*, p. 120.—Here, like most of the writers of his time, Pellow applies the term Moor in a very vague sense. All the inhabitants of Morocco, the Jews and Europeans excepted, are often so designated. This is a mistake. The substratum of the country are the Berbers, who extend all over North Africa, under the name of Berbers, Shluhs, Kabyles, Touaregs, &c., and though now good Moslems, have never yet acknowledged the Arabs' domination. It is they who form the bulk of the mountaineers who give the Sultan such ample employment for his Krupp guns and his standing army. The Arabs are the latest invaders of the country. They came when the Roman (Byzantine) power was breaking up, and are the inhabitants of the plains, being, unlike the Berbers (Brebbers), not denizens of villages or much addicted to agriculture, but, for the most part, wandering herdsmen, the Bedouins of many a familiar travel-tale. The Moors are also Arabs, but much mixed with European and other blood. They are for the greater part inhabitants of cities, merchants, artizans, officials, &c., and are the most refined of the people. Still, it is hard to draw any fast line between them and the Arabs, though for convenience' sake the term Moor is usually —or ought be—applied to the town-dwellers of the Barbary States.

(19) *Bushmough, a Native of the Brazils*, p. 121.—At that period the Portuguese held Mazagan on the coast, and, as might have been expected, many slaves were constantly escaping from

them, or were actually sold to the Moors, or in their continual skirmishes were captured from the Christians.

(20) *The Black Imperial Guard*, p. 141.—The Bokhari—so-called from Al Bokhari, on whose Korannic commentaries they were sworn—deserve all the esteem in which they were held during Pellow's time, though they are no longer the backbone of the army, and by the formation of the "Askar" or regular force of infantry, organized on a European model, are, happily, incapable of playing the part of the Turkish Janissaries or Roman Pretorians which in former times made them so troublesome. They are, however, still the Sultan's guard, and a fine powerful body of men. Pellow, it seems to me, greatly magnifies the number of the force. When they were most powerful, their headquarters were at Mequinez, and they numbered from 13,000 to 15,000; but they are now a much less considerable force. Originally formed from the Sultan's hereditary slaves, brought from the Western Soudan, their blood is now considerably mixed, but they have lost little of the physique and courage of their race. In all the engagements of the Spanish war of 1859–60 they acquitted themselves like men, badly disciplined and infamously armed as they were—and are; and at Isly these courageous negroes alone awaited the shock of the French. The Arabs and Berbers made a wild charge, fired off their flint-lock muskets, and then wheeled about, as their fashion is. But in Muley El Hassan's opinion they were too much of the nature of a double-edged tool, for they did not only form a bulwark to the throne, but when things did not always go their own way were apt to chop round and change the succession.

(21) *Mr. Russel and the Christian Captives*, p. 153.—On "Jan. 17th, O. S., 1727–8," Mr. Russel brought to the coast twelve captives, though only two of them were English, the rest being either English subjects or foreigners captured on English ships.

(22) *Muley Ismaïl and his Sons*, pp. 148, 193.—How much of these tales of fire and sword is historical it is now difficult to affirm with any certainty; for in those days, as in ours, news from

the interior of Morocco was hard to obtain, or being obtained, it
was hard to eliminate the lies with which it was so plentifully
impregnated. Yet the historians who wrote long after Pellow's
time, and were evidently unacquainted with his narrative, confirm much of what the Penryn mariner has penned. Many of
the places he mentions are still well known, and can be detected
under his phonetic and ofttimes blundering spellings. Others
are more problematical, especially the names of certain "provinces." In that curious narrative of a nameless Christian
slave whose manuscript Simon Ockley, Professor of Arabic in
Cambridge, edited (1715); in Chenier's better-known "Recherches
historiques sur les Maures" (1787); in St. Olon's "Relation de
l'Empire de Maroc" (1695); in Busnot's "Histoire du regne
de Mouley Ishmael" (1714), and, among similar narratives of
embassies which visited the country of the aged tyrant who was
Pellow's first master, in Braithwaite's "History of the Revolutions in the Empire of Morocco" (1729), may be found ample,
almost contemporary, confirmation of many of the statements
made in the preceding pages. Muley Ismaïl delighted in war and
slaughter. He would think nothing of fracturing the limbs of
an official who had offended him, and then ordering the mangled
wretch to be sewn into a bull's hide and dragged through the
camp. If a slave did not build after his notions of what was
right, he would playfully break a brick over his head, or spear
him on the spot, or even order him to have his legs burnt off
with quicklime, and then be built up in the walls. His palace
was a hot-bed of intrigues—the rival wives struggling to advance
themselves and their sons, and to ruin the children of their
rivals. Thus Muley Mohammed, the best of the many sons of
the Emperor, by the machinations of Lala Zidan, a negro
queen, was first driven into rebellion and then butchered. When
the Emperor was intent on meting out punishment, he was pre-
ceded by a guard escorting fourteen Christian slaves carrying a
copper cauldron (captured on a Portuguese ship), a hundredweight
of tar or pitch, and as much oil and tallow, and these in their
turn were followed by a cartload of wood and six butchers,
each with a knife in his hand. To this day the hands of thieves
are cut off, and, like the heads of rebels, stuck over the gates of
the interior cities, the presence of Europeans in the coast towns
preventing this literal obedience to the injunction of the Koran

touching an eye for an eye and a tooth for a tooth. The Editor numbers among his travelling acquaintances throughout the Barbary States a great many Moors who display a marked reticence to expose their right arm; and in Mogador there is a beggar who, having been proved guilty of slandering another Moslem of his own profession, was adjudged by the Kadi to have his lips rubbed with fresh capsicums! To silently draw one's finger along his lips is still so painful a reminder of that episode in his career, that he will instantly, in the midst of the most profuse flattery, disappear down the nearest lane.

But in the days of Muley Ismaïl and his successors the entrances to half the towns of the empire were simply festooned by horrible human remains. He sent, for instance, after the rebellion in the then province of Shavoia, ten thousand heads to Fez and Morocco, to be fixed upon the walls of those cities, among them being those of hundreds of the women and children whom the monster had slaughtered in cold blood. He kept an enormous number of cats—and appointed a Kaïd (Alcayde) to control their gambols, and delighted in dog-fighting. But if the dogs would not fight, or were so savage as to kill each other, then the keeper was duly cudgelled by the irritable despot. Or he would set twenty or thirty negro boys to box with each other, the lads who came off worst being severely beaten by their master. His chief amusement, however, was to superintend the slaves at work, his attendants consisting on such occasions of a black to bear his tobacco-pipe (which had a bowl as big as a child's head, and a reed-stem about two yards long), another to carry his tobacco, and a third a brazen vessel of hot water to wash his hands, and some laden with clubs to throw at his slaves upon the top of the houses or walls. When hungry, he immediately ordered a huge dish of cusscassoo, and then sitting down on the ground, ate as much as he cared for by thrusting his bare arm into the vessel and fishing up what he liked best. If tired, he simply squatted on the earth or on a heap of stones to rest himself. His caprices were endless, though not much worse than those of some of the later Sultans. One day he saw a Kaïd's wife riding upon a mule; instantly he ordered the poor woman's husband to shoot her for daring to bestride one of "those creatures of God which nourished and kept them alive." Asking another officer to whom a flock of sheep belonged, he

was told that they were the property of the person addressed.
" *Yours !* you dog," was the reply, " I thought I had been the
only proprietor in the country; " and taking his lance, this
representative of " L'etat c'est moi," ran the presumptuous Kaïd
through the body, ordering at the same time the sheep to be
given to his negro troops. A black slave, on telling him that he
wished bread, having toiled for two days on an empty stomach,
was assured that in future he should have no further occasion
for anything to eat ; and to keep his word, ordered, as a piece of
prime jocosity, the wretched negro's teeth to be pulled out.
Like the sultans generally, Ismaïl was in the habit of distributing the thinnings of his harem among his officials, a wife from
the palace being still regarded as a high honour. These ladies
are, however, apt to be what Mr. Mantilini described as " demni-
tion savage lambs." One of these even went so far as to pull
her husband's beard ; but on the henpecked Kaïd complaining,
the Emperor assured him that such a humiliation should never
occur again, for his beard should be pulled out ; which it was—
on the spot.

Muley Ahmed Ed-dehèbi (" the rich man") was a drunken
brute, as cruel as his father, but without that energy which
gave Morocco such order during his brilliant reign that a child,
it was boasted, could carry a purse from Fez to Tarudant.
One of his first acts was to order Belcaddy (Benkheddai),
who is more than once mentioned by Pellow, to be tossed
ten times, and be put in prison until he paid ten quintals of
silver ; while Bengozzy, one of his own companions, was put
to death. Having gone to prayers at the palace mosque
very drunk, he fell down and polluted the sacred building
with his vomiting. The negro soldiers whose allegiance he
had bought with some of the five millions of pounds which
he found in his father's treasury, proclaimed his brother
Abd el Malik emperor, with the results described by Pellow.
The downfall of this temporary sovereign was mainly due to
his austere arrogant manner ; for though sober he was not
much more amiable than his brother. But the real reason
for Muley Ahmed IV.—Deby, or properly El-dehèbi, to give
him his usual name—being recalled from exile in Taffilet (or
Taffilalet), was the anger of the negro troops on hearing that
the new sovereign had declared his intention of checking their

power for evil and for good. Muley Abdallah (ben Ismail) V. was as capricious and as cruel as his father. But, unlike him, was generous to excess, which fact may account for his having been deposed six times, and reinstated as often. . Yet in spite of his many rivals, and reverses of fortune, and Thomas Pellow's belief that in the year he escaped the end was drawing near,[*] this villainous ruler, who had every vice except avarice, managed to reign, after a fashion, from 1729 to 1757. (See also *Note* 25.)

(23) *Pellow's journey to " Guinea,"* p. 196.—In these days the Emperors of Morocco had regular intercourse with Timbuktoo, in which for a time they had a garrison, or received tribute in lieu of the right of keeping that expressive symbol of authority there, and, as at the present day, caravans went regularly to the Soudan in search of slaves, gums, and other commodities. It was with one of these that Pellow affects to have gone, and though, owing mainly to the lack of maps portraying the route, it is not easy to identify all of his names, yet many of them, not known to geographers until a later period, are not hard to make out. The term "Guinea" was at that period applied to all the coast north of the Cape of Good Hope and south of Morocco, so that the use of the word must not deceive. He makes, however, no pretence (as he could easily have done had he wished to tell a tale of wonder) of having reached Timbuktoo, as Paul Imbert, a French slave, did, or as Robert Adams, a sailor wrecked north of Cape Blanco, more than a century and a half later, claimed to have done, or to have made the Mecca pilgrimage as Joseph Pitts of Exeter, while in Algerian slavery, actually did in the closing years of the seventeenth century. Pellow was an uneducated man, with little idea of the geography of the regions over which he first of white men, and in some instances the only one since his time, wandered or has wandered. Had he been trying to fabricate a narrative, he would not have declared that he had reached the " Wad Nil, or river Nile," for even in those days this would have at once stamped him as a liar, the Nile rising in an entirely opposite direction. But it is now a familiar fact

---

[*] Pellow, however, was not far out in his reckoning; for one of his depositions occurred that very year.

that the Niger is known to the Arabs as the Wad Nil el
Abid, or Nile of the Slaves (Blacks), the word Nile being in that
region a common name for any large stream.   In reality, from
the fact of the caravan having seen a French vessel in the
river, Pellow and his slave-hunting comrades seem to have
reached the Senegal, the mistaking of it for the Niger being
natural enough, as the real course of the latter was not known
until many years subsequently.   Agloou, "the fishing coves"
mentioned, is a poor anchorage; but the villages in the
surrounding country are prosperous and well peopled.

(24) *The Desert between Morocco and " Guinea,"* p. 199.—This
dreadful waste of sandy billows is described in its latest details
by Dr. Oskar Lenz, who succeeded in passing it in the year
1880 on his journey to Timbuktoo, though only a small portion
of his route lay near Pellow's.   The privations endured by the
caravans are terrible.   The Arabs who carry on the trade
between that city and Mogador declare that five hundred
dollars have been given for a draught of water, and that when
the water-skins have been partially dried up in the manner
described by our author, it is by no means uncommon for the
precious fluid to be held at the rate of fourteen to twenty
dollars a drink.   In 1805—so Jackson, who carried on business
at Agadir, relates—a caravan proceeding from Timbuktoo to
Taffilet was disappointed in not finding water at one of the
usual wells, when, horrible to relate, the whole of the persons
belonging to it, two thousand in number, besides eighteen
hundred camels, perished by thirst.   Misfortunes of this sort
account for the vast number of human and other bones which
are found mingled together in various parts of the desert.

The traders at that period—1794–1808—told the same tale
as Pellow does of the "Akkabaahs," or caravans, being
directed by the guides smelling the earth.   Jackson, however,
with characteristic self-sufficiency, not always warranted by the
accuracy of his "facts," was of opinion that this was "an
artful invention of their own, to impose upon the credulity of
this superstitious and ignorant people, and thus to enhance
the value of their knowledge."   The desert pilots " possess
some knowledge of astrology and the situation of certain stars,
and being enabled by the two pointers to ascertain the polar

star, they can by that unvarying guide steer their course with considerable precision, preferring often travelling in the night rather than under the suffocating heat of the effulgent meridian sun." The references to mummies (p. 202) in connection with surgeons indicate the use of them as medicine—a purpose to which they were put in regular practice during the seventeenth century, and among empirics to a much later date.

(25) *Muley Abdullah's cruelties*, p. 226.—Scarcely a week passed, a French writer * tells us, without Abdallah putting to death great numbers of his subjects in the most horrid manner, some by nailing them to walls, others by being tied by the feet to a mule's tail, and thus dragged through the streets; others were kept incessantly employed at the most laborious work, solely to make them as miserable as possible. He even obliged the Christians and the Chaânba † (the latter being tribesmen of the Atlas, of whom Crom-el-Hajj was chief, and who ever since had been cruelly used by the Sultans) to pull down the town of Erriâdh, which obstructed the view from his seraglio. This place contained the residences of various functionaries of Mequinez, during the time of Muley Ismaïl, who had built a fine mosque in the centre, beside bazaars, baths, and a college. While demolishing this town, one of his greatest pleasures was to order his guards to drive great numbers of the labourers under walls which had been undermined and were just ready to fall, that he might see them buried alive in the ruins. In short, there was no sort of brutality in which Muley Abdallah did not seem to take a pleasure. Neither virtue, merit, nor the strictest ties of blood, put any restraint on his cruelty. Even his own mother was in perpetual danger of losing her life by his hands. One day in particular he went with a pistol to her apartment, with a design to kill her. "But she being advised of it, went out to meet him, and embracing him, spoke to him with so much tenderness, the tears at the same time falling down her

* "Relation de ce qui s'est passé dans le royaume de Maroc depuis l' année 1727 jusqu' an 1737." This curious contemporary narrative which appeared in 1742 is anonymous, but the author was probably a M. de Manault.

† In this I follow the authority of Aboulqâsem ben Ahmed Ezziâni, whose history of the events in Morocco between the years 1631–1812, have been recently given to the world by M. Houdas.

cheeks, that she softened his barbarous heart, so that he seemed seized with horror at the action he was going to commit, and denied it in the strongest manner; however, his mother thought it prudent to absent herself from his presence and court for a considerable time.

Nothing could exceed his ingratitude and cruelty to the Bashaw Hogmy, governor of Mequinez, who had been a chief instrument in setting him on the throne, and to whom he had sworn in his first transports, on his being proclaimed king, that he would never make use of a lance or fusil against him; however, taking umbrage at the great reputation of this Bashaw, and the esteem he was in with his people, on account of his great merit and virtue, he ordered him one day to come before him, and after having reproached him with accusations which had no foundation, he ordered him to sit down and pull off his turban. Then immediately a great number of boys, who had been provided for the purpose, came about him, and with pieces of lead they had in their hands struck upon his head till they had beaten it in pieces; and immediately after this, both his secretary and brother were served in the same manner.

He showed no less cruelty to eight young Alcaydes, to whose marriage he had just given his consent. It is the custom of those parts that the new-married couples (during the space of seven days) take upon them amongst their kinsfolks and friends the title of king and queen, and during this time they have a power of putting a forfeiture on those who were present at their wedding, and of throwing into the water, with all their clothes on, those who refuse to pay it. But these rejoicings are only made when the bride is found a maid; for when it proves otherways, the husband sends her back to her father's house, and the father has a right to strangle her. These eight young Alcaydes, according to custom, assumed this power during the seven days, thinking no harm; but scarce were these days of rejoicing over, but the tyrant sent for them, and having reproached them for the liberty they had taken, as a heinous crime, he ordered them to be tied by the feet to a mule's tail, and in that manner drawn through all the streets of Mequinez till they were dead.

A young Spanish slave, for whom he seemed to have a great

value, hearing that he was about to give liberty to eleven Spanish slaves, fell down on his knees, and entreated him in the tenderest and most respectful manner that he would be pleased to let his father, who was likewise a slave, and far advanced in years, be one of the number of those who were to be released; to which Abdallah made no reply. The next day the slave, with tears in his eyes, and in the most moving manner, renewed his request; but Abdallah looking upon this so natural and praiseworthy affection as a crime, ordered the slave to be immediately tossed up in the air and let fall upon his head till he expired. And as if this was not cruel enough, and as if he had been willing to punish the father for the tenderness of his son, he set the poor old man to such hard labour that he died a few days after."

His mother one day representing to him that it was contrary to humanity to put the innocent to death and beneath his dignity to be the executioner of them himself, he replied " that his subjects had no longer a right to life than he pleased, and that he knew no greater pleasure than that of putting them to death with his own hands."

The man seemed really to have been more mad than sane, and was well aware of this himself. One day he made a favourite servant the present of two thousand ducats, and told him to go far from his presence, so that he might not be exposed to the effects of his fury. The attachment of the slave to his inhuman master was, however, so great, that he refused, and in due time fell a victim to one of the Emperor's violent fits of fury, being reproached, when dying, with his folly in not having left the court when advised.

On another occasion, when passing the river Beth (Bate) at the place where it falls into the Sebou, he was in danger of being drowned, when one of his negroes at great peril to his own life rescued the floundering Prince of True Believers. The slave's only reward was to be hewn down with his master's sabre for presuming to congratulate himself on his good fortune in being able to rescue so sacred a person. " You are an infidel!" he cried, " to suppose that you have saved *me*. As if Allah stood in need of your intervention to preserve a Shereef and the son of a Shereef"—that is a descendant of Mohammed. He was said to possess judgment and courage, and a laudable freedom from the awe with which most of his countrymen regard the rascally " saints " of Morocco.   But his vices, most of them of the most hideous type, have earned for Abdallah an evil eminence in the evil dynasty of the Alides, only second to that of Muley-el-Jezîd—or Yezeed, as the name is pronounced in Morocco.   In this volume philological purism is not attempted in the transliteration of Arabic names, the rule adopted being to accept the form most generally used, and therefore most intelligible, without much regard to its minute accuracy.

(26) *The " Mahomet Woolderriva "* (p. 227) of Pellow's narrative is his illiterate way of writing Mohammed Oold el Ariba, that is the son of the Ariba, the former name of his mother.

(27) *" Muley Smine "* pp. 53, 227.—This is a name which Muley Ismaïl bore.   It ought properly to be written Muley Es-Semin, or Smahyn (the stout) ; but the rude orthography of Pellow tells in favour of his honesty.

(28) *The Fratricidal Wars of Muley Ismaïl's Sons,* p. 228.— Pellow's narrative, though it contains many minute particulars regarding the war between Muley Abdallah and his brothers, is simply such a story as might be picked up from the camp rumours of an army on the march through a country where truth is an exotic virtue, and wild exaggeration the normal condition of affairs.   Yet it is in the main correct.   Muley Ali, who was elected by the black Janissaries Emperor on the 29th September, 1734, was another of Muley Ismaïl's sons.   But he was deposed in May, 1786, in favour of Abdallah restored.   The new sovereign, besides being poor (which was no recommendation in the eyes of the negro troops), had so addicted himself to the use of " Achecha " (Hashesh), Bang, or Indian hemp—the Keef of the Moors—as to render him numb alike in body and mind.

(29) *Muley Mataddy,* p. 234.—This is apparently Muley Mustadi (El Mostadhi) another brother of Muley Abdallah, and a rival with him for the throne, who in 1738, after Pellow had left the country, was proclaimed Emperor by the negroes, and obliged Abdallah to retire once more among the mountains.

The negroes soon proving fickle, he was deposed (1740), and retired to Azila,* where he carried on a considerable trade in grain with the Spaniards, though without renouncing his imperial honours. Abdallah, with the design of cutting off his brother, laid siege to Tangier, the governor of which was an adherent of his. The city was duly taken, and the Bashaw's palace plundered after his death in battle: but his son Mohammed ben Ahmed escaped to Gibraltar with all his father's money. Meantime, Mustadi pillaged the environs of Fez, and on his return was attacked near Al K'sar by Abdallah, and forced to retreat into Sallee, where he had been so popular as governor that he was received and acknowledged as Emperor. But Rabat on the other side of the river refused to bend the knee to him. The result was a ruinous civil war between these two towns, which, under Muley Ismaïl, had become a kind of republic feudatory to the empire. For fourteen months Rabat was besieged, until Mustadi, despairing of taking the place, retired to Tedla, where he was arrested and put in irons by the Berbers in the interest of Abdallah. Another faction holding the castle of Oordega, however, released him, and transferred him to the sanctuary of Sidi El Mati, a hereditary saint who escorted Mustadi to Sallee, where he was again received with gladness, as the town was thoroughly opposed to Abdallah. Finding that it was vain to hold his own against Abdallah, he resumed his corn trade at Azila, and there continued to reside in a private station until the accession of Sidi Mohammed, when he was ordered to take up his residence in Fez, where he died.

(80) *Quack Doctors*, p. 259.—Spanish charlatans, many of them natives of Tangier and other coast towns, and therefore familiar with the language, still perambulate Morocco. The greater number of them are vile rascals, who have more trades than one, and sell poisons freely. There are, however, exceptions, among whom the Editor recalls a mild-mannered gentleman, who, after flirting with fortune as a ship-captain, a photographer, and a teacher of music, was wandering from Kasbah to Kasbah drawing teeth and tuning pianos, of which he informed me with some pride there were already thirteen in Morocco. Ophthalmia

* To Tangier, according to Aboulqâsem ben Ahmed Ezziâni, whose dates I have adopted.

and other diseases of the eye are still, as in Pellow's day, the
common maladies of the country, more especially in the South,
and it is not without interest to remark that one of the common
native remedies is counter-irritation produced by blowing pepper
into the eyes after the fashion which the highwayman (p. 247)
found so ineffectual. Now as then, purgative medicines are in
active demand, the well-to-do Moors gorging themselves to re-
pletion at every meal, even when, as a late Grand Vizier did,
they do not employ emetics in order to begin a feast *de novo ;*
while the poorer ones risk dyspepsia whenever the world smiles
brightly enough to render a gorge of cusscassoo and fat mutton
an approachable luxury. The reason why these wandering
quacks are more popular than the native doctors, is not that they
are as a rule more skilful, but simply because it is believed that
all Christians are, by the gift of God, adroit healers of sick folk.
Christ (" Sidna Aissa ")—so runs the Moslem legend—was a great
physician, and his power has descended to all his followers.
" Son of Jesus," the traveller is not unfrequently told," thou can
relieve me." But if he succeeds, not he but Allah is thanked,
for without the inspiration and permission of God man is
powerless to accomplish anything, and therefore deserves no
credit for his acts. At the same time, a rabbit or a few partridges
may be offered as a gift, and not unlikely the doctor as he sits in
his tent door may be told—as the writer was by a poor woman
whose child he had relieved—" What a pity it is that so good a
man can never enter Paradise !" This at all events, though
somewhat negative in its good wishes, is more soothing than the
not uncommon malediction of an elderly beauty whom the
infidel may happen to encounter in a narrow lane (when there
are men folk about)—" May Gehenna be your portion ! The
fire is lighted for you !" The " conjurors " with whom Pellow
had such evil luck were doubtless miracle-working " saints," or
marabouts as they are called in Algeria. The snake-charmers
and " Aissouia "—a wild religious sect who handle serpents with
seeming impunity, and indulge in a host of hideous ceremonies—
are a different class. They go annually to Soos and other
quarters to collect reptiles and scorpions. The fire-eaters and
the ordinary " Jack-Puddings " who may be seen in every market,
are a more ordinary set of performers, while the story-tellers
with their circle of admiring listeners form one of the most

interesting features in any gathering in Morocco. The itinerant doctors (or at'oubba, *sing.* t'bib) carry a leather bag containing, besides a few medicines, their surgical instruments, which usually consist of a lancet, a knife for scarifying, and a burning iron, which is used for almost every ill that Moorish flesh is heir to. That so few of their patients die may be attributed to their simple life and hardy constitutions.

(31) *The Geography of Pellow's flight*, pp. 261–290.—Some of the minor places mentioned in this narrative cannot now be identified (and indeed the writer expressly mentions that they were destroyed doing the civil and other wars), though this is chiefly owing to the country in which they were situated being still wholly or partially unknown to geographers. Many of these are, however, familiar, though, at the time Pellow wrote, not on any map, or on those to which it is extremely unlikely either he or his editor had access, and then under names so differently spelt from his, that this fact tells in favour of the authenticity of his narrative. As the interest of this work is mainly in the adventures it describes, I have not thought it necessary to try and localize all of them. But as a test of the writer's *bona fides*, this may be done here and there, in addition to the names already identified in foot notes.

The " Waddonfeese " (p. 262) is, for instance, the Wad-Enfisa (or 'Nfis), a tributary of the Tensift. " Rosselelwad " is still the name of a village and district—or " parish " as Pellow puts it— the Ras-el-Wad in Sus (p. 265), while Tarudant (Territrent) is a well-known town. At one time there was a considerable trade with this place, but it is now so fanatical that no Europeans visit it, and since the decay of Agadir it has fallen into ruins, and is without much commerce or industry, though surrounded with olive, orange, and date gardens. From information obtained through the European officers of the Sultan's army, it appears that the place is about 690 feet above the sea, and contains between six and seven thousand inhabitants, including a considerable number of Jews and Berbers, the latter of whom, armed to the teeth, swagger along its narrow filthy lanes, eyeing the stranger with a ferocious glare, and wreaking vengeance on any enemy whom they may encounter, almost with impunity from the badly organized police of this whilom residence of the Shereefs, and the centre from which they carried on a religious propaganda among the neighbouring tribes. "Arhallah" I take to be a corruption of Aouara or Haouara; and Gesseemah is most likely Exima, a tribal (Ouled) village and "parish" in the position assigned to it. Santa Cruz or Agadir (this name, which means in the Berber language a protecting wall, being applied to several other places) is a picturesque fortress perched on a spur of the Atlas, about 990 feet above the sea. Up to the year 1760, when Sidi Mohammed ben Abdallah founded Mogador (*Note* 87), owing to the difficulty he found in exacting his dues at the Sous port, as well as to punish the rebellious Sousees, Agadir was in the enjoyment of considerable intercourse with Europe. But it is now fallen entirely into decay, the fishing village of Fonti at the base of the fortress being a miserable place, and the inhabitants so bigoted that when, during the expedition of 1882 against Sidi Hussein of Tazelronalt, the Sousan religious chief, the Sultan authorized grain ships to discharge here, the people refused to sell sheep to the crews until the authorities compelled them to "feed the infidel" in spite of the Korannic injunction to the contrary. In 1773, Sidi Mohammed ordered all the foreign merchants to leave, and since that date, with the exception of a brief interval (1792–1797), it has been closed to sea-borne commerce. "Terroost," or Tourazt, is not an uncommon Berber name, though I do not identify the particular village so named. "Hahah" is a well-known province. Between Agadir and the north a spur of the Atlas must be crossed, either by the Hamserout or the Bebaouan passes.

The method of preparing the locust (jeraad) for food (p. 276) is that still practised. They are considered by the Moors very stimulating food.

"Zumineeta" (Zesomeeta, or Zummeeta, as it is called in Tripoli) is made of barley which has been a little malted, coarsely ground, and sometimes mixed with dates, and is eaten in the form of dough with salt, argan or olive oil, and with water also. Barley meal and water or milk is the ordinary morning diet of the country people, who know it as "El hassûa." The barley is ground to the size of fine shot, and simmered over a slow fire. This food is regarded as so particularly wholesome and cooling, especially during fever time, that the Sultan himself (as did Muley Suliman and his father, Muley El Jezíd) always lays a foundation of it before drinking the fine hyson which he loves. Its health-giving qualities are celebrated in a little tale told by the southern tribesmen. A wandering doctor arrived in a strange country, and after saying the morning prayer, inquired after the way the people lived, and with what food they broke their fast. On being told that it was El hassûa, he rose, saddled his mule, and bade them good-bye. " Salaam u alikoum ! Peace be with you. For if you eat El hassûa in the morning, you have no need of a doctor!" This meal is prefaced by a brief grace consisting of " Bismallah " (" In the name of God "). But every act of the Moor is flavoured with piety. Even the street hawker is careful to preface the calling of his wares by some preparatory objurgations to attract the faithful. " God is gracious ! Beans, fried beans ! " " In the name of Muley Idriss ! Roast Chestnuts ! " " In the name of Sidna Mohammed Al Hadjj ! Pop corn !"; and I can recall among the most agreeable of street cries, after a hot ride over the dusty plain where Dom Sebastian met his doom, hearing in the filthy Soko of Al K'sar El Kebir, the welcome shout, "In the name of Sidna Ali-bou-Rhaleh! Melons, nice sweet melons !" The familiar tale of the Stambouli who invoked custom for his figs "in the name of the Prophet !" which has amused Europe for a century, scarcely tickles a resident of Morocco. For this or something similar is what he hears every day of his life (p. 276). " Idogurt " is, we have already noted, Ida-ou-gort, not far from Mogador; and Shiedmah and Abdah are still the designations of provinces.

The Argan tree is the source of the argan oil, so extensively used in the cookery of Southern Morocco, though there is an unfounded belief in some parts of the country that it engenders leprosy (p. 279). " Saphee" is the modern Saffi (p. 278) or Asfi, a town which, after having been in the hands of the Portuguese for more than a century, was voluntarily deserted by them in 1641. It contains a number of sanctuaries (Zaouias), the burial-places of holy men, where criminals finds a safe refuge. The " Rabat " or quarter on the cliff south of the main town is a veritable City of Refuge, so that, as in Pellow's day, it is " the great rendezvous " of undesirable characters.

" Willadea " (p. 282), or El Waladia, is a town 85 miles south of Mazagan, of which we seldom hear nowadays, though in former·

times it was a place of some trade. It is situated on an extensive plain, and were not the entrance to its harbour obstructed by rocks, the cove might be capable of containing a large fleet of vessels. The town itself is small, and encompassed by a square wall, but it contains few inhabitants, there being almost nothing for them to do, as no Europeans live there, and no caravans arrive as ships never come. During the usurpation of Crom-el-Hajj (1648–1652) this place, called in a contemporary document "Houladilla," was occupied, and employed as a base for the siege of Saffi. "Marcegongue" (pp. 229, 282, etc.) is a curious corruption of Mazagan, now the principal outlet for the maize of the rich plains behind it. This town was held until 1769 by the Portuguese, who, on abandoning it, founded Villa Nuova de Mazagan in Brazil. The "River Tammorot" (p. 285) is clearly the Wad Tammerekt which appeared on no map for nearly 65 years after Pellow mentioned it (I believe) for the first time ; and not to attempt the identification of every village, the "mountain Idoworseern" (p. 286) is probably the Djebel Ataneen, and "Gorrasurnee" (p. 275) the Idiaugomoron, while "Jibbil Neddeed" (p. 290) is, of course, Djebel Hadid, the Iron Mountain, north of Mogador. The "high mount called Itatteb" (p. 288) is evidently Itata, S.S.E. of Mequinez. The "Monsieur Pedro Pollee" who entertained Pellow (p. 280) was most likely Pierre Pillet, a renegade who, as mentioned in our introduction, was, under the name of Abd-el-Adi, for a short time governor of Sallee. Espousing the cause of Abd-el-Malik, he was beheaded, and his corpse suspended by the heels from one of the gates of the town which he had ruled, though the date of this tragedy not quite agreeing with Pellow's narrative, leaves us open to doubt whether the identification suggested is correct.

(82) *Mecca Pilgrims,* p. 288.—"Elhash" is a fairly phonetic form of El Hājj, or Hadjj, the courtesy title with which every Moslem is dignified after having made the Mecca Pilgrimage. However, in common with many of the old writers, Pellow blunders in making Mecca the burial-place of the Prophet, instead of Medina. It was, of course, his birthplace. All the princes of the Imperial house are styled "Muley" (Maûlái, Mulai, Maulay, Moulé, Mole), "My lord," or master, a fact of which Defoe seems to have been ignorant when he names the

Moor in charge of Robinson Crusoe's master's boat "Muley, or
Moley." "Sidi" means much the same thing, but is accounted
even more respectful, and is universally applied to saints, and in
the abbreviated form of Sid (or Cid) to all of the faithful named
after the Prophet—which means to about half of the Moroquin
population.

(33) *Tea Drinking*, p. 297.—Though there is a good deal of
coffee drunk by the humbler Moors in their shabby coffee-houses,
which are not, as in Turkey and Egypt, frequented by the better
classes, the Moors of Morocco, as a people, differ from most
other Moslems in preferring tea to coffee, and green tea to any
other variety of the herb. They infuse it with large quantities
of sugar, and flavour it, in lieu of cream, with mint, citron
leaves, orange blossoms, ambergis, &c. The amount drunk
at a sitting is never less than three cups or glasses, and
as the sittings mean six times a day, and as often more as
favoured visitors call, it may well be believed that more tea per
head is consumed in Morocco than in any other part of the
world. Yet up to the year 1660, at earliest, the Moors were
perfectly ignorant of what may now be termed the national
beverage. For in a paper of that date written by Monsieur
Charant, the French merchant " who lived twenty-five years in
the kingdom of Sus and Morocco," it is expressly mentioned
that though some of the less devout do not forbear by stealth
to drink wine, nay brandy, "which both the Christian slaves and
Jews sell," such drinks as coffee, thee, and chocolate they know
not in those countrys what they are," though the writer adds
that he heard they are much used in England. Coffee in an
especial degree is there drunken in " great store " to prevent
drowsiness. " And as for thee and chocolate (some think) they
strengthen nature, revive and refresh the spirits, when weakened
by overmuch study."

(34) *English Gunpowder*, p. 300.—To this day, a pound of
English gunpowder is one of the most acceptable gifts which
can be made to a Moor, as it is not allowed to be imported for
sale, and the native article is very poor.

(35) *The Woled (or Ooled) Aboussebàh Arabs*, p. 288.—The
curious account Pellow gives of the great band of marauders

he encountered refers, I am of opinion, to the inroad of those
Arabs which about this period added to the intestine troubles
of Morocco. They claim to be sprung from Shereefs (the
" Xeriphs " of Pellow), and are very warlike. During the civil
war following the death of Muley Ismaïl — not during Sidi
Mohammed's reign as Jackson declares—they left their sandy
deserts in Sous, and, to the number of about 7,000 men, overran
the southern parts of the empire, until, with little or no opposition, they reached the provinces of Abda and Shiedma, where
Pellow met them. Here they had a battle with the Woled-el-
Haje and other tribes of the fertile country north of the river
Tensift, but were so completely victorious that they almost
exterminated their enemies, and holding their ground against all
opposition, took possession of the depopulated territory. But
their predatory disposition made the country so unsafe that
Sidi Mohammed outlawed the whole clan, and ordered them to
leave the country in which they had settled. This order was
forced to be obeyed by the Sultan's army, who drove them south,
the natives of the provinces through which they had to flee
plundering and murdering so many that only about half of the
tribe reached the Sahara in an impoverished condition.

(36) *Allalben-Hammedush* (p. 278) *or Elebenhamedush* (p. 290).—
I cannot find any mention of this " castle " or Kasbah of Ali ben
Hamedûsh, as it would be called in Morocco, on any map or
document prior to Pellow's day, or since, unless the point named
" Ben Hamuda" on Gråberg di Hemsö's" chart is the same place.
Nor indeed is it mentioned by any traveller since that day, with
one exception, and this exception is a striking proof of the
general accuracy and authenticity of the Penryn mariner. For
Dr. Gerhard Rohlfs, who had no knowledge of this book, casually notes that though he was unable to find the town called
Rabat el Kus which so many geographers describe at the mouth
of the Tensift, not far from its banks " are the romantic ruins of
an old castle, called Kasbah Hammiduh, situated on some abrupt
rocks in the midst of a forest. It was probably erected to guard
the mouth of the river." This is clearly the same place described by Pellow, and perhaps it is also the "square castle built
in the reign of Muley Ishmael to defend the passage of the
river," which, in Chenier's day (1767) contained only a few

families, though that usually accurate writer does not mention
the name it bore. I have not visited the place, but a correspon-
dent of whom I made inquiries writes that the "Kasbah of Hamdoosh " is an extensive ruin, not unlike that of Old Tangier, but
of greater extent and in better preservation. Granaries, battlements, and rooms can still be traced. It was evidently intended
as a check upon the Portuguese fort at the mouth of the river,
though this also has now almost vanished. But it is incorrect to
suppose that it was built by Sidi Mohammed, as this sovereign
(the founder of Mogador) lived after Pellow's day.

(37) *Markadore*, p. 806.—This curiously spelt place appears to
have been Mogador, the well-known southern port of Morocco.
At that time the Portuguese monopolized most of the coast trade,
and, as the "Portuguese fort" on the shore of Mogador Bay
shows, had fortified places on other parts of the Atlantic shore
than that which they actually held. For it is an error to believe
that the fort in question dates no further back than the beginning of this century, or was built on behalf of the Sultan by
Genoese engineers, as is sometimes stated. In reality, it was
erected to keep intact the communications with Agadir, and to
protect the coasters who called in here. Nor is it any more
accurate to take for granted that because Sidi Mohammed ordered
a town to be laid out on the spot by M. Cornut, a French engineer (a native of Avignon), who was for ten years in his service,
there was no previously existing place, or that the Europeans
first named it Mogador at that date, now more than 120 years
ago, though S'oueïra—"the image" or the picture—is the Moorish name. The Touraine Capuchin Fathers, writing in 1644,
expressly mention that there was a fort on the island, and that
in 1628 Abd-el-Malik II. had intended to employ the Christian
slaves in the erection of fortifications around the Bay. But long
before that period there was a native town there, without pinning our faith to the suggestion that this was the site of the
Tamusiga of Ptolemy, or of a more modern place marked on
various seventeenth-century maps as Sufega or Suriga. But it
is very doubtful whether S'oueïra is a corruption of that word,
as some ingenious antiquaries have imagined. The name is in
reality of modern origin, and in the Berber language Tasourt,
their designation for the town, has the same meaning. On the

northern side of the Tensift river, amid sands and marshes, there are the ruins of another small town which also bore the name of S'oueïra: it was deserted long ago.

"Mogador," though doubtless derived from the tomb or sanctuary of Sidi Mogdul or Mogdor in the vicinity of the town, is of very much older date, Hodius's chart of 1608 having "I. Domegador" marked on it, and this is copied from others of a more remote period, and in documents as early as 1660 "Mogator" is repeatedly referred to as a place of trade. The sanctuary of Sidi Mogdul—the guardian saint of the town—is of very ancient origin, so remote indeed that both the Jews and the Moors contend for the saint having been one of their people, and do him equal honour. In 1604 Captain John Smith made a voyage to "Sancta Cruse, Cape Goa (*Ghir*) and *Magadore*." But though the Sidi-Mogdul legends are connected with a ship coming from the sea, I am unable to discover any foundation for the notion that he was a wrecked Danish captain, far less, as Mr. Harris puts it so circumstantially, "a Scotchman McDougal," who in the Middle Ages lived among the natives, whose old village is still near the town, and taught them many useful arts. The Arabs, it is true, are fond of making saints out of rather flimsy material. Between "Morocco and the Atlas" Monsieur Charant, who lived in the country before the year 1660, notes that there is a place called "Gomet" (probably Aghmat, the old capital of the Almoravides), where a monument exists which the Moors in . his day pretended to have been St. Augustine's, "whom they call Sid Belabech," and every one who has visited the site of Carthage will remember the white native village of Sidi Bou-Saeed, a spot so holy that until lately no Christian was allowed to live in the place. Yet Sidi Bou-Saeed is affirmed by the Arabs to have been St. Louis, who on his death-bed became a convert to Al-Islam, and is interred there under that name. However, the historical difficulties regarding Sidi-Mogdul have never interfered with the esteem in which he is held. He is the patron saint of Mogador, and when I was there in 1886, the muleteers were hastily driving their animals into his sanctuary on a report getting abroad that the governor would be pressing them for the service of the French minister, who was then in the town on his way to the city of Morocco, on one of those useless "diplomatic missions" which prove so expensive to the villagers, who have to defray the cost of the sumptuous journey of the " 'bashdor " and his friends though in the polite parlance of an official report these useless jaunts are described as being at the cost of the Sultan!

(88) *Argaireens*, or *Argireens*, pp. 130, 306.—" Argiers " was one of the old names of Algiers, the word being evidently a corruption of the Spanish " Argel." The French " Alger," and its modification " Algier," are also in use by the older writers.

(89) *A " Tartan " and a " Snow,"* pp. 304, 308.—These were names applied at that date to particular builds of vessels. A " snow," for instance, as my friend Captain Warren, R.N., informs me, was " a brig which set her boom mainsail on a trysail mast, instead of, as in the present way, on the mast itself." A " tartan," Commander Robinson, R.N.—who also has obligingly favoured me with some notes on the subject—remarks, is a small coasting vessel peculiar to the Mediterranean. It has only one mast and a bowsprit; the principal sail, which is extremely large, is extended by a lateen-yard. This is a long spar used to extend the three-cornered lateen sail upon; it is slung about one quarter from the lower end, which is brought down to the tack, while the upper end is raised in the air at an angle of about forty-five degrees. When the wind is aft a square sail is generally hoisted on the tartan, like a cross-jack. This craft—now seldom seen—does not appear to have differed considerably from the " felucca " so familiar in the Mediterranean. Its ancient name was " targia," which suggests the possible derivation of the name. " Can it have come," Commander Robinson suggests, " from Tarhish or Tarragona ? I find also that an ancient term for a vessel of any kind which carried a cargo, as distinguished from a vessel built for fighting only, was ' tarita.' "

(40) *Mamora or Mehedia*, p. 313.—This is now a poor neglected though picturesque place, with a shoaled-up harbour at the mouth of the Sebou River, with no trade except the catching of the shebbel, or shad, the only good fresh-water fish of Morocco. From 1614, when Don Louis Fajardo captured it for the King of Spain, to 1681, when the weak, dispirited garrison surrendered

it to Kaïd Amor-Hadou on behalf of Muley Ismaïl, the town
was a fief of His Catholic Majesty. But it was never of great
importance, though it did more business then than it has ever
done since. The object of Spain in seizing upon it was to root
out the nest of pirates it had become, and it is said by contemporary writers that there were at the time more Christians
there following the business than Moors. This confirms Captain
John Smith's assertion (p. 11), that the Morocco Moors were
taught the art of sea-robbery by English outlaws, and that they
in their turn (reversing the usual legend) initiated their countrymen exiled from Spain in what was subsequently their principal
trade. But no sooner did Mamora get free of the Infidels than
it returned to its evil ways. For here on the 13th of June, 1685,
Thomas Phelps and Edmund Baxter, escaping from "Machanes"
(Mequinez), helped to burn "two of the greatest Pirat-Ships
belonging to Barbary."

(41) *Passing the Straits of Gibraltar*, p. 315.—The frolic
described is evidently a survival from the days when the
Carthaginian mariners sacrificed to the gods on passing what
a pillar at Gibraltar even in Edrisi's day proclaimed to be the
limits of navigation. The ceremonies have been long discontinued,
though something of the kind is practised on novices who for the
first time pass "the Line," and among the Arctic whalers on
May Day, as I have fully described elsewhere.*

(42) *Gibraltar*, p. 320.—General Sabine was the thirteenth
governor of Gibraltar, viz., from 1730, when he succeeded
General Clayton, to 1739, when General Columbine took his
place. The excessive precautions taken to prevent any Moor
from entering the fortress may seem absurd to those of us who
remember the picturesque crowds of Barbary folk lounging in
the Waterport Street, the little steamer from Tangier full of
Moslem egg and fowl merchants, and the forty or fifty Moors,
most of them native-born subjects of her Majesty, resident on
the rock. But in 1738 treachery was abroad, and the fortress
had only recently stood its thirteenth siege. To this day all
comers are questioned, those of British nationality being alone
permitted to tarry without certain inoffensive formalities, touching guarantees for their good behaviour. The other gentlemen

* "Countries of the World," vol. i. pp. 103-107.

24

mentioned by Pellow were officials at the time of his story, as an examination of the Colonial records proves.

(48) *The Moorish Ambassador*, p. 827.—This envoy was El Hajj Abd' el Kâdr Perez, Admiral of Sallee. He was succeeded by "Abroggly," who came back with Mr. Consul Russel from England in 1727. At a later date several others arrived on various missions, among others Tahar Fenishe, in the reign of George III. It is therefore far from accurate to state, as is still mentioned in some "works of reference," that the ambassador from Sidi Mohammed ben Abd-er-Rhaman, who arrived in June, 1860, was the first "since the time of Charles II." One of the early English envoys to the Court of Morocco —Sir James Losely, Captain Nicholson, Lord Howard, or Captain Kirk of "Kirk's Lambs, for statements differ—being obliged to appear barefooted before Muley Ismaïl,"* Mohammed Ben Hadou Ottar, the Moorish Envoy who was sent to Charles II., was compelled to submit to the indignity of being received at court without shoes, turban, or fez.

Morocco is, however, even yet the one country with which we have diplomatic relations, where the Christian envoy has to submit to more or less degrading observances at the hands of the Moslem ruler. An ambassador is received by the Sultan in the courtyard of his palace, the "Prince of True Believers" sitting haughtily on horseback while the envoy of a great power stands humbly bareheaded at his side, presenting to him the members of his suite, and expressing the diplomatic commonplaces suited to the occasion. He has not even the protection of an umbrella from the burning sun, though the Sultan has borne over his head the great silken paraschute which is so much the emblem of his authority that when he entered Tetuan and Tangier in the summer of 1889, a notice was issued that no person in the crowd waiting to receive him was to put up their sunshades. Slaves also go on either side of him with silk handkerchiefs flicking the flies from his hands and face. Should the Embassy be afterwards favoured with a more private interview, it takes place in a kiosque in the garden, and even

---

* As late as the reign of Sidi Mohammed ben Abdallah, there were difficulties over the foreign diplomatists not taking off their shoes or prostrating themselves in presence of the Sultan.

then this distinction is not always accorded, and chiefly in order
that the presents which invariably accompany an embassy should
be presented and explained to the Sultan. Such gifts, though
possessing in the eyes of the giver no more meaning than those
sent by one European sovereign to another, are sedulously represented to the ignorant Moors as tribute sent by the Infidels to the
Leader of the Faithful, and should be discontinued, more especially
as the courtesy accorded to an envoy is apt to be in an exact
ratio to the value of the gifts he bears. In any case the Powers
ought at once to insist on being received in the person of their
envoys on the same terms that the Sultan's ambassadors are
when he sends, as he has of late years been fond of doing,
representatives for the purpose of condoling with, or congratulating, his brethren in the West. These envoys are usually two
or more in number, and as they are compelled to defray the
expenses of their mission, the selection of a dignitary for this
duty is as often considered a punishment as an honour. For if
the Ambassador in Chief does not spend lavishly, he is certain to
be represented by his colleagues and rivals as lowering the dignity
of their Lord and Master by behaving niggardly before the Infidels. The return presents usually consist of a horse to the ambassador and a sword to each of his suite. The horse is not very
often a Barb of the first quality, but it is accompanied by a
" permit," without which no horse, mule, camel, cow, goat,
sheep, or donkey is allowed to go out of the country; so
that the animal can be sent to a profitable market on the other
side of Gibraltar Strait. Time was, when no Christian or Jew
—not even a Consul—could enter holy cities like Saffi or Fez
without dismounting from their animals, and even yet, the same
invidious formality, *plus* taking off their slippers, is demanded
from Jews when they enter the Moorish quarters in the interior
towns, or pass a mosque. Last century and well into the
present one, no Christian or Jew could enter the Moorish
quarters of Fez without a permit from the Emperor; and to this
hour, for either to try and pass the street in which is situated
the mosque of Muley Idris would be to endanger the life of the
rash intruder. As for attempting to visit the town of Muley
Idris, and other sacred spots—no one as yet has openly ventured
on that dangerous experiment.

All the other Barbary States have long ago abandoned any

official efforts to differentiate between the Infidel and the followers
of the Prophet, Tripoli, indeed, being the only one of them
with the exception of Morocco which is not directly or indirectly
under Frankish rule.   Algeria is a colony of France, so that the
days are over when the insolent pirate-chiefs treated Consuls
with contumely, found fault with their presents, and insisted on
more frequent changes in order that this form of tribute should
come less sparingly.   Tunis also, though a '' Protectorate," is to
all intents and purposes a dependency of France.   But there are
men still young who can remember when no person except the
Bey could drive in a four-wheeled carriage, and not far from the
Kasbah was a gate called Bab-es-silsilah—through which until
sixty or seventy years ago it was death for a Christian to pass.
But these were in the happy times when—

'' Nsara fe Senaara !	'' To the hook with the Nazarene !
Lehood fe Sefood ! ''	To the spit with the Jew ! ''

was a maledictory couplet of something more than academic
import.   No Christian can enter any mosque in Morocco, or
with one exception any in Tunisia.   But the exception is
sufficiently remarkable, for it happens to be that of Sidi Okba
in the sacred city of Kairwan, which, a few years ago, no
unauthorized infidel could visit unless he was prepared to be
stoned or even worse treated.   Nowadays, you can trundle over
the plain between it and Susa on iron rails, and the keeper of
the Great Mosque holds out his hands for the five-franc piece as
if he had been bred to the vergership of an English cathedral.
Morocco is still, in the interior at least, not very different from
what it was a thousand years ago.   But '' Tunica ricca ed on-
orata sede " has fallen from its high estate.   For the Nazarene
sits in the seat of the Bey, and a Juge d'instruction interprets
the law.   Newsboys and shoeblacks ply their trades in sight of
Rubbatinos railway station, and over the blood-sodden soil,
where less than a century ago Christian slaves toiled under the
Turkish lash, Arab cabmen drive furiously.   You can take the
train to Carthage, and the diligence to Utica and Sicca Veneria.
And all day long past cafés where cogging Greeks bargain over
their absinthe is heard the hoarse cry of the tramway conduc-
tor—'' Place Bab Carthagène !   Four karrobas all the way ! ''

INDEX.

A.

Abdallah, Muley, *Frontispiece*, 226, 252, 346, 352, 354, *et passim*
  ,,   ,,   his cruelties, 226, 354, 355, 356
Abd-el-Malik II., 346
Abd-el-Malik (ben Ismaïl), 351
  ,,   Muley, his death, 183
Abd-el-Mumin, Muley, 341
Abd-er-Foolan, a black governor, 161
Abd-er-Rahman Medune, 50
Abd-es-Slam, an English renegade, 103
Aboulqâsen's history, 354
Aboussebah Arabs, incursion of, 288, 364, 365
Abramico, the Sultan's agent at Gibraltar, 318, 320
Acton, Chevalier, destroys or disperses Sidi Mohammed's fleet, 17
Adams, Robert, 352
Africa and Europe, contrast, 8
Agadir (*pl.*), 304, 360, 361, *et passim*
Agloou, 353
Agoory, 343, *et passim.*
Ahmed Sceikh, Muley, 25
" Aissa Sidna," 359
Aissouias sect, 359
Aït-Hassan, 189
  ,, Zemour, 189
  ,, Wadyl, 95
Akkabaahs, or Caravans, 353
Al K'sar el Kebir, 362
" Allalben-Hammedush," 278, 365

Ali, Muley, 357
Amarisoo, Kasbah, 192
Ambassadors to Morocco treated slightingly, 370, 371
Ambassadors, Moorish, to England, 368, 370
Amsmiz, 87, 260
Animals, wild, of Morocco, 87, 346
Aouara, 361
'Aoodya Lalla, 97
Arabs, 120, 347
Archid, Muley, 134
" Arcby," Muley, 334
Argan oil, 278, 279, 362
Argaireens, 366, 368
" Arhallah," 361
Army, Moorish, 115, 343
Ar'scid, Muley, 134
" Aselami," renegade Jews, 31
Ataneen Djebel, 363
Attar, Ben Hadou, 74
Azamoor, 43, 155 156 (*pl.*)
Azila, 9, 14, 29, 358

B.

Bab-Mancoor-el âlj, 53
  ,, es-silsah and Christians in Tunis, 372
Barbary States, decay of, 372
Baxter, Edmund, 369
Beaver, Mr., 319
Bebaouan Pass, 221, 361
Bebash, 85
Belabech, 367

Ben Hamuds, 365

" Hattar, 336, 337

Beni-boogaffer, pirate village, 39

" Hassan tribe, 335

" M'tir tribe, 119

" Snous, 130

" Zibbah, 112

Berbers, 347

Beth River, 84, *et passim*

Betton, Thomas, 27, 28

Bishop, a pirate of note in Morocco, 12

Black Imperial Guard, 141, 348

Bled-Shereef, 347

Blois, Madamoiselle de, 25

Boisselin, a French renegade, 33

Bokhari Guard, 141, 348

Booty from Guerida, 101

Building mania of Muley Ismaïl and his successors, 19

Bou Azza, Muley, 184

" el Roseo, Kaïd, 152

Bou-ragrag River, 335

Bou-Saeed, Sidi, near Carthage, 367

Boyd, Captain Henry, 339

Brooks, Francis, 342

Brooke, Sir Arthur, quoted, 40, 41, 42

Bu (Bou) Sacran (*pl.*), 52, 211

Bushmough, a frisky slave, 121, 347

Butler, Mr., 40

C.

Captive, Scottish, romantic tale of, 23

Captives driven into interior, *pl.*, 52

" English, in harems, 25

" escape of, 27, 29

" how treated, 18, *et seq.*

" ransom of, 27, 28

" toil of, 68, 69, 70

Caravans, great loss of, in desert, 353

Carr, a renegade, 32

Carthaginian Mariners, and Pillars of Hercules, 369

"Caultsnab," 67

Cautery, actual, in Morocco, 340, 360

Cellis, an English pirate, 11

Ceuta intended by Muley el Yezeed as a pirate station, 15

Chaban, a renegade, assassinates Muley Abd el Malik II., 346

Charrant, Monsieur, 334, 341, 367, &c.

" on tea-drinking in England, 364

Chaânaba tribe, 354

Christ, a great doctor, 359

"Christians" in Morocco, 9

Clayton, General, 369

Clinton, an English pirate, 11

Columbine, General, 369

Conti, Princess de, and Muley Ismaïl, 25, 26

Convicts escaped, renegades, 44

Cornut, builder of Mogador, 32

Costermongers, Moorish, 362

Crom-el-Hajj, 346, 354, 363

Cunningham, Rev. Mr., 319

Cuscussoo, 22, 68, *et passim*

D.

Damker, a Dutch pirate of note in Morocco, 12

Dâr Debibeg, palace built by Christians, 20

Dâr-el-Bastyoon, 53

Dâr-es-Solt'âna, 335

Darmusultan, 335

Dayat-er-Roumi, 195

Defoe, ignorance of Moorish titles, 364

Delaval, Admiral, 72

Delgarnoe, Captain, 335

Demnat, 241

Denooa, 111

Desert between Morocco and Guinea, 199, 353

Disguise, danger of, 43

"Djellabia, Wooden," 339

Doctors, Moorish quack, 259, 358, 359, 340

Douls, Camille, the late, 40

Douvia, Lalla, 26

Draa River, 206

Dyspepsia in Morocco, 359

E.

Ed-Dehebi, Muley Hamid, 346, 351
Ed-doukkáli, Salêm, 204, 225
Edinburgh, Lord Provost of's daughter and Barbary pirate, 24
Edinburgh and Sallee Rovers, 24
Ehiah Embelide, 89, *et passim*
El 'Arby Ben Abou-Oold Emjiotlee, 150
Eleben-hamedush, 290, 365
El hassuâ, 361, 362
  ,, Mati Sidi, a saint, 358
  ,, Valid, Muley, 25
Embassies in Morocco useless, and wastefulness of, 367, 368
Enkees-wad, 195
Erriadâh quarter of Mequinez, 354
Europeans, indignities to, 37
Es-Shereef, Muley, 25
Executioner, an English, 103
Exima, 361

F.

Fez, 161, 186, *et passim*
  ,, time when no Jew or Christian could enter Moorish quarter without Imperial permit, 37
  ,, time when Jew or Christian forbidden to enter on horseback, 371
Fleet, Moorish, 215
Flemming, an English pirate, 11
Fnsira, 84
Fonti, 361
Fûm-el-bungh, 112
Fûm-el-Karoo, 94
French Military Commission, 45, 344

G.

Gabdad, 84
"Garnoe," 335
German Surgeon in Moorish Army, 115
Gerygra River, 111
"Geseemah," 361
Gibraltar, 8, 9, 369
  ,, Straits of, 8, 369

"Gomet," St. Augustine's tomb believed to be there, 367
"Gorrasurnee," Mount, 275, 363
Graham, Colonel, 45, 46
Gray, Andrew, Scottish pirate, 25
Grub Street and the Sallee Rovers, 34
Guerrou River, 334
Guinea, vague meaning attached to, 352
Gunpowder, English, 300, 364
Guzlan, march to, 112, 342

H.

Habíb ben Baruk and Mr. Butler, 40
Habid, Wad-el, 98
Hadaha, 130
Hadid Djebel, 363
Hahah, Province, 361
Hajj (or Hadj), title of, 363
Hamdoosh, Kasbah, 366
Hamid, Muley (Ahmed IV.), 134, 346
  ,, Losmee, 225
Hamseduh Kasbah, 365
Hamerostu Pass, 361
Harbours of Morocco, shoaling up of, 15, 16
Harris, Mr., and Sidi Mogdul, 367
Hartan, Kasbah, 218
Hassan, Muley El, 345, 348, &c.
Haunsell, Jusef, a rebellious conjuror, 203
Hay, Sir John Drummond, and Riff Pirates, 39
Henna, use of, 76, 340
Hharùn, Muley, 134
"Highland Lad" transport, 42
Hisciam, Muley, 26
Hogmy, Bashaw, 355
Horses, Moroccan, 83, 340
Howard, Lord, 370
Hudson, Sir Jeffrey, Charles I.'s dwarf, a slave, 23
Hussein, Sidi, 361

I.

Ida ou Gort District, 277
Idiaugomoron, 363
"Idoworseern," Mount, 281, 363

Imbert, Paul, 352
" Immintackcamost," 221
" Ingliz Bashaw," 45
Inspector Privateer wrecked in Tangier
    Bay, 15, 35
Invelg-Khamis, 193
Irish Sultana, story of, 26
Ismaïl, Muley, his children, 338
    „   „   cruelties of, 63, 338,
            349
    „   „   habits of, 134–148
    „   „   palace of, 59, 338
    „   „   sons, wars of, 148, 193,
            348, 357
    „   „   his wives, 338
" Itatteb," Mount, 238, 363
Itata, Mount, 363
" Itchacam," 191
" Itehuzzan," 189
" Itemoor," 189
" Itewoossey," 212

J.

Jackals, 89, 340
Jackson, Mr., his dogmatism, 353
Janissaries, Black, 348
Jbad-Kasbah, 84
Jews, degradation of, 371
    „   malignity of, 28
    „   offices held by, 336
    „   town for, built by Christian
    slaves, 20
Johnson, William, a renegade, 324
Juan, Maestro, 26

K.

Kairwan, changes in, 372
Kareebs, Moorish boats, 39
Keef, 357
Kirk, Captain, 370
Khoneta (or Yoneta), Lalla, 25, 299

L.

Larache, 9, 14, 29
Lenz, Oskar, 353
Lions in Morocco, 109, 342
Locusts as food, 276, 361
Lorshia, 52, 334

Loscly, Sir James, 370
Lundy Island, Sallee Rovers lying
    under, 16

M.

Macaulay, error of, 11
Maclean, Kaïd, 343
Mamora, a kennel of European pirates,
            9, 13, 14, 15, 340, 368
    „   forest of, 335
Marakesch, or Morocco City, *pl.*, 97
" Markadore," 306, 366
" Marcegongue," 229, 282, &c.
Matamoras, 21
Maundevile, Sir John, and the
    "sarrazines," 346
Mazagan, 135, 363
Meakin, Mr. Budgett, 38
Meat, price of in 1738, 283
Meat Bir Oo Bir, 195
Mecca, mistakes about, 363
    „   Pilgrims, 283, 363
Mediuna District, 193
Mehedia (Mamora), 313, 368
Memeran, a Jew, 337
Mequinez, Pellow's journey to, 50–53.
    „   description of, 53, 185 (*pl.*)
Mercenarian Fathers, 27
Merchants, selfishness of, 28
Mils, 193
Mocquet, Jean, 341
Mogador Island, 345
Mogador, history of, 366, 367, 368
Mogdul, Sidi, 367
Mohammed Ben Araby, late Grand
            Vizier, of Jewish origin,
            31
    „   Muley, 349
    „   Sidi, 26, 361, 366
    „   Sidi, audience of, *pl.*, 135
    „   Wad Nuni, governor of
            Saffi, 306
Morocco, appearance of coast, 8, 9
    „   changes in, of late years, 42
    „   city, 341, 342, *pl.*, 97
    „   „ golden globes of, 99,
            340, 341
    „   ethnography of, 347

" Morocco Land " in Edinburgh, 23

Morocco, only independent Barbary
State, 372

„ stability of, 46

„ still much as it was, 46,
371

Moorish buildings erected by captives,
344

„ towns, 9

Moors, 120, 347

Mosque, Kutubia, 341

'Mshrah Dallia, 195

'Mshael, a Black Bashaw, 183

'Msida, 88

Mtooga, 95

Muley, title of, 363, 364

Mulootjibbilly, 224

Multorria, 191

Mustadi Muley, 234, 357

N.

Navy, Moorish, 32, 43

" Nazrani," 44

" Neddeed Jibbil," 290, 363

Nicholson, Captain, 370

Niger, 353

Nil Wad, 352

Norbury, Captain, 145

Nun Wad, 195

O.

Officials, robbery of, 342

Omar, a Scotchman " Reis," or captain of a Moorish zebek, 32

Om-er-R'bia, 98

" Oodali," Christian renegade, 31

Oold-el-Ariba, Mohammed, 357

Ooled Aboussebah Arabs, 288, 364, 365

Oudah, Lalla, 97

" Our Lady of Mercy," Fathers of, 27

P.

Peacock, Captain, 322, 324

Pellow's book, 37

„ · „ proofs of its authenticity, 37, 38

„ journey to Mequinez, 50, 337

„ „ Morocco City, 196,
352

Pellow, mention of him in Braithwaite's narrative, 35, 36

„ in James's " Straights of Gibraltar," 35

Perez Abdel Kâdr, 370

Petrobelli, a Triestan employed by Sidi
Mohammed, 32

Piety of Moors, 362

Pillet, Pierre, a renegade, 32

Pilots Desert, 353

Piracy, Moorish origin of, 10, 11

„ decay of, 15, 33

„ in Morocco, suppression of,
38, 89

„ nature of, 10 *et seq.*

„ recent cases of, 39, 40, 41,
42

Pirates, English, in Morocco, 12

„ Riff, 39

Pitts, Joseph, 352

Phelps, Thomas, 342, 369

Pietrasanta, a Tuscan employed by
Sidi Mohammed, 33

" Pollee, Pedro," 280, 363

Poison, fear of, in Morocco, 342, 344

Portuguese in Morocco, 347

Presents to Sultan regarded as tribute,
371

Pretorians, Black, 348

Princes of Morocco numerous and
poor, 346

Provinces of Morocco, uncertain limits
and number of, 343

Pursser, an English pirate, 11

Pye, Captain, 320

R.

Rabat, 9, 50, 262 (*pl.*), 304, 333, 334

" Rabat " of Saffi, 362

Ras-el-Wad, 360

" Raval," 334

Redemptorial Fathers, 27

Religion the dividing line in Morocco,
9

Renegades, 29, *et seq.*, 44, 45, 46, 345

„ descendants of, in Fez,
Agoory and other towns,
31

Renegades, their treachery against each other, 169

Reis Hadjj ben Hassan Houet Shivi, a Moorish captain, 16

Riff Pirates, 39

Riffians drink wine and eat pork, 345

Ripperda, Duke of, a renegade, 32

Robinson, Commander, on the vessel called a " Tartan," 368

Rohlfs, Gerhard, 365

" Rosselelwad," 265, 360

" Roumi," 44

Russel's, Mr., Embassy, 153, 348

S. .

Sabine, Governor, of Gibraltar, 320

Saffi, 278, 362, *et passim*

Safeegosoolz, 195

Saffi, time when Jew or Christian forbidden to enter on horseback, 371

St. Louis believed to have become Moslem, 367

Sallee-Rabat, 9, 30, 262 (*pl.*), 333

Sallee Rovers, 9, *et seq*.

Salletines' ways of life, 13

Sampson, Captain, 319

Sanctuaries, 362

Saulty, Count Joseph de, 45

Savoy, Marquisate, bought by Ward, an Anglo-Moorish pirate, 12

Scottish girl, romantic story of, 23

Sebou River, 368

Sebastian, Dom, 20, 362

Seersceta, Lalla, 26

" Segosule," 285

Sejea Hambra, 195

Senegal River, 353

Shademah Province, 290

Sharrot River, 84

Shatel-Arbi, 64

" Shot, Larby," 64

Shaw, Mrs., a renegade, 25

Shelley, Captain, 215, 217

Shereef-es-Muley, 25, 117

Sherf-el-gusooli, 95

Sherrers, Palace of, 59, 338

Shinget, 196

Shoarumlah, 219

Sidi Amara, 111

Sidi Bou Azza,

  ,, el Bamsoo, 119

  ,, Hamid ben Moosa, 195

  ,, Hussein, 361

  ,, Ra'hal, 101, 111, 244

  ,, el Fileli, 102

  ,, title of, 364

Slavery in Morocco, suppression of, 88

Slaves, Christian, at work, *pl.*, 211

  ,, keeping shops, 345

  ,, Moors caution in purchasing, 71

  ,, narratives of, 33, 34

Sma Hassan Tower, 9

Smine, Muley, 53, 227, 357

Smith, Captain John, 11, 367

Snow, a vessel, 304, 308, 368

S'ouera, or Soueïra, Moorish native of Mogador, 26, 345, 366, 367

Sous (Souze, or Sûs) Province, 39, *et passim*

Spanish War of 1859–60, 348

Spartel, Cape, 42, 315

Spha, Muley, 54

Stewart, Commodore, 65, 72, 339

Sufega or Surega, 366

Suliman (S'liman), Muley, 38, 361

Sultans, Drunken, 345, 346

Sultan, how treated, 73

Surgery, Moorish, 70, 339, 359

T.

Tabia, 19, 20

Taffilet and the Imperial Family, 120, 346, 347

Tahar Fenishe, 370

Taib, or Tabia, 19, 20

Taleb, an interpreter of the law, 260

" Talgror," supposed Province of, 86, 840

Tammerket Wad, 363

" Tammorto " River, 285, 363

Tamsaloaht, 252

Tamusiga of Ptolemy, 366

Tangier, 29

  ,, Bashaw of, 319

Tanisna, Kasbah, 81

Tartan, a vessel, 304, 308, 368

Tazourt, Berber name of Mogador, 366

Tazelronalt, 361

Tea-drinking, 297, 364

Tedla, 235

Telfil (" Teffilifille "), 335

Temple, Sir Greville, quoted, 41

Temsna, Province, 80, *et passim*

Tensift River, 101, 290, 367

    ,,   Bridge, 20

Terodant, 360

Terrijet, 159

" Terroost," 361

Tetuan's, Bashaw of, son's love of wine and pudding, 345

Tezza, or Tazza, 130

Tlemcen, 147

Tobacco forbidden, 345

Toobin, Captain, 293, *et seq.*

Tourazt, 361

Trinitarian Fathers, 27

Tunis changes since French Protectorate, 372

U.

Umseet el Kashib, 221

V.

Valid-el Muley, 25

W.

Wad-Enfisa, 360

" Waddon Enkeese," 195

" Waddonfeese," 262, 360

Waladia, El, 362

Ward, a pirate of note in Morocco, 12

Warren, Captain, on vessel called a " Snow," 368

Wazan, Grand Shereef of, 345

" Willadea," 282, 292, 362

Wilson, Captain, 292

    ,,   Sir Daniel, 25

Windus, Mr., pockets picked by Muley Abdallah's guards, 345

Windus, Mr., his buttons cut off by domestics of Muley Abdallah, 346

Wine-drinking, 119, 344, 345, 346

    ,, sent as present to Muley Eddehebi, 346

" Wishaddah," 130

Wives, European, of Sultans, 25, 26

" Woolderriva, Mohamet," 227, 357

" Wolelsager," 52, 335

Wounds, how treated, 344

Y.

Yezeed (or Jezid), Muley, 26, 27, 346, 357

Ymin Tanood, 95

Yoneta (or Khoneta), Lalla, 25, 299

Z.

Zaouias, or Sanctuaries, 362

Zebek pirate, *pl.*, 335

Zeitoun, Wad-el, 130

Zenboudj-el-Aousat, scene of Muley Ismaïl's defeat by Dey of Algiers, 136

Zemmur tribe, 189, 335

Zidan, Lalla, 349

    ,,   Muley, 14, 25, 29, 30

Zooyet Benus, 112

Zouyet et Handore, 112

" Zumineeta," 276, 361

Zummith, a kind of food, 80

UNWIN BROTHERS, THE GRESHAM PRESS, CHILWORTH AND LONDON.

CPSIA information can be obtained at www.ICGtesting.com
Printed in the USA
LVOW11s1707031013

355315LV00012B/281/P